THE ROMAN EMPIRE

THE ROMAN EMPIRE

Economy, Society and Culture

Peter Garnsey &
Richard Saller

University of California Press

Berkeley and Los Angeles

First published in 1987 by
University of California Press
Berkeley and Los Angeles

Library of Congress Cataloging-in-Publication Data

Garnsey, Peter
  The Roman Empire.

  Bibliography: p.
  1. Rome—History—Empire, 30 B.C.–284 A.D.
Social life and customs
I. Saller, Richard P.   II. Title.
DG276.G36 1987   937'.07   86-25029
ISBN 0-520-06066-0 (alk. paper)
ISBN 0-520-06067-9 (pbk. : alk. paper)

Printed in Great Britain

Contents

Abbreviations   vii
Map   viii
Introduction   1

Part I

1. A Mediterranean empire   5
2. Government without bureaucracy   20

Part II

3. An underdeveloped economy   43
4. The land   64
5. Supplying the Roman empire   83

Part III

6. The social hierarchy   107
7. Family and household   126
8. Social relations   148

Part IV

9. Religion   163
10. Culture   178

Conclusion   196
Bibliography   204
List of emperors   225
Index   227

To the memory of
Moses Finley

Abbreviations

Most of the abbreviations are those of *L'Année Philologique*. In addition the following may be unfamiliar to some readers.

AE	*L'Année Epigraphique*
Acta Ant.	*Acta Antiqua Academiae Scientiarum Hungaricae*
BAR	*British Archaeological Reports*
CIG	*Corpus Inscriptionum Graecarum*
CIL	*Corpus Inscriptionum Latinarum*
EMC/CV	*Echos du Monde Classique. Classical News and Views*
IG	*Inscriptiones Graecae*
IGBulg.	*Inscriptiones Graecae in Bulgaria repertae*
ILAlg.	*Inscriptiones Latines de l'Algérie*
ILS	*Inscriptiones Latinae Selectae*
P&P	*Past and Present*
PIR	*Prosopographia Imperii Romani*
RHDFE	*Revue Historique de Droit Français et Étranger*
RIB	*The Roman Inscriptions of Britain*
SEG	*Supplementum Epigraphicum Graecum*
SHA	*Scriptores Historiae Augustae*
Syll³	*Sylloge Inscriptionum Graecarum*, 3rd ed.
TAM	*Tituli Asiae Minoris*
ZSS	*Zeitschrift der Savigny-Stiftung für Rechtsgeschichte* (Romanistische Abteilung)

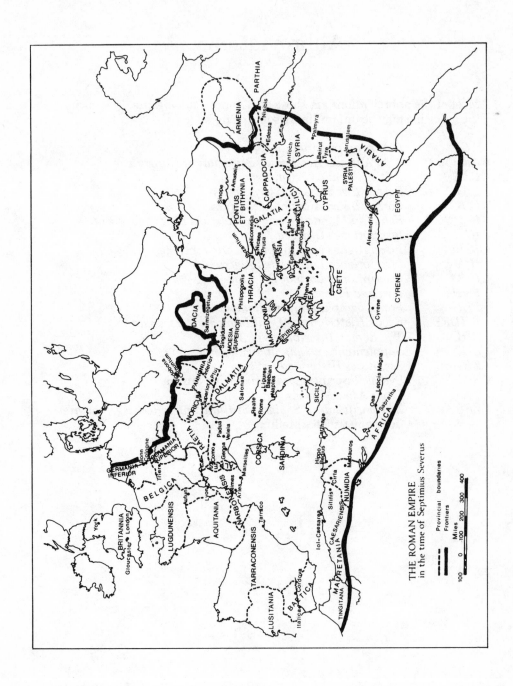

THE ROMAN EMPIRE
in the time of Septimius Severus

Provincial boundaries
Frontiers

Miles
100 0 100 200 300 400

Introduction

The Roman empire at its zenith in the period of the Principate (roughly, 27 BC to AD 235) covered vast tracts of three continents, Europe, Africa and Asia. It encompassed countless cultures, languages, climates and diets. It included nomads and sedentary farmers, primitive tribesmen and cultivated urbanites, bandits and Platonic philosophers. How was it ruled? What forces of cohesion held it together? What was the outcome of the confrontation of imperial and local institutions, customs and values in the provincial setting? How did the society and culture of the imperial capital itself adapt to foreign (especially Greek and Oriental) influences and to the requirements of emperors? What difference did it make to Romans, Italians and provincials that monarchy had replaced oligarchy?

This is not a conventional history of the Roman empire. The structure is thematic not chronological, and the standard topics of Roman history (politics and the constitution, central administration and the military) are not the focus of attention, but are integrated into a study of the society of Rome as a whole. 'Society of Rome' in our usage encompasses the political, social, economic, religious and cultural life and outlook of the inhabitants of the Roman empire.

The study of Roman imperialism and the transformation of imperial society and culture properly begins in the metropolis, but the challenge lies in the description and analysis of Romanization and the identification of its limits in the provincial context. The subject calls for treatment on a grand scale. Our book is limited in scope, being a general introduction to the main issues.

No synthetic analysis is available of many of the themes here treated. In particular, cultural history is fragmented by the specialized interests of its practitioners. 'Economy and society' is not virgin soil, and much of our discussion summarizes and responds to current debate. We also cover unfamiliar terrain. The family and household, personal relationships and the material implications of Roman rule for the subject populations have not hitherto received systematic analysis. On the other side, we make no claim to completeness of coverage. The book is idiosyncratic in the sense that selection of both themes and documentation is influenced by our own interests and areas of competence. The enterprise will have been worthwhile if we have succeeded in extending the conventional bounds of Roman history and provoked thought and stimulated the imagination in the process.

1

This book could not have been composed without exposure to the recent work of a large number of scholars. We single out two prolific and influential writers: Fergus Millar, whose work over a wide range of subjects and historical periods is of singular importance; and Moses Finley, inspirational author, teacher and adviser of the young, to whose memory this book is dedicated. Substantial parts of the book were read and improved in earlier draft by Keith Hopkins, Dominic Rathbone and Dick Whittaker, in addition to Moses Finley and Fergus Millar. Others who have given advice include Graeme Clarke, Ian DuQuesnay, Janet Fairweather, Richard Gordon, Richard Hunter, Henry Hurst, Janet Huskinson, Simon Price, Joyce Reynolds, André Tchernia, Andrew Wallace-Hadrill and Gregory Woolf.

P.G.
R.S.

PART I

CHAPTER ONE

A Mediterranean Empire

The setting

Contemporaries explained the rise of Rome in terms of the moral
character, political institutions, military talent and good fortune of the
Roman people.[1] Writers of the era of Augustus (31 BC – AD 14) adduced
also the physical environment of Rome and Italy. Livy, the historian
from Padua, referred to the central position of Rome in Italy, its
serviceable river and not far distant sea (5.54.4), while Strabo, the
historian and geographer from Amaseia near the southern shore of the
Black Sea, spoke of the location of Italy in the heart of the inhabited
world: 'Further, since it lies intermediate between the largest races on
the one hand and Greece and the best parts of Libya on the other, it not
only is naturally well-suited to hegemony, because it surpasses the
countries that surround it in the valour of its people and in its size, but it
can also easily avail itself of their services because it is close to them'
(286). Pliny the elder, writing in the mid-first century AD, praised the
productivity of the Italian peninsula as Varro had done a century before
(Varro 1.2; Pliny, *HN* 37.201-2, 3.39-42).

In the eyes of Strabo these natural advantages were not peculiar to
Italy, but were a possession of the Mediterranean region as a whole: 'Our
interior sea has a great advantage in all these respects [over the exterior
sea]; and so with it I must begin my description. And far greater in extent
here than there is the known portion, and the temperate portion and the
portion inhabited by well-governed cities and nations. Again, we wish to
know about those parts of the world where tradition places more deeds of
action, political constitutions, arts, and everything else that contributes
to practical wisdom; and these are the places that are under government,
or rather under good government' (122). In fact for Strabo it was less the
Mediterranean as a whole that possessed signal qualities than the
European part of it: 'But I shall begin with Europe, because it has
contributed most of its own store of good things to the other continents;
for the whole of it is inhabitable with the exception of a small region that
is uninhabited on account of the cold' (126). Strabo's message is in line

---

[1] Strabo 286; cf. Varro 1.2. On Italy, also Pliny, *HN* 37.201-2; 3.39-42. Brunt (1978), 164ff.
assembles the texts, mainly from Livy, Cicero and Polybius, on non-geographical causal
factors.

5

with the political ideology of the Augustan age, which stressed the
cultural unity of Greece and Rome.

In asserting the superiority of Mediterranean, or southern European,
civilization, Strabo does not fall back on environmental determinism. In
this he is parting company with his major source, Posidonius, and a
stream of authors going back to the fifth-century BC Hippocratic corpus.[2]
Whereas his contemporary Vitruvius talks of the balanced temperament
of the Italian peoples, lying 'in the true mean within the space of all the
world' (6.1.10), Strabo is interested in the 'diversified details with which
our geographical map is filled', including the favourable positions of
cities and peninsulas and the broken texture of coastlines (120ff.). In the
case of Italy, he points to the length of the peninsula, the extension of the
Apennines down much of its length, and the not unrelated climatic
variation which ensures a variety and comprehensive range of foodstuffs.

This is Strabo at his most percipient. Regional variation in climate is a
dominant feature of the landscape of Italy and the northern
Mediterranean as a whole, which experiences many deviations from the
'pure' Mediterranean type.[3] This means that given the good
communications and developed exchange relationships that are easily
established in the setting of the Mediterranean, individuals, families and
communities could survive all but the worst natural catastrophes. We
should not expect any ancient source to produce a balanced account of
conditions of life in the Mediterranean. We hear nothing from Strabo
about endemic weaknesses of the Italian and the Mediterranean climate.
These include the maldistribution of the rainfall that prevents summer
growth for root crops; the unreliability of the drought-breaking autumn
rains which hinders planting and germination; rainfall variability during
the growth period of the plant; the low level of rainfall in certain regions
(for example, in the northern Mediterranean, Apulia, much of Sicily, and
south-east Greece), coinciding with a very high rate of variability.
Moreover, Strabo obscures the fact that Augustan and early imperial
Italy was not and could not be economically self-sufficient, given the
distribution (and perhaps also the absolute level) of the population.
There are no reliable demographic data from antiquity, but Rome and
the cities of Italy may have contained about 30 per cent of the population
of the peninsula or around two million people, half of them concentrated
in the capital.[4] The task of feeding so many non-producing consumers
was beyond the underdeveloped agricultural economy of Italy in the
Roman period. Of course Rome had been steadily and inexorably
tightening its grip on external sources of supply in the Mediterranean for

[2] Thomson (1948), 106ff.

[3] See Walker (1965), Part I; Braudel (1975), vol. I, part I, 1-4. With special reference to
antiquity, Semple (1932); Cary (1949).

[4] According to an estimate of Hopkins (1978a), 68-9, 32 per cent of the six million
inhabitants of Italy were urban residents.

two centuries before the inauguration of the Principate. It was left to Augustus to extend the tentacles of Rome far beyond the Mediterranean basin, and in particular in the European sphere.

The Roman empire at its peak in the early third century AD comprised not only the Mediterranean peninsulas, islands, coasts and substantial tracts of the interior (to the fringe of the Sahara, to the river Tigris), but also Europe as far north as southern Scotland and the Rhine and Danube (with the addition of a slice of southern Germany across the Rhine and Dacia across the central Danube). The most extensive advances under the Principate were made in Europe during the rule of the first emperor, Augustus. His generals pushed the northern frontier from the Alps to the Danube and finally pacified the Iberian peninsula.[5]

Augustus achieved much less than he intended. He appears to have nurtured the grandiose ambition of advancing beyond the Rhine to the China sea, that is, to the ocean in the East. A map of the world begun by his right-hand man Agrippa, completed under the direction of the emperor and displayed by him on a portico in Rome, showed this distance to be no more than three and a half times the breadth of Gaul, east to west.[6] An expedition to China over the Elbe, if it had ever been launched, would probably have been even more of a shambles than that of Augustus' prefect of Egypt, Aelius Gallus, into Arabia, since they shared a profound ignorance of geography (Strabo 780-2; Pliny, *HN* 6.159-62). As it was, the military effort was stalled between the Rhine and Elbe; the Germans, formidable opponents in any case, were able to exploit Roman ignorance of the terrain.

Beyond the motive of sheer conquest, strategic and sometimes economic considerations played some part in shaping the campaigns of militarily active emperors.[7] In the case of Augustus these motives help to explain, on the one hand, the conquest of the previously untamed Cantabrian and Asturian tribes of the interior of the Iberian peninsula, with the object of tapping the mineral resources of the mountains and enhancing the security of the coastal plains and river valleys; and, on the other hand, the absence of a campaign in Britain, thought to be poor in resources and no great threat to Gaul (Strabo 115-16). The annexation of Britain in AD 43 was a distraction from the political embarrassments of Claudius' accession and early years; it was not that wise men in Rome had revised their view of the value of the country. The conviction that Britain was not worth anything to Rome lingered on (Appian, *BC* pref. 5).

Elsewhere, the eastern frontier was the main theatre of war. Persia

[5] See *CAH* X ch.9,12; XI ch.4,6 for standard accounts of conquest and frontier development. Also Luttwak (1976); G.B.D. Jones (1978).

[6] Klotz (1931); Dilke (1985), ch.3.

[7] The motive of (universal) conquest is stressed by Brunt, *JRS* 53 (1963), 170-6, Wells (1972). On imperial decision-making in strategic matters, see Millar (1982).

exercised a fatal attraction for the more militarily ambitious emperors, as it had done for a succession of would-be emulators of Alexander the Great in the closing decades of the Republic, most notably Crassus, Caesar and Antony. Trajan (AD 96-117) followed up his two Dacian wars and eventual annexation of Dacia with a vigorous campaign east of the Euphrates, which led to the establishment, briefly, of the provinces of Armenia, Parthia and Assyria (Adiabene, beyond the Tigris). His motive, according to the historian Cassius Dio (68.17.1), was a desire for glory. The expedition of Lucius Verus in AD 167 deep into Parthian territory was punitive rather than annexationist, but Septimius Severus established the provinces of Mesopotamia and Osrhoene beyond the Euphrates in the late 190s. Cassius Dio, a contemporary, was not convinced of the permanence of these conquests: 'Severus ... was in the habit of saying that he had gained a large additional territory and made it a bulwark for Syria. But the facts themselves show that it is a source of continual wars for us, and of great expense. For it provides very little revenue and involves very great expenditure; and having extended our frontiers to the neighbours of the Medes and Parthians, we are constantly so to speak at war in their defence' (75.3.2-3). Dio's words were prophetic, for within a few years the last of the Severans, Alexander, marched east to inaugurate an apparently never-ending cycle of armed confrontations with the aggressive Sassanids, who had lately risen from the ashes of the Parthian dynasty and were determined to restore the ancient Persian empire in all its former glory. Persia/Parthia was a case apart. Most emperors, whatever the nature of their official pronouncements, valued consolidation and stability above expansion and concomitant insecurity. The *limes*, a strategic system based on linear frontiers, its characteristic features regular forts, walls, palisades, fences and roads, was a product of this preference.

The Roman empire, then, extended far beyond the Mediterranean world. Yet throughout the period of the Principate, from about 27 BC to AD 235, the political axis and cultural base of the empire were to be found in the Mediterranean.

Rome, Italy, and the political elite

Rome in the age of Augustus was the seat of emperors, the court and administration and the residence of close on a million people. Rome was essentially a parasite city, feeding off the manpower and wealth of Italy and the numerous provinces that made up the Roman empire. The dramatic growth of the capital city in the two centuries before Augustus, in the course of which its population may have quintupled, was achieved by high levels of immigration of destitute Italian peasants and enslaved provincials. Under the Principate, the influx from largely provincial sources continued and had to continue at a significant, if lower, rate, if the population was to stabilize at its Augustan level. Again, the expensive grain distributions, public works programmes and entertainments of the city of Rome were financed from imperial taxes and rents from public properties carved out from the territory of other states.

These revenues were drawn in large part from the provinces. Italy was not a province and was exempt from the direct tax on property and persons. This privileged status was retained until the end of the third century when Diocletian introduced a provincial administration into Italy and imposed a property and capitation tax.

Italy's special status was however gradually undermined in the course of the Principate by the influx of upper-class provincials into the senate and into the second rank of the Roman aristocracy, the equestrian order.[8] By the early third century Italians had lost their absolute majority in both orders. Moreover, provincials had replaced Italians as emperors by the turn of the first century. Trajan, Hadrian and Marcus Aurelius were of Spanish stock, the family of Antoninus Pius was Gallic in origin, and the Severan dynasty had its roots in the local aristocracy of Lepcis Magna on the cost of Libya. Nevertheless, Italians held more than their share of important posts throughout our period. Moreover, it was the Mediterranean regions not the northern provinces that shared with Italy the direction of the empire.

The Roman and Italian elite only slowly and reluctantly opened its ranks to provincials, and remained very selective in the areas allowed representation. Only Latin-speaking western provincials were received into the senate until late in the first century; thereafter individual Greek-speakers, mainly from the coastal and riverine areas of Greece and Asia Minor, were admitted, but most provincial senators were from the West, especially from the Mediterranean regions of the Iberian peninsula, France and the north African provinces.

The progressive but eccentric emperor Claudius gave encouragement to the politically ambitious leaders of the Aedui of Autun, traditionally the most loyal of the tribes within the Three Gauls (that part of Gaul conquered by Julius Caesar in the 50s BC, as distinct from the Gallic province fashioned out of Provence and the Rhône valley in the 120s BC). Claudius ruled that the Aedui and their fellow countrymen were eligible for membership of the Roman senate, and he pressed his view on the senate itself. If we wish, we can credit Claudius with a concept of the unity of the Roman world, a world in which the conquered, whatever their race, profited as much as the conquerors from the Roman peace. It is not in fact easy to extract this vision from the exceedingly tentative and engagingly pedantic speech that survives in part on the so-called Lyon tablet and also in summary form in Tacitus (*ILS* 212; Tacitus, *Ann.*

---

[8] See Sherwin-White (1973), 259ff. with bibliography; Saller (1982), ch.5.

11.24-5.1). Claudius' conceptions were certainly much more advanced than those of the majority of senators, who, to judge from the speech itself, were disinclined to accept non-Italians of any kind into their ranks. But his intervention had very little effect on the composition of the senatorial order. Apart from Iulius Vindex who as governor of Gallia Lugdunensis rebelled against Nero in AD 68, and perhaps his father, there are no known senators from the Three Gauls in the Julio-Claudian era (Augustus to Nero).

In this same period a few Gallic chieftains, men like C. Iulius Victor (who advertised his Celtic origins on inscriptions: son of Congonneto-dunus, grandson of Acedomopas), are known to have served in or around their own province as army officers of equestrian rank. From the Roman point of view this was a limited reward for loyalty. Such men had typically held the post of provincial high priest of the imperial cult.[9] Their employment in positions of authority in the army was evidently considered a relatively safe gamble. It must also have seemed logical to make use of Gauls as leaders as well as rank-and-file soldiers in the native, 'auxiliary', regiments. However, Gauls did not command the troops of first rank, the legions. Nor did army officers move on to imperial administrative posts; the Gallic financial official (procurator) C. Iulius Alpinus Classicianus is a rarity in the Julio-Claudian period. The judgment that 'down to AD 69 the admission of Gallic gentry to the Roman administrative class was proceeding normally' is unjustified.[10]

No breakthrough was made by Gaul or the northern provinces as a whole in the hundred years that followed.[11] A mere handful of senators and equestrian military men are known (and the latter did not pursue full careers in the imperial service) to be set alongside an ever-increasing list of provincial senators, officials with responsibilities for finance, and army officers from the Mediterranean provinces.

It is difficult to fit into this pattern the career of one Marcus Valerius Maximianus from Ptuj in Yugoslavia, the Trajanic colony of Poetovio in the province of Upper Pannonia.[12] We know nothing of his education, but can assume that it played little part in his rapid promotion to equestrian and then senatorial rank, by special appointment of the emperor Marcus Aurelius. What influenced Marcus in his favour was his distinction as a soldier and leader of men, shown in a succession of special military missions. In the reign of Marcus (AD 161-80) the Roman world was given

---

[9] Victor: *CIL* XIII 1042-5, 1037; cf. *AE* 1888, 51,170. Consult Devijver (1976-1980), vol.3, Geographica A 1143ff., C 1153ff., etc.

[10] Sherwin-White (1967), 55. Classicianus: Tacitus, *Ann*.14.38.

[11] Pflaum (1950), 183ff., 186,190ff.; Devijver (n.9); Millar (1964), 184ff.; Sasel (1982), Burnand (1982), and contributions by A.R. Birley and W. Eck in the same volume; Alföldy (1978); Drinkwater (1979), and for a fuller treatment, Drinkwater (1983).

[12] *AE* 1956, 124, with Pflaum (1960), no. 181 bis + add.; Mócsy, *PW* Suppl. s.v. 'Pannonia' IX. 2.713-4.

a preview of what the tribes across the northern frontier could do if they got together. A coalition of German tribes poured across the Rhine and penetrated as far as north Italy. The flimsiness of the defence line, and no doubt the weakness of the high command, were exposed. Maximianus (a Danubian, not a Gaul or Briton) may have been a rare bird; there are few known parallels.[13] We are not justified in inferring that it was part of Marcus' regular strategy to promote to senatorial rank first-rate military men from frontier provinces, so that he could award them army commands without breaking the convention that such commands were for senators.

Septimius Severus is commonly credited with the more radical step of appointing equestrian prefects to the command of his newly created legions, thus beginning a trend that culminated in the virtual exclusion of senators from army commands by the end of the third century. He is also thought to have changed the pattern of promotion, in that he made it easier for the ordinary soldier to rise through the ranks and hold a commission. As in the case of Marcus, so with Septimius Severus: one must be careful not to exaggerate the scale of his innovations or even their innovatory character.[14] Decisive change did not precede the collapse of the Severan dynasty in 235. In the century that followed, the direction of the Roman empire was placed firmly in the hands of military men from the Balkan provinces. In our period, however, the domination of the Mediterranean governing class was undisturbed.

The causes are multiple, and sometimes intangible. Local loyalties were a salient factor. They operated within the Mediterranean sphere as well. It would be absurd to dub as failures the numerous local politicians who did not engage in public careers outside their cities and provinces – including men as distinguished as Dio of Prusa in Asia Minor, Plutarch of Chaeronea in Greece, and Apuleius from Madauros in Africa.[15] That would be to underrate the strength of local patriotism and the willingness of leading men to satisfy their ambitions at home. To these considerations we can add, with varying degrees of applicability, distance from Rome, inadequate financial resources and, among the better informed, an appreciation of the uncertainties and perils of politics in the capital. But especially in the northern provinces social and cultural considerations are crucial: the relative weakness of urbanization and the values associated with it and therefore the maintenance of traditional structures and ways of life. These factors operated in both directions, to rebuff those who sought imperial careers and to discourage those who were in principle eligible.

[13] 'In the course of the next sixty years Danubian senators are far to seek' Syme (1971), 180. Cf. the meteoric rise and sudden fall of Aelius Triccianus in the next generation, *PIR*[2] A 271.

[14] Campbell (1984), 408-9 with bibliography.

[15] A.H.M. Jones (1974), ch.5; C.P. Jones (1971) (1978); d'Escurac (1974).

The sources do not catch for us either the stifling of ambition at source or its rejection by emperors and their advisers. But contemporary literature, the creation of spokesmen of the imperial political and cultural elite, reveals attitudes that help to explain the absence of Northerners from high office and the Mediterranean orientation of the empire throughout our period.

Civilization and its limits

Two of Augustus' strategic aims, the conquest of the North, and the reconciliation of the Greek world to Rome, present a sharp contrast. Less than two generations earlier, Roman rule in the eastern Mediterranean had barely survived the rebellion of Mithridates VI of Pontus and his Greek-speaking allies. The fearful revenge taken by the Romans and the succession of civil wars that they proceeded to fight on Greek soil did nothing to lessen Greek hostility to Roman rule. Yet this period of crisis in Greek-Roman relations also witnessed two related, positive developments: the progressive acknowledgment by educated Romans of the superiority of Greek culture, and the forging of links of mutual interest between individual Roman and Greek aristocratic families. Augustus' aim and achievement were to foster the mutual dependence of Romans and Greeks and thereby secure the empire and broaden its base. In this he was aided by men of letters from the Greek-speaking parts of the empire. Among those who moved to Rome it is Dionysius of Halicarnassos, with his message that Romans were actually Greek in origin and culture, who catches the eye. However, the most rounded vision of the unity of the Graeco-Roman world, and the fullest exploration of its cultural limits, is provided by Strabo, a man from the Pontus whose ancestors had been active partisans of Mithridates.[16]

The distinction between the civilized and uncivilized is a recurring motif in Strabo. This distinction embraces, in the first place, the division between plain and mountain. Civilization was an urban phenomenon, centring on the *polis*, the self-governing town or city-state; and the urban life with which Strabo was familiar, in southern Europe and Asia Minor, was concentrated in a narrow coastal fringe hemmed in by impressive and daunting mountain ranges. (In the south and south-east it was the desert that limited the penetration of urban civilization.) Strabo presents a picture of Europe as a continent in which plain and mountain coexist, the inhabitants of the plain preserving a dominant role with the aid of the political authorities: 'The whole of it is diversified with plains and mountains, so that throughout its entire extent the agricultural and civilized element dwells side by side with the war-like element; but of the

---

[16] Bowersock (1965); Crawford (1978).

two elements the one that is peace-loving is more numerous and therefore keeps control over the whole body; and the leading nations too – formerly the Greeks and later the Macedonians and the Romans – have taken hold and helped' (127).

Elsewhere we are told how the Romans 'helped' not just by taming the wild men of the hills, but by bringing them down to the valleys and converting them into sedentary farmers. Thus, when the Romans extended their advance into the interior Iberian peninsula in the reign of Augustus, the symbol of their success was held to be the abandonment by the conquered tribes of their hill-top refuges and their resettlement as communities of farmers in the plain, preferably within the territory and juridical and fiscal control of an urban centre. The strategy was apparently successful among the Turdetani of Baetica, the southern Spanish province (151), less so among the Lusitani and the northern tribes, who after the conquest still lived on goat's milk, ate acorn-bread for two-thirds of the year, drank beer not wine, used butter not olive oil, and exchanged by barter (154). Strabo was aware that goods were exchanged between mountain and plain, that for example the Ligurians brought down to Genua flocks, hides, honey and timber and took back olive oil and wine (they drank for preference milk and a beverage made of barley). But it was his conviction that the mountain peoples were forced into such exchange relationships by the poverty of their own territory, and that their natural instinct was to plunder (202). Throughout antiquity mountains preserved their reputation among the cultured urban elite as the haunt of the brigand, the barbarian and the savage, man and beast.

Besides the mountain – and in the south the desert, whose nomadic inhabitants 'are driven by poverty and by wretched soil or climate to resort to their kind of life ... being more often root-eaters than meat-eaters, and using milk and cheese for food' (833 cf. 839) – the north of Europe removed from the Mediterranean was condemned as uncivilized. The comment of Diodorus the Sicilian on the Celts of Gaul is typical: 'Since temperateness of climate is destroyed by the excessive cold, the land produces neither wine nor oil, and as a consequence those Gauls who are deprived of these fruits make a drink out of barley which they call *zythos* or beer, and they also drink the water with which they cleanse their honeycombs. The Gauls are exceedingly addicted to the use of wine and fill themselves with the wine brought into their country by merchants, drinking it unmixed, and since they partake of this drink without moderation by reason of their craving for it, when they are drunken they fall into a stupor or a state of madness. Consequently, many of the Italian traders, induced by the love of money that characterizes them, believe that the love of wine of these Gauls is their own godsend' (5.26.2-3).[17]

---

[17] Cf. Strabo 155,186,197 on the Celts of north Gaul. Cicero, *pro Font.* 27-36 criticized the Gauls, but also disapproved of all provincials. See Brunt (1978), 185ff. Romans had not

Diodorus was writing shortly before the great period of expansion under Augustus. Strabo lived through this period: 'At the present the Romans are carrying on a war against the Germans, setting out from the Celtic regions ... and have already glorified the fatherland with some triumphs over them' (287). Strabo's words imply that Rome's mission in the North was essentially one of conquest rather than the spread of Graeco-Roman civilization.[18] In another passage the impact of Rome on the way of life of the conquered barbarians is tacitly recognized: 'The Romans too took over many nations that were naturally savage owing to the regions they inhabited, because those regions were either rocky or without harbours or cold or for some other reason ill-suited to habitation by any number. Thus they not only brought into communication with each other peoples who had been isolated, but also taught the more savage how to live under forms of government' (127). The approach of the Roman government was essentially pragmatic, its cultural objectives limited. The frontier peoples were to be tamed, neutralized and exploited. The exposure of conquered barbarians to a superior way of life was part of this policy, but a means to that end, not an end in itself.

Strabo's cultural prejudice is allied to ignorance. He knew that the expansion of Rome (rather than the industrious research of geographers) had significantly increased men's knowledge of the North (14; 117-18),[19] but did not himself tap these new sources of information. Thus in his discussion of Gallic geography Strabo seems more interested in scoring off Pytheas the geographer from Marseilles of the fourth century BC than in learning from Caesar. One must of course be careful when evaluating geographers of antiquity to avoid making anachronistic judgments. The ancients lived with only a partial knowledge even of that part of the world with which they were familiar. Estimates of the length and breadth of the Mediterranean and distances within it varied greatly, while Pliny miscalculated the length of Italy, his home country, by about 400 Roman miles (*HN* 3.43). In antiquity distance was measured in travel-time, which was far from constant, especially at sea. No one therefore would have been surprised let alone shocked by Strabo's apparent lack of interest in seeking to acquire and pass on precise information, as exemplified in the following passage: 'Now a country is well-defined when it is possible to define it by rivers or mountains or sea; and also by a tribe or tribes, by a size of such and such proportions, and by shape where this is possible. But in every case, in lieu of a geometric definition, a simple and roughly outlined definition is sufficient. So, as regards a country's size, it is sufficient if you state its greatest length and breadth;

---

forgotten the *terror Gallicus*, the shock of the sack of Rome in about 386 BC. See Peyre (1970).

[18] See n.7 above.

[19] See Thomson (1948), 192ff.; Pédech (1976), 150ff.; cf. Lasserre (1982).

and as regards shape, if you liken a country to one of the geometric figures (Sicily for example to a triangle) or to one of the other well-known figures (for instance, Iberia to an oxhide, the Peloponnesos to a leaf of a plane tree)' (83). The Roman army imposed a modicum of order by laying down and measuring out in Roman miles or a local equivalent an arterial road system, and by building up a body of reasonably accurate information on particular localities. But outside the military, confusion reigned and was tolerated.

In Strabo's case the ignorance, which most men shared, of the basic geography of non-Mediterranean Europe was compounded by lack of interest, no doubt a by-product of his cultural bias. Strabo accompanied his patron the prefect of Egypt, Aelius Gallus, on his exploratory voyage down the Nile, but did not penetrate north (or west) of Italy.

For a provincial's appreciation of the empire in the golden age of its development, the middle of the second century AD, it is customary to turn to Aelius Aristides, the sophist and rhetorician from the town of Hadrianoutherae inland from Pergamum in Asia Minor. It was Aristides who hailed the fulfilment of Claudius' dream of the *orbis Romanus*, of Rome as the *communis patria* of the world. 'You have caused the word "Roman" to belong not to a city, but to be the name of a sort of common race, and this not one out of all the races, but a balance to all the remaining ones. You do not now divide the races into Greeks and barbarians ... you have divided people into Romans and non-Romans. Yet no envy walks in your empire. For you yourselves were the first not to begrudge anything, since you made everything available to all in common and granted to those who are capable not to be subjects rather than rulers in turn' (26.63,65).

The most convincing aspect of Aristides' oration 'To Rome' is its firm Hellenocentricity. Rome's great achievement in the eyes of the Greek world and Aristides its representative was to promote a renaissance of Hellenic urban culture and civilization: 'Now all the Greek cities flourish under you, and the offerings in them, the arts, all their embellishments bring honour to you, as an adornment in a suburb' (26.94). 'You continually care for the Greeks as if they were your foster fathers, protecting them, and as it were resurrecting them, giving freedom and self-rule to the best of them' (26.96). The unity of the world under Rome symbolized by the spread of the Roman citizenship was a secondary consideration. Aristides pays lip-service to the Roman/non-Roman distinction, slipping back easily into the traditional division of the world between Greeks and barbarians. Roman citizenship was only sparsely distributed in the Greek East, even among the provincial upper classes. In the province of Lycia/Pamphylia in south-west Asia Minor, fewer than half of about a hundred known holders of the provincial high priesthood, the highest local office, were Roman citizens before the turn of the second century AD. Caracalla, the elder son of Septimius Severus, changed all this by conferring citizenship at a stroke on almost all free inhabitants of the empire by an edict of AD 212. Meanwhile, Aelius Aristides all but ignored the non-Mediterranean world. Its existence is acknowledged only by a brief reference to frontier warfare and the constant reminder of the cultural cleavage between Greeks and barbarians, whose education at the hands of the Romans is compared with horse-training (26.70,96).[20]

The opinions of Cassius Dio from Nicaea in north-west Asia Minor (not far from Strabo's Amaseia near the south Black Sea coast, and even closer to the inland town of Hadrianoutherae, Aristides' birthplace) are of particular significance.[21] He was a senator, a member of the Roman governing class; he lived right at the end of our period and might therefore have been expected to reflect two centuries of social transformation in the frontier regions. We might note in passing his total ignorance of the geography of Britain, the scene of a war waged by Septimius Severus in 208-11 (76.12.5; cf. 39.50.2), and his curiously selective ethnography, which is entirely devoted to the wild and colourful Caledonians and Macatae against whom the military effort was directed. Only the barest recognition is afforded the non-hostile, even friendly, province of Britain from which Severus launched his expedition (76.12.1-13.4). But it is Dio's treatment of the Pannonians that deserves the closest scrutiny. Dio had served as legate of the Danubian province of Upper Pannonia and therefore, as he himself insists, was writing from knowledge (49.36.4). The Danubian army constituted the largest concentration of frontier troops in the empire, about ten legions plus auxiliary regiments. In unstable times this army was a potent political force. In 193 Septimius Severus held Upper Pannonia as governor and was carried to power on the backs of the Danubian legions. Before long, the army, which drew its recruits from the region, would promote men of local origin who had risen through the ranks. Maximinus, a huge and heroic soldier from the province of Lower Moesia who replaced the last of the Severans, Severus Alexander, was merely the first of a series of Balkan emperors culminating in the great conservative reformer Diocletian.

Cassius Dio has nothing to say of the consulship (in about 187) or earlier career of Maximianus the soldier from Ptuj or its implications for the future, though he is interested in the irregular progress of one Aelius Triccianus. If Dio's account of his career is complete, this rank-and-file

---

[20] See the commentary on *Oration* 26 by J.H. Oliver, 'The Ruling Power', *Trans. Amer. Phil. Soc.* 43 (1953). For Greeks and barbarians, *Or.* 26.96, 100; cf. 35.20,36 (authorship and date uncertain). It is perhaps implied that Romans were to be interpreted as honorary Greeks. For an explicit evocation of this theme, see Dion. Hal. 1.89.1-2. For Lycian priests, see Magie (1950) App. II E. 1609-12. Around 25-30 per cent of Asian priests (*archiereis* and asiarchs) are aliens or Aurelii.

[21] For Cassius Dio, Millar (1964). Syme (1971), ch.11-12 is best on Maximinus and his successors and the strategic significance of the Balkans.

soldier in the Pannonian army became in succession doorkeeper of the legate of Pannonia, prefect of one of the new Parthian legions (under Caracalla, AD 198-217), prefect of the legion stationed on the Alban mount (under the short-lived emperor Macrinus, in AD 217-18), senator by special adlection, and governor of Pannonia Inferior before his death by order of the emperor Elagabalus (218-22). Dio brands him an upstart and implies that his promotion had attracted criticism. But something is said in his favour: he died because he had annoyed the men of the Alban legion with the strictness of his discipline.[22] About ten years later ex-legionary soldiers were baying for the blood of another ex-governor of a Pannonian province for precisely the same reason (the same words are used). The man concerned – it was Dio himself – after having served as consul for the second time in AD 229, abandoned Rome and Italy forever for his native province on the advice of an emperor, Severus Alexander, who could honour but not protect him (80.4.2ff.). The threat came from the soldiers of the praetorian guard, who had once been men from Italy, Spain, Macedonia and Noricum 'of rather respectable appearance and simple habits' but, since the triumphant entry of Septimius Severus into the city in 193, had become Danubians 'most savage in appearance, most terrifying in speech, and most boorish in conversation' (75.2.4-5). Nursing a bad leg and his dignity in Bithynia, Dio produced this considered opinion of the Pannonians as a race: 'The Pannonians dwell near Dalmatia along the bank of the Danube from Noricum to Moesia, and live of all men the most wretchedly. Both their soil and climate are poor; they cultivate no olives and produce no wine except to a very slight extent and of a very poor quality, since the climate is mostly extremely harsh. They not only eat barley and millet but drink liquids made from them. For having nothing to make a civilized life worthwhile, they are extremely fierce and bloodthirsty' (49.36.4).[23]

Of writers from the western Mediterranean, Tacitus (perhaps a native of the old Gallic province of Narbonensis) is the most important source on Germany, Gaul and Britain.[24] Within his sphere of interest, however, he was very selective. Rome's opponents held considerable fascination for him, especially the Germans, whose customs and institutions are given extended treatment in a monograph. He had an eye for heroic leadership, and derived wry pleasure from ascribing to Rome's most dangerous opponents, whether Arminius the German, Civilis the Gaul or Boudicca the Briton, virtues that he believed the Romans as a people had abandoned – in particular, love of liberty. Once enemies became subjects, however, Tacitus lost interest in them. The unconquered and perhaps unconquerable Germans receive monographic treatment, not the conquered Gauls.

[22] Cassius Dio 78.13.3-4; 79.4.3. Full refs. in *PIR*[2] A 271.
[23] Cf. Herodian 2.9.11; 4.7.3; 7.1.1ff.
[24] Syme (1958), esp. 453ff.; Sherwin-White (1967), ch. 2; Thomson (1948), 242ff.

In a well-known but unique passage (*Agr*.19-21), Tacitus outlines the Romanizing policy of his father-in-law Agricola in the province of Britain, of which he was governor in AD 78-84. Agricola saw his brief as to lead British tribal chieftains and their sons to live an urban life, receive a Roman education and adopt Roman customs. The motive is clear, to turn a nation of warriors into peaceful subjects. The passage is damning of the British tribal aristocracy, characterized as people 'without settled communities or culture', easily roused to war. Once introduced to urban life, they fell for its baser attractions, and imagined in their innocence or ignorance that they had found civilization. On the contrary, they had given up liberty for slavery, under the artful supervision of the Roman authorities.

The same passage obliquely acknowledges that the identical process had been going on in Gaul. Agricola is alleged to have thought that British native intelligence more than made up for Gallic training. A casual detail in the *Annals* of Tacitus under the year AD 21 comes to mind: sons of Gallic chieftains in pursuit of a Roman education at Autun (Augustodunum) were taken as hostages by the rebels C. Iulius Florus and C. Iulius Sacrovir (3.41.3). The item conveys a message about the limits of Romanization. Here the cause of Gallic liberty won a symbolic victory over the slavery of Romanization. The rebels were tribal chieftains, beneficiaries of Rome (they bore the names of Caesar), who had presumably themselves been exposed to a version of the Roman provincial educational system. Of some more dangerous enemies of Rome it was written that they 'possessed not only a knowledge of Roman discipline but also of the Roman tongue, many also had some measure of literary culture, and the exercise of the intellect was not uncommon among them'. This appraisal of the Pannonian rebels of AD 6 by the underrated contemporary historian Velleius Paterculus (2.110.4) has puzzled modern commentators, but Tacitus would have seen the point (and ignored the exaggeration).[25]

The rebels of AD 21 were put down relatively quickly. But Romans must have wondered whether the balance could ever be tipped permanently against Gallic liberty. Doubts would have been confirmed by the events of 68-70, when first Iulius Vindex and then Iulius Civilis raised the banner of revolt. The former was a provincial governor. In the account of Tacitus, the Roman general Petillius Cerialis, eventual conqueror of Iulius Civilis, declared before the assembled Treviri and Lingones that the gulf between Romans and Gauls had been bridged. Gauls were in command of legions, conquerors and conquered were partners in empire. The claims are hollow. They would have convinced or attracted few Romans.

The pacification process in the British and Gallic provinces was

[25] See Mócsy (1983).

incomplete in the age of Tacitus (he died in the 120s). 'More like Italy than a province' was the elder Pliny's verdict on the old Gallic province of Narbonensis, essentially the south of France (*HN* 3.31). Uncertainty over Tacitus' own origin (south France or north Italy?) is symbolic. Almost two centuries of occupation and pacification, colonization and immigration, building on the climatic resemblances with and physical proximity to Italy, had produced a remarkable similarity of institutions and culture. But the rest of Gaul, and Britain, remained essentially unchanged. Their basic structure was tribal, not urban. But without thoroughgoing urbanization, there was no prospect of an integrated Graeco-Roman-Celtic society.

What however of the men of Illyricum, the great central land mass of the Balkans? We have to wait a century and a half for an appreciation of the men who saved the Roman empire in the third century. The African Aurelius Victor, a governor in Pannonia in the mid-fourth century, wrote: 'Their fatherland was Illyricum; and although they had little concern with liberal culture, yet seasoned in the hardships of the farm and the camp, they proved best for the state' (*Caes.* 39.26). Velleius' educated rebels had become Victor's ill-educated heroes.[26]

We might, in sum, have imagined that the perspective of commentators and observers would have altered, as information on the North was acquired and disseminated, and as Rome was seen to be making an impact on the northern peoples. In fact, it is impossible to detect in literature any softening of attitude or any positive response to cultural and political change in the area from north-west Gaul and Britain to the Lower Danube. From Strabo to Cassius Dio, from the beginning to the end of our period, the cultural elite of the empire drew a firm line between what they saw as the Mediterranean core of the empire and its barbaric periphery. In particular, the conquest of the North did not in their view produce a broader cultural unity. Rome broadened its governmental and cultural base, but not to the extent of assimilating the North.

[26] Den Boer (1972), e.g. 87ff.; Bird (1984), ch. 5-6.

CHAPTER TWO

Government without Bureaucracy

Introduction

The Romans controlled an empire far flung by any historical standards. They did not, however, develop an imperial administration that matched the dimensions of the empire. A rudimentary apparatus of officialdom sufficed a government whose concerns were limited to essentials. The basic goals of the government were twofold: the maintenance of law and order, and the collection of taxes. Taxes were needed for wages, military expenses and to provide shows, buildings and handouts of food or cash in the capital city. To achieve these very limited aims the early emperors took the Republican system of senatorial administration and expanded it, creating more posts for senators, but in addition employing for the first time in positions of public responsibility non-elective officials, men from the equestrian order, or lesser aristocracy, and, more controversially, slaves and freedmen of their own household.[1]

Expansion in the number of posts and diversification in the social background of officials do not in themselves entail a more rationalized or bureaucratic administrative system. The functions of government remained essentially the same. The emperors brought in no sweeping social and economic reforms, and were not interested in interfering to any substantial degree in the lives of their subjects. Hence there was no dramatic increase in the number of centrally appointed officials. The Roman empire remained undergoverned, certainly by comparison with the Chinese empire, which employed, proportionately, perhaps twenty times the number of functionaries.[2] Meanwhile the operation of patronage rather than the application of formal procedures and rules determined the admission and promotion of administrators, who were not and never became 'professionals'.

Again, there was substantial continuity in administrative practices. The limited financial ends of the government were achieved without recourse to economic *dirigisme*. The state did not seek to exercise control over the production and distribution of goods. There were no state factories, no state merchant fleets, and although the emperor's landed possessions steadily grew as property was confiscated, legated or simply

[1] Millar (1967) remains the best introduction to the subject of government.
[2] Hopkins (1983b), 186.

left vacant, the resources required by the state came in the main not from the imperial properties but as tax from the provincial population.

A fiscal policy was needed, though not an elaborate one. The nature of the tax system that evolved in the early empire reflects the restricted purposes it was intended to serve: it was unstandardized, undersupervised and it underwent little change.[3] Thus the diversity of local procedure that was a hallmark of the Republican taxation system – so that for example the main direct tax (*tributum*) was paid by Spaniards in the form of a lump sum and by Sicilians as a quota of produce (a tithe) – did not disappear under the Principate. It remained the Roman custom where possible to follow the practices established by the previous rulers in any particular area, whether Carthaginians, Seleucids or Ptolemies. Emperors instituted regular provincial censuses, gradually phased out the Republican system of letting out contracts to private companies for the collection of direct (and later indirect) taxes, and in general raised taxes more effectively than any Republican government had done, and from a much larger empire. But these developments were not part of any drive for administrative uniformity such as might be associated with bureaucratic government.

If the government's fiscal policy was only rudimentary, it is not clear that it can be said to have had a regular monetary policy at all.[4] When faced with financial emergency or simply a pressing need for more cash, the central authorities tended to fall back on another solution, the debasement of the coinage. It is difficult to accept that emperors and officials, their attention fixed on the short-term advantages of debasement, appreciated the long-term consequences. They possessed only a limited empirical understanding of economic concepts and the working of the economy.

Central and provincial administration

There were around forty provinces in the Roman empire governed by a thin spread of centrally appointed officials. The proconsul of Africa stood over a vast expanse of territory comprising much of modern Libya, Tunisia and eastern Algeria, while his counterpart in the province of Asia governed the western coast of Turkey plus a substantial tract of land in the interior. Each official was assigned a single junior senatorial magistrate with financial responsibilities (quaestor). He took with him an advisory panel of friends or protégés (including one or more senatorial legates as potential deputies) and a small staff of minor officials of low rank (freedmen or slaves).

for each province

---

[3] A.H.M. Jones (1974), ch. 8, with Brunt's addenda.
[4] Contrasting views in Crawford (1970), Hopkins (1980), Lo Cascio (1981).

Government under the Republic was by proconsuls, ex-magistrates of senior standing (praetors or consuls) appointed by lot by the senate. Augustus took responsibility himself for those provinces where a continuous military presence was required, and entrusted them to officials appointed by him, of whom the most important were also of senatorial status (*legati Augusti*).

The organization of personnel was somewhat different in those provinces under the emperor's control, but the numbers involved were no greater. In the major provinces, with the exception of Egypt, the emperor appointed a legate to govern in his stead from among the ex-praetors and ex-consuls, while the responsibility for finance fell to a procurator rather than a quaestor, an equestrian rather than a senator. Another group of provinces was governed by equestrian appointees, again responsible directly to the emperor. Foremost among these was Egypt, controlled by a prefect and lesser equestrian officials, and the only province with legions to be regularly governed by an equestrian.[5] The other equestrian provinces were small enough to be run by a procurator, who heard legal cases, managed financial affairs and commanded auxiliary units of the army, if any were assigned to the province.

The number of officials of senatorial rank employed in the provinces experienced no significant increase in our period. In the late first century and early second century we begin to hear of officials with judicial responsibilities, but this was clearly not an empire-wide or a permanent phenomenon. Two jurists are known to have held the post of *iuridicus* in Britain in the last decades of the first century, and one man with no special qualifications, the future emperor Septimius Severus, was apparently *iuridicus* in one of the Spanish provinces in about AD 177. Hadrian is said to have appointed four *iudices* of consular rank for Italy. In later reigns these were renamed or superseded by *iuridici*. Italy, not officially a province, was traditionally controlled by the consuls and the senate, but by the late second century jurisdiction in Italy as in Rome had been taken over by other officials more closely associated with the emperor. The urban prefect of the city of Rome, a senior senator, had jurisdiction up to the one hundredth milepost, and beyond this, the praetorian prefect, a high-placed equestrian official. The *iuridici* fit into the picture as subordinate judicial magistrates; their emergence in Italy is one of several signs that Italy was losing its special status and being gradually brought into line with the provinces of the empire.[6]

From the same period, the late first century AD, city curators (*curatores rei publicae*) begin to be appointed in some cities with financial responsibilities. Again, the curators are likely to have been

---

[5] Brunt (1975a).

[6] *Iuridici*: *ILS* 1015, *CIL* IX 5533, *SHA Sev.*3.4, *Hadr.*22, *Ant.Pius* 2, *Marcus* 11; Appian, *BC* 1.38, *CIL* V 1874 etc., with Eck (1979), 247ff.

[handwritten margin notes at top: "proconsuls - junior / legati - procurators / procurators / prefects"]

employed only to a limited extent, and the post was far from being the exclusive property of senators.[7]

It was in the equestrian administration that the greatest changes took place, not only growth but also the unification of disparate elements into a single hierarchy. In the empire at large one development was the appointment of equestrians to govern Egypt and several minor provinces. In the latter such officials had at first a military title, prefect, and predominantly military duties. Their appointment and their brief is testimony to the determination of the emperors to bring to heel hitherto unsubjugated peoples within their empire (as in the Alps, central Sardinia or Judaea). The replacement from the reign of Claudius of prefect by procurator, a civilian title, was designed to reflect the success (sometimes as in Judaea more apparent than real) of the pacification process in the areas concerned. Secondly, emperors appointed equestrians (and sometimes freedmen) with the title of procurator of Augustus as their financial agents, with the task of superintending the imperial properties. Thirdly, procurators appear in the provinces as tax officials, collecting customs dues, the inheritance tax and other indirect taxes. The officials in these last two categories were potentially influential, and sometimes acted as a counterweight to the senatorial officials, but they cannot be said to have increased the administrative burden on the cities.

[handwritten margin notes: "equests as procurators military"]

Finally, the military function of the equestrian order should be stressed. There were around 360 posts annually available for senior officers of equestrian rank: prefectures of cohorts, military tribunates and prefectures of *alae* (cavalry units). Progression through this series of posts, which were already being termed the equestrian *militiae* by the reign of Augustus' successor Tiberius (Velleius Paterculus 2.111), was a necessary precursor to the tenure of posts in the civil administration. The careers (and, because of mortality patterns, the lives) of many equestrians proceeded no further. Military service must be seen as the basis of the equestrian career.[8]

Developments in Rome and in the imperial court affected both equestrian and senatorial careers. The emperors gave the city of Rome for the first time a continuous administration. By the end of the reign of Augustus there existed a 'police' force, a fire department and an office for the grain supply. These prefectures fell to a senior senator and two equestrians (*praefectus vigilum, praefectus annonae*). Another leading equestrian was appointed praetorian prefect, commander of the emperor's elite bodyguard, the praetorian guard. Because of his proximity to the emperor and control of troops in the vicinity of the

---

[7] On city curators, see Burton (1979), Duthoy (1979), Jacques (1984).

[8] See esp. Nicolet (1984). For early posts see Sherwin-White (1940), A.H.M. Jones (1960), 115-25. On procuratorial jurisdiction, dating from Claudius, Brunt (1966b). On the political significance of the creation of the equestrian administration, Brunt (1983).

capital, the praetorian prefect's power was considerable: to hinder its abuse two prefects were usually appointed.[9]

The structure of the central financial administration has been the subject of debate, much of it stemming from the various possible meanings of the word *fiscus*. The main treasury, the *aerarium*, into which provincial taxes flowed, was headed by a pair of prefects who were chosen by the emperor from the ranks of former praetors. Similar officials were appointed over the military treasury (*aerarium militare*) created by Augustus to provide benefits for veterans on retirement. Much of the fiscal responsibility, however, lay not with these men, but with the emperor's freedmen and then from the middle of the first century with a high-ranking equestrian procurator (*a rationibus*), who with a staff of imperial freedmen and slaves kept accounts of the empire's revenues and expenditures.[10] It does not follow from the fact that these accounts were kept by the emperor's slaves and freedmen that there was no division between public finances and those of the imperial household.[11] But in the end the distinction between the two may not have been of great practical importance, because the emperor subsidized the public treasuries with his own steadily increasing private wealth, and was empowered to draw on funds from the public treasuries for the administration of his provinces.

It remains to consider the roles of the emperor, his advisers and personal staff in the administration.[12] The emperor was ultimately responsible for policy decisions and the appointment of imperial officials, but in reaching his decisions he took advice from those around him. The good emperor, in the eyes of the aristocracy, found his advisers in his council (*consilium principis*), a group of leading senatorial and equestrian friends.

This council also advised the emperor in his legal capacities as a judge both of appeals and in the first instance, and as a formulator of new laws.[13] Some emperors, most notably Claudius (but also Nero and Commodus), aroused the aristocracy's anger by allowing themselves to be swayed by imperial freedmen, slaves or wives. In the case of freedmen and slaves, their power was a natural result of the access they gained to the emperor while helping him carry out routine duties, such as receiving reports from provincial officials and writing replies, and responding to petitions for favours or justice from cities and individual subjects.

[9] Vitucci (1956), with review by Cadoux, *JRS* 49 (1959), 152-60; Baillie-Reynolds (1926); d'Escurac (1977); Durry (1938).

[10] Boulvert (1970); Weaver (1972), pt. III.

[11] For example, emperors made ordinary private wills; they were not, in those, bequeathing public funds. For the debate, A.H.M. Jones (1960), 99-114; Millar (1963); Brunt (1966a).

[12] Millar (1977), ch.3.

[13] Crook (1955); Millar (1977), 110ff., 507ff.

However, the emperor also dealt with many letters and petitions personally.

We can see the essentials of this administrative system in operation already under Augustus: the employment of senators by the emperor in new administrative posts, filling out the senatorial career and bringing it more closely under imperial control;[14] the employment of equestrians and freedmen to non-elective posts as officials and agents, dependent on the emperor; the use of the imperial household, in effect, the emperor's domestic servants, as supporting staff. In later reigns greater order was introduced into the non-senatorial sections of the administration. By the early second century the procuratorial administrative posts (then about 60 in number) were divided into three categories according to the salary of the office-holder. A career structure comparable to that of senators could now be held to exist, with the great prefectures at the top and the lowest ranking procurators at the bottom.[15] Similarly, a clearly defined hierarchy of posts can be discerned in the imperial household itself (*familia Caesaris*). A slave on the clerical staff might hope for manumission and promotion to the position of record-keeper (*tabularius*) and finally to a freedman procuratorship.[16] Imperial freedmen and slaves continued to provide the permanent support staff of the administrative system.

For an understanding of how this administrative organization worked and where the power lay, it is important to know how the office-holders were appointed. The emperor ultimately made all the above-mentioned appointments except to the proconsulships and quaestorships, but it must still be asked how he made his decisions. This is an important question because it shapes our view of how bureaucratic the administration became under the Principate. Numerous scholars have held that during the second and early third centuries bureaucratic rules governed appointments and promotions to the point where the process became almost automatic, leaving the emperor little discretion.[17] Senatorial careers do exhibit certain patterns: ex-praetors holding senior posts in the emperor's service were usually promoted to the consulship while their contemporaries in the senate usually were not; moreover the emperor preferred to use men without consular ancestors as legates to govern his provinces. These regularities, however, do not constitute automatic promotions: the variety in the number and order of offices held, as well as the decreasing number of posts available at each succeeding level of promotion, suggest that emperors must have used their discretion in the appointment of senators and equestrians. In

---

[14] Morris (1964) (1965).

[15] See however Millar's review of Pflaum's work in *JRS* 53 (1963), 194-203.

[16] Weaver (1972), 224ff.; Boulvert (1974), 111-98, reviewed by P.R.C. Weaver, *Antichthon* 13 (1979), 70-102 and G.P. Burton, *JRS* 67 (1977), 163ff.

[17] See e.g. Birley (1953); Pflaum (1950); Eck (1974).

addition, our literary sources of the first and second centuries speak not of rules, but of personal factors, such as patronage, as being decisive in imperial appointments.[18]

In regard to promotions, and in other respects, the central administration of the Principate represents an advance in bureaucratic organization over the Republic, but the extent of the advance must not be exaggerated. The administration at its top levels remained amateurish. Senators and equestrians spent only a part of their working lives in office, they received no special training for their duties, and in the course of their careers they did not develop specialist expertise.[19] If there were any administrative 'professionals', they were the emperor's freedmen and slaves. Moreover, the numbers remained small enough (around 350 elite officials in Rome, Italy and the provinces in the Severan period) to make unnecessary the development of a hierarchy of responsibility: for the most part each senatorial or equestrian official was responsible directly to the emperor.

no political heirarchy

Cities

The secret of government without bureaucracy was the Roman system of cities which were self-governing and could provide for the needs of empire. The period of the Principate witnessed a striking multiplication and expansion of autonomous urban units, especially in those parts of the empire where cities had been few. Roman pragmatism rather than Greek cultural idealism lay behind this development. It was a characteristic Greek view that higher civilization was only attainable within the framework of the *polis*. The Romans were not equally dedicated to this belief, even when they fell under the influence of Greek culture. No Latin word for city (*civitas, municipium, colonia, res publica*) has the ideological potency of *polis*, while Latin literature can easily give the impression that the city was viewed as the seedbed of immorality rather than the seat of civilization.[20] As organizers of empire, the Romans rated most highly the administrative function of the city, without however losing sight of its potential role as a centre of Romanization in newly conquered and incompletely pacified areas. We shall inquire in a moment into the mechanisms by which cities performed their administrative tasks. First, it is necessary to explore, on the one hand, the diverse statuses of cities and, on the other, the common features that set cities apart from the countless subordinate communities in the empire.

[18] Saller (1982), ch.3; de Ste. Croix (1954).
[19] Campbell (1975) (1984), 325-47; Saller (1980).
[20] On the Greek view of the polis, see Martin (1984), ch.1. Contrast Varro 2 pref., 3 pref.

City statuses

The different statuses and privileges of cities were a heritage of the period of the Republic. The *colonia* and the *municipium* were standard in the West, but, especially in the case of the *municipium*, rare in the East. The *colonia* was essentially an extension of Rome. It was a community of Roman citizens established with a standard form of constitution modelled on that of Rome. Outside Italy colonies tended to be settlements of retired soldiers, but when veteran colonies were discontinued, in the early empire, *colonia* became an honorific title conferred by special grant, linking a city in its title with an emperor but carrying no substantive privileges.[21]

A *municipium* in theory possessed greater freedom than a *colonia* because it used its own laws and magistrates. This is reflected in the 'surprised' reaction of the early second-century emperor Hadrian to the request of the people of Italica in southern Spain (his town of origin) for 'promotion' from *municipium* to *colonia* (A. Gellius, *NA* 16.13.4-5). Italica was not alone in its ambitions: at least 120 Italian cities, more than a quarter of the whole, had converted from *municipia* to colonies by the end of the third century.[22] Hadrian was being perversely pedantic. The miscellanist Aulus Gellius, who recorded Hadrian's remarks made in a speech to the Roman senate, is not being unusually percipient when he comments that the two categories of city were virtually indistinguishable, but *colonia* had the higher status. The essential point is that *municipia* grew and spread in Republican Italy, and were exported overseas under the empire, in quite different historical circumstances. To put it simply, municipal status was won by Italy from Rome by dint of a bloody 'civil' war (the so-called Social War, war against the allies, of 91-89 BC), but was imposed on the western provinces as a standard Roman form of constitution for the purpose of consolidating Roman power. For this reason in Italian *municipia* Roman citizenship was the possession of all free inhabitants, but in the corresponding cities abroad it was bestowed as a rule only on the most eligible provincials: in some communities magistrates and ex-magistrates, in others local councillors (some of whom had held no magistracy).

Apart from the chances afforded prominent individuals for self-advancement, these 'chartered' cities, colonies or *municipia*, had no special material privileges, unless they were brought into line with all Italian cities by the award of 'Italian rights' (*ius Italicum*) carrying exemption from the land tax. Septimius Severus rewarded in this way his native city of Lepcis Magna, Carthage, and Utica in Africa, and civil war

[21] On the legal status of cities, see Sherwin-White (1973); A.H.M. Jones (1940), 113-46; Magie (1950), e.g. 966 n.85, 967 n.88; Nörr (1966); Millar (1977), 394-410; and n.23. On veteran colonies, Mann (1983); Keppie (1983).
[22] Keppie (1983), 211; Salmon (1971), 161-3.

partisans Tyre, Heliopolis and Laodicea in Syria (among others), but other emperors were much less generous (*Digest* 50.15.1).

The constitutions of the rest of the cities of the empire were as diverse as the cities themselves. The cities ranged all the way from the Greek *polis* with its elaborate and time-hallowed constitution to the tribal capital of Gaul and Britain, which tended to ape Roman constitutional practices. Within the cities there existed a number of privileged categories. Federate cities (*civitates foederatae*) were so called because they had struck treaties with Rome establishing their rights. Free cities (*civitates liberae*) were theoretically exempt from interference by the provincial governor. Free and immune cities (*civitates liberae et immunes*) possessed the additional privilege of immunity from taxation. Tax-exempt cities were always very rare, while the number of free cities declined in the course of the late Republic and early empire. A mere handful of western cities enjoyed free or federate status at any time. This goes back to the fact that in the West, outside the areas where Etruscan, Greek and Phoenician influence was strongly felt, the growth of cities was a late and largely unspontaneous development, coinciding with the spread of Roman power. Most provincial cities in the West were either new creations or grew up on or near the site of earlier communities of lesser significance. Thus the typical western city was always in principle subject to outside interference. In the East, in contrast, the Romans had to establish a *modus vivendi* with numerous city-states having proud and long-standing traditions of sovereignty. Nevertheless privileges were dispensed only selectively in the East. They were typically the reward for conspicuous service to the winning side during the civil wars staged by Roman generals in the eastern Mediterranean in the course of the first century BC. Thus for example Aphrodisias was rewarded with freedom and immunity by Octavian (Augustus) in 39 BC for its loyal support of the Julian cause after the death of Caesar.[23]

Cities and villages

Cities, despite their diverse traditions and character, did have something in common that distinguished them from communities of lower degree. A city was essentially a self-governing urban community, with a regular constitution centring on a council and magistrates and a rural territory under its jurisdiction and control. This is a political/administrative definition, squaring with the attitude of the central government, if not with that of representatives of the Greek-speaking or Hellenocentric elite, whose definition would have included cultural institutions, amenities and public buildings, whether purely decorative or utilitarian. However, when the Roman authorities are found making decisions as to the status of a particular community, practical considerations come to

[23] Reynolds (1982), docs. 6-13. On free and immune cities see also Bernhardt (1971).

the fore, in particular the potential viability of the community in economic and demographic terms. The interplay of formal and material requirements can be followed in the documents.

In an inscription of Orcistus, a town situated on the borders of Galatia in central Asia Minor, the citizens are shown seeking from the emperor Constantine an upgrading from village to city (*ILS* 6099). This was a lapsed city; as evidence of its former status, it was urged that it had once elected annual magistrates, had a council and a full complement of ordinary citizens; and that it still had baths, statues and aqueducts. It was also thought worthwhile to inform Constantine that Orcistus was a Christian community. But the crucial point to establish was that a city on the site would be a practical proposition. The emperor was informed that there was a plentiful water supply, and that the community stood at the meeting-point of four roads. The distance from the neighbouring cities is given precisely, perhaps with a view to showing that there was room in the region for another city with a territory of reasonable size. Orcistus was a dependency of one of those cities, Nacola, and judged its rule oppressive. It was standard practice for a city to exact financial contributions, services and manpower for its own benefit from the communities under its control.[24] As Strabo wrote of Nîmes (Nemausus) in Gaul: 'It has subject to its authority twenty-four villages that are exceptional in their supply of strong men, of stock like its own, and contribute towards its expenses' (186). Here we catch a glimpse of the way cities went about providing the imperial government with its revenue.

A second inscription from Galatia concerns the town of Tymandus, which petitioned an unknown emperor for the status of city (*ILS* 6090). We do not have the petition itself, but an imperial letter to an official. This states explicitly that it was the assurance of the Tymandeni that they could provide a sufficient number of local councillors that decided the issue in their favour.

A third inscription, dated to AD 158, shows Antoninus Pius in correspondence with a newly established city in the Strymon valley in Macedonia (*IGBulg*. IV 2263). The city was permitted to strengthen its financial base in two ways, by imposing a poll tax on free citizens in its territory, and by expanding its local council, or *boulê*, of 80 men, all liable to an entry-fee. A council of 80 reasonably wealthy men suggests a relatively substantial population base, and is something of a surprise in a remote Thracian village. Pius had presumably supplemented the existing population by drafting both rich and poor from nearby settlements, to create a community better endowed in population and resources than any pre-existing one. Nine villages contributed residents to Pizos on the Thracian sector of the *via Egnatia* when it was established

---

[24] On the city-territory relationship see Frederiksen (1976).

by Septimius Severus and Caracalla in AD 202 (*IGBulg.* III/2 1690). In rather different circumstances Augustus had herded Achaeans into Patrae and Aetolians into Nicopolis (Pausanias 7.18.7-8,10.38.4). Roman city-foundation from early days had a strongly coercive aspect.

That is not to say that communities such as those established in Macedonia and Thrace were invariably successful. No inscription from the site of the city in the Strymon is known after AD 238. It may be that our anonymous city soon after this date slipped back into its previous condition as an anonymous village. Some cities in rural areas of provinces such as Moesia Superior and Dalmatia had a history of this kind.[25] Such communities may never have acquired the outward form of cities or become centres of administration or social activity, partly no doubt because the councillors, who were intended to be the mainstay of the new foundations, preferred to live in their villages or on their estates. They had the name and status of cities but otherwise were not distinguishable from the independent villages that commonly prevailed where city life was underdeveloped, as in the interior of Syria or in central Asia Minor.[26]

Social and cultural considerations, therefore, played their part in influencing the success or failure of a city. But the inscriptions suggest that the decision of a Roman emperor as to the status of a community was closely related to his assessment of the adequacy of its economic and demographic base.

Nevertheless such criteria were not applied throughout the empire or in all periods. There were villages within the substantial territory of Trier in Gaul that were larger than the smaller cities of Italy or Britain.[27] Similarly in Greece a number of cities retained their status because propped up by Leagues, if they were not saved from downgrading by their past fame.[28] Thebes in Boeotia was one of the latter, in Strabo's view not even a significant village: it was underpopulated, its buildings were dilapidated or in ruins, its economy was weak and its culture in decay (402). That it was officially a city is indicated by Strabo's own account, which contains scattered references to settlements and geographical features incorporated in its territory. When Pausanias saw Thebes in the mid-second century it had a few hundred inhabitants who had retired to the Cadmeia, but was still a city (8.33.2). The same writer knew that Panopeus in Phocis was a city but was doubtful whether it deserved the title. It did have a territory and magistrates, or at least personages who

---

[25] Mócsy (1970), 164; Wilkes (1969), 356-7.

[26] Jones (1940), 285ff.; Harper (1928).

[27] On Trier, Wightman (1970), 128ff.; for Britain, Frere (1978), 292.

[28] For Thebes in decline see also Strabo 180, Dio Chrysostom, *Or.*7.121, Pausanias 9.7.6; as a model of greatness, see Plutarch *Mor.* 811 BC. Both the Boeotian and the Phocian League had by the end of Tiberius' reign become part of the wider Panachaean or Panhellenic League based on Patrae. See Bowersock (1965), 87ff.

represented the city in the Phocian assembly; on the other side, it lacked magistrates' offices, a gymnasium, an agora, fountains and respectable housing (10.4.1ff.).

The political division between city and village was conspicuously out of tune with economic and cultural realities in Egypt. The capitals of the administrative districts, or nomes, were only late given municipal institutions, limited self-government, and jurisdiction of a sort over their hinterlands by Septimius Severus at the beginning of the third century. Alexandria, one of the largest centres of population in the whole empire, lacked a local council until this time. The explanation can only be political and fiscal. Alexandria had a very bad record for civil disturbance involving the Jewish and Greek populations. Moreover, the Romans had inherited from the Ptolemies a complicated and oppressive bureaucratic structure, unique to Egypt, that it suited them to perpetuate because of the enormous agricultural resources of the province. Municipal or quasi-municipal government came to Egypt only when the Severans saw the advantage to themselves of spreading more widely the burdens of administration among the better-off members of the subject population.[29]

Self-governing cities were also slow in coming in the heartland of Africa Proconsularis, the other great grain surplus producing area of the empire, before the Severan period.[30] The primary explanation is the scale of imperial interest and presence in the area, which included the Medjerda valley behind Carthage, the location of extensive imperial properties. Administration and control, traditional functions of such communities, were in large part accounted for in this area by the imperial authorities in Carthage and on the domains. When eventually civic status was granted, the size of the imperial estates, the number of communities and their proximity to one another ensured that the newly chartered cities would have exiguous territories and therefore little opportunity for growth.

Other factors, and especially the influence in Rome of powerful expatriates of senatorial or equestrian status, may have played a part in postponing the fragmentation of the huge territory of Carthage, or for that matter, that of its counterpart in Numidia, Cirta. The operation of patronage could, however, work against the interests of the large cities. Four communities within Carthage's vast territory, Avitta Bibba, Bisica, Thuburbo Maius and Abthugni, became *municipia* in the reign of Hadrian, thus outpacing numerous others of equal insignificance that in most cases had to wait for the Severan period or later for promotion. We may suppose that Hadrian was influenced by the pleas of patrons of the communities or of other important individuals, as Pius certainly was

[29] On Egypt, Bowman (1971); A.H.M. Jones (1971).
[30] On the Carthaginian territory, Pflaum (1970a), at 109-10; Gascou (1972), 226ff.; Garnsey (1978), 244ff.

when he granted the status of city to Gigthis in southern Tunisia. But emperors did not always need prompting. Byzantium, Antioch and Neapolis in Palestine happened to support the wrong side in the civil war that led to the elevation of Septimius Severus and lost their civic rights in consequence. At the same time other cities, such as Tyre and Laodicea, neighbour and rival of Antioch, received 'Italian rights' and therefore tax exemption. The village in Syrian Auranitis that produced the emperor Philip was renamed Philippopolis in AD 244 when it achieved the status of a colony. In short, the initiative of individuals, imperial whim or other chance factors rather than a deliberate policy originating in Rome might determine on which side of the line a community fell, or for that matter, and even more so, the special status and privileges, if any, that it held.[31]

To sum up, the distinction between city and communities of lower status in the Roman context is at base one of political constitution and relationship to the surrounding territory. In the Greek East where the political landscape was already fully formed in the islands, coasts and river valleys Roman intervention took the form of minor adjustment to existing settlement hierarchies, and the promotion of new foundations in the underurbanized hinterland. In contrast the West (especially in North Africa and the Iberian peninsula), and to a much lesser extent the North, witnessed the remarkable spread of Roman cities. Here decisions had to be made with some frequency as to the status of individual communities and the shape and extent of their rural territories. Intense diplomatic activity involving the local elites formed part of the background. The communities were not and could not afford to be passive. Their fortunes depended upon the ability of their leadership to mobilize support in high places or if necessary argue their cases in person before a governor or an emperor. The documents cited above from the East show the kind of arguments that weighed with the Roman authorities. In the West the Romans were looking in addition for concrete evidence from pacified barbarian tribal communities of a reorientation of their political loyalties and culture. Empire-wide, the broad objective was the same, to build up a structure of centres of local government that could render practical services to the imperial power.

Functions of cities

The primary goals of the imperial administration were the collection of taxes, the recruitment of soldiers and the maintenance of law and order, but the cities from time to time were required in addition to respond to requests for animals for transport, hospitality for visiting officials, or shelter and equipment for soldiers. In addition to these state-imposed

[31] Herodian 3.6.9; cf. Cassius Dio 74.14.3-5 (Byzantium; rights restored c. 201); Pflaum (1970a) on Avitta Bibba, etc.; *ILS* 6780 (Gigthis).

burdens, local governments had to shoulder the regular 'parish pump' jobs of city administration: supervision of aqueducts, repair of buildings, provision of fuel for public baths, preservation of public order (a local responsibility especially in provinces where no soldiers were stationed), staging of religious festivals and games, furnishing of embassies and legal representation.[32]

The key institution that enabled the cities to meet the demands of the government and their own needs was the liturgical system. This was a system by which the more well-to-do members of a community saw to the performance of essential services and responsibilities by payment in cash or kind or by personal service. The wealthy also gave of their time and money in performing the regular magistracies of their city, and some, a small minority, made benefactions over and above what was expected of them as liturgists and magistrates.

The phenomenon of public expenditure by individuals has economic, political and social implications.[33] Private munificence was necessitated by the weakness of city finance. But it suited the rich that city finances should be weak. The alternative of regular taxation was unattractive, because it did not carry political, social and perhaps economic rewards. The system of liturgies rendered legitimate the domination of local society and politics by the rich: if local politicians are required to be benefactors, whether by custom or by law, then political office is effectively restricted to the rich. At another level, the system enabled the rich to compete with each other for prestige, honour and office. To put it in another way, there was a close relationship between the liturgical system and public munificence in general and social differentiation within the local aristocracy. The legal sources of the second century AD reveal the existence of men whose wealth and social standing placed them above other local aristocrats as civic leaders. Moreover, the social inequality within the governing class that this implies is sometimes referred to in the context of liturgies. For example, we hear in a rescript of Hadrian to the city of Klazomenai in the province of Asia of embassies classed as more important for which only the most prominent people should be chosen (*primores viri*) rather than those of lesser eminence (*inferiores*) (*Digest* 50.7.5.5). Honorific inscriptions convey the same message, that a small group of dominant families monopolized those offices and liturgies that both were intrinsically important and brought the greater opportunities for self-advancement. The irony is that mounting central government interest and interference in city finances had the effect of accentuating differences in wealth and status that were

---

[32] On all these matters Liebenam (1900) and A.H.M. Jones (1940) are still fundamental. See also, for the West, Langhammer (1973), and, for Italy, Eck (1979).

[33] The classic treatment is by Veyne (1976). See also, for the Hellenistic period, Gauthier (1985).

already present in the municipal upper class, and reduced the capacity of the class as a whole to fulfil its liturgical obligations.

Emperor, governor, cities

The task of extracting the surplus resources of the provinces was handled by the cities. But could the cities be relied on to collect the taxes and fulfil their other obligations, and was a monarchical government likely to take this on trust? It might be supposed that a central administration of the kind that we have described, centrally organized and controlled, and ready to contemplate modest expansion and diversification where crucial needs were served not at all or only inefficiently, was likely to take a more active interest than its Republican predecessor had done in local administration and in particular in the tax-collecting operation.

The appearance from the late first century of city curators, centrally appointed from the senatorial or equestrian order or the local elite, has already been noted. Their sphere was primarily financial administration, and their typical tasks were control of investment of city funds, management of city lands, enforcement of the payment of debts owed to the city or of pledges of financial expenditure made (*Digest* 22.1.33; 50.10.5 etc.). The sources rarely show us curators in action, we know little of their doings, and they are likely to have been employed only to a limited extent in our period. Their emergence is nevertheless a sign of central government concern over the state of municipal finance.

But other evidence suggests that the emperor and his advisers manifested this concern not by multiplying the officials who were active in the provinces, but by supervising more closely those who were already there. This means, in the first place, the provincial governor, and secondly, local government officials themselves.

Governors with consular or praetorian rank possessed *imperium*. A holder of *imperium* by tradition had the power to command an army and full jurisdictional authority. But the concept was ill-defined, and this was not unintended. The Romans were inclined to give their high officials wide discretionary powers, and to provide safeguards against their use in the case of certain privileged categories of people, in the first instance Roman citizens. A precise definition of powers might have limited their scope and flexibility. This imprecision was exploited in the reverse direction by emperors who were rather less interested than the senatorial oligarchy of the Republic had been in preserving magisterial and pro-magisterial initiative. Under the Principate a governor was likely to possess only so much power and independence as he was allowed by emperors.

Both the powers and independence of governors were reduced under the Principate, and the crucial steps were taken by Augustus. The subordinate position of governors vis-à-vis the emperor was institutionalized early in his reign in the grant to Augustus by the senate and Roman people in 23 BC of power superior to that of other provincial officials (*maius imperium*) (Cassius Dio 51.32.5). This among other things settled the issue of whether a governor held any military power independent of the emperor. Thereafter no one could command an army unless with the authority of the emperor. The control of armies by proconsuls, as distinct from imperial legates, was phased out, and the rewards of military success – the acclamation 'imperator' and the award and celebration of a triumph – were monopolized by the emperor.

The coming of the empire also made a difference to the jurisdictional authority of the governor.[34] Under the Republic the power of a magistrate or pro-magistrate with *imperium* to inflict full punitive sanctions was limited in respect of citizens. In particular, appeal, *provocatio*, was a Roman citizen's peculiar prerogative. The first emperor was disinclined to bestow benefits on citizens exclusively, and his successors showed a similar tendency not to discriminate against aliens. The distinction between *honestiores* and *humiliores* that first makes an appearance in legal texts in the early second century is a status distinction that cuts across the citizen/alien division: there are citizens and non-citizens on both sides of the line. The differential treatment of the two broad status groups is spelled out most clearly in the area of penalties, but it is likely to have extended to all aspects of judicial affairs. It may even have been possible for some aliens, those of high status, to have their cases taken to a higher authority than the governor, namely the emperor or a deputy. Citizens appear to have been able to apply to have their cases referred to a court at Rome in the first instance or on appeal after sentence. It is unnecessary to believe, as some have done, that citizens acquired an automatic right from about the turn of the first century AD to have their cases transferred to Rome from the court of the governor, who now lost the power to try them, at least in capital cases. On the other hand, it is clearly attested in the legal documents that by the Severan period governors had lost the power to execute a man of high status, and apparently also a citizen of any status. All such cases involving the death sentence had to be referred to Rome.

Another aspect of imperial supervision and control of provincial administrators is the issuing of instructions, *mandata*, to governors, proconsuls as well as legates of the emperor. This practice was apparently initiated by Augustus himself, and shows that he was not merely interested in asserting his superior authority on an ad hoc basis.[35] Unfortunately our only detailed knowledge of the content of *mandata* is

[34] For restrictions on governors and privileges of citizens and *honestiores* see Garnsey (1968b) (1970).

[35] See Burton (1976), concerning *mandata* to an Augustan proconsul. The differences between 'public' and 'imperial' provinces are minimized in Millar (1966).

derived from the younger Pliny's untypical experience from about AD 109 as a special emissary of the emperor Trajan with the rank of legate in the normally proconsular province of Bithynia/Pontus (*ILS* 2927; Pliny, *Ep*.10). If we took Pliny as a model governor, we might find it easy to believe that gubernatorial actions were as a rule closely monitored by emperors. His general brief[36] was to try to bring to heel a province that had established a reputation for maladministration, corruption and civil disorder. But he also received a number of specific instructions, which he incorporated in an edict, ranging from the examination of city accounts to the suppression of potentially subversive associations; a minor persecution of Christians was an unintended consequence of this clause in the edict (*Ep*. 10.96-7). However, a normal governor, in particular a proconsul, might not have received such detailed instructions, nor have reported back to his emperor so regularly seeking advice, approval or sanction for his actions. Moreover, although Pliny's successor Cornutus Tertullus had the same status and responsibilities (*ILS* 1024), there is no sign, and no likelihood, that there was a significant multiplication of special legates in proconsular provinces in the second century.

Nevertheless, not only the governor's formal powers but also his discretionary authority were significantly reduced in our period. An anecdote from the reign of Hadrian suggests that part of the responsibility lay with the governor. At a drunken gathering in Spain, a young man was tossed in the air from a military cloak and died of injuries received in the fall. The governor punished the offenders lightly, but apparently unnecessarily asked the emperor to comment. Hadrian was thus given the chance of overruling the governor (he did not do so), and of penning the jurisprudential maxim: 'even in the case of more serious offences, it is of concern whether the action was intentional or accidental' (*Mos.Rom.Leg.Coll*.1.11.1-3). But it would be idle to blame governors for the erosion of their powers. The root cause is to be found in the arrival of monarchy, which deprived the senate of its central authority in the state, silenced its more independent members and replaced them with a new breed of deferential senators of undistinguished backgrounds, of whom Pliny may be taken as representative.[37]

The identification of standard patterns or general trends in governor-city or emperor-city relationships is equally difficult. Pliny's contacts with the cities of Bithynia-Pontus are no more likely to have been typical than his dealings with Trajan. His *Letters* record a quite unusual degree of interference on the part of the governor in the administrative affairs of the cities, both those few that possessed special rights and the majority that did not. Pliny had been ordered to examine the accounts of all the cities in his province, including those privileged

---

[36] See Sherwin-White, *Commentary*, 526ff.
[37] Syme (1958), ch.6-8. See also Tacitus' ideal senator of *Agr*. 42.4.

cities, such as 'free and federate' Chalcedon and Amisus, that would normally have escaped such intervention. There is nothing to suggest that these occasions were anything but unusual.[38]

But Pliny's treatment of the ordinary subject cities was equally untypical. The more conscientious governors in all periods would have made it their business to check municipal accounts. It was always within their discretionary authority to do so. More than one and a half centuries earlier Cicero had carefully investigated the accounts of the cities of Cilicia.[39] But neither Cicero nor the standard proconsul of the period of the Principate, including Pliny's predecessors in Bithynia, would have received instructions as Pliny had to investigate city accounts systematically throughout the province, and to make this his chief concern. Moreover, no rule was ever enacted to the effect that cities should regularly submit their accounts to governors.

The power of the cities to regulate their own finances was restricted by imperial directive in at least two respects. No city was to levy new taxes without special permission of the emperor (*Cod.Iust.* 4.62.1), and no new public buildings were to be erected at public expense without the emperor's licence (e.g. *Digest* 50.10.3 pr-1). The first regulation was probably issued early in the empire, perhaps in the reign of Augustus, as is implied in a reply of the emperor Vespasian to the city of Sabora in the south Spanish province of Baetica that requested a new site and amendments to local tax arrangements. Vespasian confirmed those taxes that were conceded by Augustus, but ordered the community to approach the proconsul if it wished to impose new ones, 'for I cannot make any decision if I have no advice on this matter' (*ILS* 6092). The second rule can be seen evolving in the late first and early second centuries. Already before Pliny arrived in his province it had become regular and perhaps compulsory to sound out the proconsul before embarking on a building project (Dio Chrysostom, *Or.* 40.6, 45.5-6). In the reign of Antoninus Pius, a generation after Pliny's legateship, a rule was formulated making imperial permission a prerequisite.

The interest of the Roman authorities encompassed not only the vetting of building projects but also their completion. At Claudiopolis in Bithynia, Pliny had to exact entry-fees from some newly admitted city councillors so that a massive bath-project could get off the ground (*Ep.* 10.39). But a project might be held up because of the withholding of contributions pledged voluntarily, as in the case of the redevelopment scheme at Prusa sponsored by Dio Chrysostom the philosopher/politician a few years before the arrival of Pliny (Dio Chrysostom, *Or.*47.13-16,19).

---

[38] For a special commissioner for free cities in Greece see Pliny, *Ep.* 8.24. Inspection of the accounts of all cities by a special commissioner is recorded once for Syria (*ILAlg.* II 645) and once for Tres Galliae (*AE* 1920, 43). See also *Forsch. Eph.* II 24; cf. *JOAI* 27 (1932), Beiblatt 21ff. (Ephesos, Asia).

[39] Cicero, *Att.* 6.2.5.

Here the legal position was less clear, because private rather than public funds were in question, until Trajan ruled that pledges of expenditure made by private individuals in favour of their cities had to be fulfilled, if not by themselves, then by their heirs (*Digest* 50.12.14). Thereafter, an ambitious politician who sought to buy his way to office with a pledge of some bounty would have to make good his promise. Two inscriptions of the early 160s from Cuicul in north Africa show unfulfilled pledges of a statue, and of a hall with statue and columns, being honoured by order of a legate of Numidia.[40] Such rulings, and others on bequests for games, hunts and other spectacles,[41] show that the voluntary benefactions as well as the obligatory contributions of the local aristocracy came under scrutiny and at least partial control, and in about the period that we have already identified as one in which imperial anxiety as to the state of local finances was expressing itself in sporadic intervention. A parallel, roughly contemporaneous and much more significant development is the increasing regulation of the whole liturgical system by the central government and its representatives. Liability to serve, exemption from service and the distribution of liturgies among those eligible are all addressed by a stream of imperial rescripts, establishing rules where previously there had been lack of regulation or simply confusion.[42]

The risk of misinterpreting these interventions and exaggerating the scale of the interference is reduced if two points are borne in mind. First, the imperial rulings were invariably elicited by interested groups and individuals. Similarly, when governors became involved in appointments, as they did from time to time, it was only on receipt of appeals from aggrieved nominees or councils attempting to nominate them. The involvement of the governor, and even more so, the emperor, in the affairs of the cities remained sporadic, limited and ad hoc throughout our period.[43] It was out of the question that the central government should attempt to exert direct and continuous control over local administration. The governor was best placed to do so, but his term was too short (one year or three), his sphere of responsibility too large and his supporting staff too small.

Secondly, the imperial rulings fell far short of a rash of general enactments that drastically undermined the autonomy of local government institutions. Above all, the emperors failed to produce new institutions and offices. (The far from ubiquitous city curator stands alone.) Nor for that matter did they reform old ones. The transformation of traditional Greek-style councils with changing memberships into

---

[40] *CIL* VIII 2353; 20144 + Leglay; texts and discussion in Garnsey (1971), 119ff. *Pollicitatio* has a whole title to itself in the *Digest* (50.12).

[41] *ILS* 5058,5186,5377, 5878; *AE* 1888,126; *Digest* 50.8.6.

[42] See Millar (1983a); Nutton (1971).

[43] The circumstances in which governors became involved in local affairs are very diverse. They included subsistence crises and other emergencies. See ch.5.

Roman-style permanent councils was a gradual process and was not imposed by the central authorities.[44] More generally, no attempt was made by Roman governments to eradicate the many differences which persisted between city constitutions in the Greek world. When a Roman official tampered with a local constitution (leaving aside the suppression or suspension of the systematically distrusted popular assemblies, the last vestiges of Greek democracy) it was by invitation. This is the origin of Marcus Aurelius' intervention in Athens over the recruitment of the council of the Areopagus. It is interesting that Marcus stood by the traditional regulation that only men of good birth should be admitted, defending it against Athenian attempts to undermine it by adlecting freedmen into vacancies.[45]

The treatment of privileged cities conveys the same impression. What happened in Bithynia/Pontus under Pliny, when the accounts of Apamea and Sinope (colonies), Chalcedon and Amisus (free and federate cities), traditionally immune from inspection, were checked by order of the emperor, was merely the temporary suspension of privileges. As Trajan explicitly states in a reply to his legate, loss of privilege was not in question (Pliny, *Ep.* 10.48, 93). If Aphrodisias is any example, the threat to the special status of a city came not from emperors – who regularly confirmed traditional privileges in return for a demonstration of loyalty – but from tax-collectors acting on their own initiative, or from rival communities within the province. In practice, of course, real civic independence was unattainable within the Roman empire. This is why Aphrodisias thought nothing of asking emperors for curators to investigate their 'neglected' finances or for that matter for earthquake relief. The best that a city could hope for was favoured ally status, and to hold on to such privileges as it possessed by careful cultivation of each succeeding emperor. The uniquely informative Aphrodisias dossier shows no change in this situation over almost three centuries, from Augustus to Decius.[46]

No emperor, in sum, was interested in introducing a substantially larger and more highly organized bureaucracy at any level, or in reorganizing local government systematically. Nor was there any need to do so. Despite more or less endemic corruption in the localities, tax revenues forwarded by the cities were adequate for the limited goals of the central government. Civic office was still by and large attractive to the wealthy.[47] Local patriotism, civic autonomy and the tax system that

---

[44] Here we differ from the canonical account of Jones (1940), ch. XI, 170-91, who both speeds up the development and attributes an active role to Roman officials: 'In Asia the character of the council had already by Cicero's day been transformed: the members now sat for life ... The final step was taken by Pompey' (p.171).

[45] Oliver (1970).

[46] Reynolds (1982).

[47] Garnsey (1974).

was built on them eventually fell victim to the insecurity of the post-Severan era and the multiplication of taxes and exactions for military purposes that were features of that age. The replacement of the local aristocrat by the governor in the honorific epigraphy of the period after AD 250 is symptomatic of the change that had overtaken the city. The governor had become 'the arbiter and saviour of its fortunes'.[48]

[48] Nutton (1978), at 221. Brown (1978), ch.1 is a brilliant evocation of the change in the atmosphere of local government.

PART II

CHAPTER THREE

An Underdeveloped Economy

We know little in detail about the economy of the Roman world. There are no government accounts, no official records of production, trade, occupational distribution, taxation. A systematic account of the Roman economy is therefore beyond our reach. Economic historians, more even than those historians with traditional interests, must set themselves limited objectives and be imaginative and discriminating in their pursuit of them.[1]

We begin with a simple model of the Roman economy, arrived at by setting that economy against the background of other, better known, pre-industrial economies. The next step is to ask how far it is possible to progress beyond a broad characterization of the Roman economy as underdeveloped toward a delineation of the peculiarly Roman form or forms of underdevelopment, and by which of the several available methodologies and approaches. In a final section the economy's capacity for growth is explored with reference to the period of the Principate.

A simple model

The Roman economy was underdeveloped. This means essentially that the mass of the population lived at or near subsistence level. In a typical underdeveloped, pre-industrial economy, a large proportion of the labour force is employed in agriculture, which is the main avenue for investment and source of wealth. The level of investment in manufacturing industries is low. Resources that might in theory be devoted to growth-inducing investment are diverted into consumption or into unproductive speculation and usury. Demand for manufactured goods is relatively low, and most needs are met locally with goods made by small craftsmen or at home. Backward technology is a further barrier to increased productivity. Finally, there is no class of entrepreneurs who are both capable of perceiving opportunities for profit in large-scale organization of manufacture and prepared to undergo the risks entailed in making the necessary investment. In ancient Rome, small-scale handicraft industry was predominant. Some goods were made in quantity,

[1] For an introduction see Finley (1985a) and, more briefly, Hopkins (1983a). On sources and methodology, Finley (1985b).

43

notably pottery and textiles. But little technical expertise or accumulation of capital was required for their production. They were in constant demand as basic and inexpensive consumer goods. However, no one producer or group of producers could be sure of a steady or expanding non-local market.

In Rome as in other pre-industrial economies, commerce received some of the capital that could not find an outlet in industrial enterprise. But the riskiness of trade acted as a disincentive to potential investors. In addition, transport facilities were backward. Land transport was slow and costly, even as it was after Roman times, when the collar harness and nailed shoes were invented. Water transport was altogether cheaper and faster, although goods could not be moved with speed and efficiency in all seasons until the invention of the steamship in the nineteenth century. Most agricultural areas inevitably aimed at subsistence rather than the production of an exportable surplus. In the case of manufactures, too, proximity or ease of access to markets was essential. The emergence of Pisa and then Lyon as centres for the production of fine tableware illustrates the problems faced by the potters of Arezzo in the early decades of the first century AD in selling their product on the northern frontiers where the Roman army offered a ready market. In general, the backwardness and expense of transport and the relatively low level of demand limited opportunities for profitable investment in commerce.

Trading profits were attracted into land and money-lending. Money-lending brought the better return. Interest rates were especially high where the risks were great, as was the case with nautical loans and loans abroad (an empire afforded opportunities for exploitation). Money-lending was also unproductive: loans to aristocrats, for example, were used for purposes of consumption rather than land improvement and increased productivity.

Land investment offered security and a steady income. In modern developing countries, the scale of speculation in land suggests that many of those who have wealth find alternative opportunities for investment limited, or consider anything but a marginal investment in trade (or industry) unsafe or undesirable. In such societies, as was the case in pre-industrial Europe, land is valued also as a source of prestige and political power. The conversion of profits won in commerce into landed wealth often heralds the arrival of a new family in the ranks of the aristocracy. In such cases, the acquisition of property may be followed by the purchase of office and the forging of marriage connections with the upper class. The process of assimilation into the aristocracy might take one generation or more. As regards Rome, the best-known example of the merchant turned landowner is fictional, the freedman Trimalchio in Petronius' mid-first-century AD novel; and he, notoriously, failed to found a family that might have secured the status that was denied to

Trimalchio himself. Freedmen were barred from political office. However, as many inscriptions from Italy and elsewhere demonstrate, sons of freedmen could enter a city council and hold magistracies and priesthoods on the basis of their father's wealth and generosity. The source of their wealth is not generally specified on these inscriptions, which are intended to be honorific; nor is the form in which it was invested.

Finally, in pre-industrial societies the prevailing value system is that of a landed aristocracy. A prosperous merchant class, the source of whose wealth was not land, and whose success rested on enterprise and skill rather than traditional precepts and modes of behaviour, provides a potential threat to aristocratic values. But successful merchants fall easy prey to the dominant ideology: they buy or marry their way into the aristocracy and seek political office. Only the rise of a class of industrial owners, who possess social prestige and economic power independently as profit-makers and employers of labour, endangers the traditional social order.

In ancient Rome there was no prospect of the emergence of such a class. Moreover, economic realities, in particular the limitations of the market, virtually ruled out the possibility of the formation of a competing social hierarchy based on commercial wealth. Nevertheless, the landed aristocracy perceived a threat to their supremacy in the growth of commerce that followed Republican Rome's expansion beyond Italy. It is this which explains the reactionary and defensive tone colouring Roman social attitudes from the early second century BC, when Latin literature begins. Treatises on agriculture and morality defend landowning as the safest occupation (the least likely therefore to impoverish the aristocracy and weaken its position) and as the most honourable (the most conducive to the lifestyle appropriate for the senator), and manifest hostility in differing degrees to trade as a source of income. The theme surfaces in Cato's *On Agriculture* of the mid-second century BC, and is taken up more than a century later in Cicero's *On Moral Duties* and then, more cursorily, in Varro's *On Farming*. It is not a purely Republican phenomenon; Columella in the mid-first century AD affirms in stronger terms than any preceding writer the superiority of agriculture over trade.

The limitations of an analysis of the kind we have just attempted are obvious. The search for points of similarity between societies, when coupled with the tendency to pass over differences both between and within societies, produces a picture of any particular society that is grossly oversimplified. The arguments are set at a high level of generality. Thus, for example, the supremacy of agriculture over other forms of investment and income has been established, but only at a very general level. A sceptic might question whether it is in fact possible to offer a more penetrating analysis of the role of agriculture, and of its importance in relation to other sections of the economy, on the basis of the existing, non-quantitative, evidence. A discussion of some recent contributions to the debate on this central issue will enable us to evaluate the various ways employed by ancient historians (optimists rather than pessimists by inclination, with few exceptions) to circumvent this problem.

Methodologies and debates

In the revised edition of his *Ancient Economy*, Moses Finley challenged conventional historiographical methods and assumptions in typically uncompromising fashion: 'Any analysis of the ancient economy that pretends to be more than a mere antiquarian listing of discrete data has perforce to employ models (Weber's ideal types).' In his recent *Ancient History: Evidence and Models* this message is reinforced with a detailed analysis of the weaknesses of the ancient evidence. 'The ability of the ancients to invent and their capacity to believe are persistently underestimated. ... The insufficiency of primary literary sources is a continuing curse.' Written documents 'constitute a random selection in both time and place, and they often lack a meaningful context.' Archaeology cannot uncover 'economic structure' or the 'social mode of production', and is too often used to provide support for the literary tradition. So we come full circle. Finley's critique of the ancient sources is not to be mistaken for blanket condemnation, while his models are by definition simplified and capable of refinement and emendation, largely by reference to the primary evidence. But the contrasts between existing historical methodologies are as striking, and the fragility of much conventional historiography is as genuine, as he has indicated.[2]

We begin by considering an argument relating to the nature of the Roman economy that has been very influential despite the patent weakness of its empirical base. A.H.M. Jones suggested that the tax revenue derived from agriculture 'was something like twenty times' that derived from trade and industry in the late Roman empire, and went on to assert a rough correspondence between this apportionment and the economic structure of the empire.[3]

Jones' calculation, according to which the contribution of trade and industry to the imperial revenues and to the overall wealth of the economy amounted to around 5 per cent, was arrived at by a comparison of the payments made by the northern Mesopotamian city of Edessa to the *collatio lustralis*, often called a trade tax, in the late fifth century, with the returns in land tax from the Egyptian nomes of Heracleopolis

[2] Finley (1985a), at 182; Finley (1985b), ch. 1 and passim. For a more orthodox approach to the sources, not specifically those for economic history, see Crawford (1983).

[3] Jones (1964), 465.

and Oxyrhynchos in the sixth century. Apart from doubts about the legitimacy of this comparison (tentatively aired by Jones himself), one might question the value of an equation that includes among revenues from 'trade and industry' levies on usurers and prostitutes, who were subject to the *collatio*, while excluding tolls, sales taxes and above all customs dues, that were collected separately. There are more fundamental objections. Any estimate of the value to the state of agriculture, on the one hand, and trade and manufacturing, on the other, that is based on their relative contributions to tax revenues, will be worthless unless we can compare, first, the rate of taxation, and secondly, the extent of state ownership, and hence the scope of a taxable private sector, in each section of the economy. Needless to say, such information is lacking, whether for the late or the early empire.

Jones' argument represents an attempt to evade the problem of the non-existent quantitative data by conjuring up isolated texts of special significance. There are a few such texts bearing on trade, for example, the Vienna papyrus that documents the extraordinarily high value of a cargo of nard, ivory and cloth imported into Egypt from India, and invites inferences concerning the cost of investment in the trade in luxuries, and its profitability.[4] Another valuable document, which needs careful interpretation, is the emperor Diocletian's price edict of AD 301.[5]

In contrast, any attempt to establish the significance of trade and manufacture in the economy with reference to texts allegedly bearing on upper-class economic activity would be inhibited by data that is qualitatively as well as quantitatively deficient. The patient collection of stray items from diverse sources might just about be justified if the individual pieces of evidence were self-evidently valuable. But, to cite a typical case, there is no reason for accepting that a particular Roman senator had invested in trade through an ex-slave or slave unless we can be sure about the precise nature of the economic activities of the alleged middleman, establish firm links between the parties, and show that a sharing of risks and profits was entailed.[6] As yet no text has yielded this kind of information, just as documentary evidence for the direct involvement of senators in trade is lacking. What can be said, on the basis of diverse, mainly non-literary, sources, is that individual aristocrats (and emperors) were proprietors of large warehouses, brickyards and pottery works, or the source of loan capital invested by third parties in, among other things, shipping. As owners rather than exploiters, as lenders on fixed interest rather than direct participants, they avoided whatever risks and ignominy were associated with direct

---

[4] Harrauer and Sijpesteijn (1985).
[5] Giacchero (1974); cf. Hopkins (1983b), 102ff.
[6] See D'Arms (1981); Pleket (1983); cf. Garnsey (1981).

and public investment in trade and manufacturing.[7]

Such evidence justifies the negative assertion that not all members of the high elite were completely uninvolved in trade or manufacture. But there is nothing very radical about this finding, and the key questions remain: how many individuals, and what proportion of their wealth? Any over-optimistic answers would run up against the reality of the substantial investment of senators and other rich men in rural property, and the survival in law and convention of opposition to senatorial involvement in trade.

There remains a further, critical, issue. So far the assumption has gone unchallenged that insofar as we can piece together the sources of wealth of the rich, we can reconstruct the sources of wealth of the empire at large. But Polanyi, and more recently, Finley, have reminded us that not all commodity movement in antiquity is properly described as trade in the sense of market exchange. In particular, the transport of goods by order of or under the control of the state, 'redistribution', or 'administered trade', was of singular importance under the Roman empire. Insofar as rich investors were caught up in the transport to the city of Rome or the Roman armies of massive quantities of goods, especially tax grain, this would tell us little about the importance of trade in the Roman world.[8]

The argument about the economic activities of the rich is mirrored by, and closely associated with, the debate over the nature of the economic life of cities, the seat of most men of means in the Roman empire. Again the implication is that the issue of the character of the Roman economy at large will be illuminated, and again it is possible to proceed by means of a conventional methodology, the accumulation of information about the economic life of particular cities. Here the problem, supposing one can hit upon a relatively well-documented area, is to convince anyone that the results have a general significance. Thus, for example, it is uncontroversial that the economy of some cities was based on trade rather than agriculture. The question is rather whether such cities were exceptional.

This is an appropriate point to turn to a consideration of less conventional approaches, and, in particular, the construction of explanatory models, whether quantitative or non-quantitative. Perhaps the most familiar and influential model concerns the urban economy. This is the 'consumer city', adumbrated long ago by Sombart and Weber and revived and publicized by Finley. According to this model, the ancient city was primarily a centre of consumption, in contrast with the medieval city, which was primarily a centre of production. By a consumption city is meant 'one which pays for its maintenance ... not

[7] Rickman (1971); Helen (1975), Setala (1977), with Champlin (1983); Andreau (1983) (1985), with Rougé (1980), at 293 and Tchernia (1985), at 8-9.
[8] Polanyi (1957) (1968), with Humphreys (1978), 31-75; Finley (1985a).

with its own products, because it does not need to. It derives its maintenance rather on the basis of a legal claim such as taxes or rents, without having to deliver return values'.[9]

The essential power and truth of the consumer city model can be admitted; so can its role of confirming the supremacy of agriculture in the economy. The city was both the base of the major landowners, who were also the wealthiest residents, and the centre and focus of their expenditures, which were funded in large part by their rural investments. Whether the model reinforces the minimalist view of the role of trade and manufacturing is another matter. The model, any model, is not a statement about reality, which is much more complex and problematic. The minimalist view is such a statement, and must be tested along with others. In fact there is some room for manoeuvre within the limits set by the model. Thus, for example, it can be argued, with the aid of familiar literary sources, that city elites were not merely holders of rural property, but also invested in urban property to a considerable extent. Without rejecting the crucial importance to most ancient cities of the flow of income from the countryside, one might want to recognize that there were income-creating activities taking place in the 'internal' urban economy, activities access to which, and often control over which, were provided by ownership of urban property.[10]

This last argument is instructive for its implication that 'model-building' and 'empirical' data collection and analysis can be complementary rather than competing methodologies. No model will carry conviction unless it can be shown that it bears resemblance to the historical reality. With this in mind we may consider some further arguments that carry negative implications for the minimalist thesis.

An argument of Hopkins[11] runs as follows: A ship of 400 tonnes can be calculated, with the aid of comparative evidence, to have cost 250-400,000 sesterces to build and a further 185,000 sesterces to load with wheat. The Romans are known to have built ships of 250-450 tonnes from the first century BC. Only the rich could have afforded to build and run such ships. Those who invested in them must have included the richest men in the empire, the Roman elite. This is the argument, in bare summary form.

Now, in our period, such large ships (most Roman ships were smaller) were used for the transport of goods, principally wheat, to Rome, from Egypt and north Africa. Rome was a special case. Emperors attracted shippers into the service of the food-supply (*annona*) with tax and insurance benefits, benefits that were available, however, only to bulk suppliers. Most of the grain imported in this way, we may suppose, was

---

[9] See Finley (1981), ch. 1 (p.13 for citation from Sombart); Hopkins (1978b), 68ff.; Goudineau (1980), 66ff.; Leveau (1983), with reply of Goudineau pp.283-7; Leveau (ed.) (1985).
[10] Garnsey (1976).
[11] Hopkins (1983b).

state-owned, having the status of tax or rent. The extent of profit over and above that allowed for in the contract (an unknown) would have depended on the amount of (subsidized) trade a shipper was able to carry on alongside his function of transporter of state goods. As for upper-class participation: senators might have been involved, though the class of men who had the means to invest as individuals or groups was much larger than the senatorial order. But in any case, the involvement of rich investors, whatever their status, would tell us more about the importance and character of 'administered trade' (as earlier defined), than the scale of trade in the sense of commercial exchange in the Roman world. In sum, the implications of Hopkins' argument require further exploration. However, unlike the conventional method of text-by-text analysis, it is of a kind to raise the level and the tempo of the debate.

In a second, more elaborate, argument, Hopkins asserts for the period of the Principate that the exaction of money taxes in central provinces of the empire for expenditure on the frontiers stimulated a large volume of long-distance trade, as taxpayers sold produce to raise cash. This, the imposition of money taxes, is one of the mechanisms by which the monetary economy of Roman Italy spread to other areas of the empire, in Crawford's recent account; Crawford adduces also the spending power of soldiers paid in coin and the need of ambitious local aristocrats to raise cash to spend in Rome. These hypotheses force an examination of the relative importance of money taxes as opposed to taxes in kind, the character of the army supply system, the nature of army pay, the political horizons of local aristocrats and their strategies as landlords. In comparison with the Hopkins/Crawford model, we envisage a more significant role for taxes and requisitions in kind in army supply, lower spending capacity among soldiers, who received little of their pay as cash (see Chapter Five), lower political horizons among local aristocrats (and therefore less adjustment of their economic behaviour) and, in general, less penetrating monetization of local economies.[12]

A third argument[13] relates to the central issue of demand. The bulk movement of essential commodities beyond the local market, whether basic foodstuffs such as grain, wine, olive oil and salt, or other essentials such as metals, wood for fuel and construction, other building materials and clothing, was stimulated by deficiencies, whether natural or man-made, permanent or periodic. The unequal distribution of resources from one region to another, the regular though not precisely predictable crop failures, the destructive or disruptive action of men and states, generated trade. This argument too opens the door to wider questions: how to balance trade narrowly defined as market exchange against other forms of exchange (administrative trade, reciprocity), how to weigh

[12] Hopkins (1980); Crawford (1985), at 279; cf. Crawford (1986), 65-6.
[13] Garnsey (1983b), 1-2; adumbrated by Hopkins (1980), 103. See Hopkins (1978b), 52ff. on trade in textiles.

household production (of textiles, for example) against local and non-local exchange (in its several varieties). If there is to be a way forward, then it lies in proposing models that revolve around large issues of this kind, and in testing them, insofar as is possible, against the available evidence.

Growth and its limits

So far we have been operating with an essentially static model of the Roman economy. It remains to ask whether the model can accommodate a measure of economic growth.

A general argument for economic growth under the Principate might run as follows: the accession of Augustus inaugurated an era of relatively stable government, the basic condition for economic recovery and expansion. The new regime was dedicated to the cause of civil peace and the pacification of Rome's enemies. The success of this policy furthered internal economic development, and, insofar as it expanded the territory under Roman control, extended the economic horizons of the empire. The settlement of substantial numbers of Italian soldier colonists in northern Italy and abroad promoted the recovery of central and southern Italy, now relieved of intense pressure on the land, and furthered the development of more thinly populated areas of the empire, particularly in the West. Augustus lacked a clear and coherent policy of stimulating economic expansion, but he did create the conditions under which economic life could flourish. After his reign the *pax Romana* was by and large uninterrupted. Apart from the civil wars of 68-69 and 192-93 and the plague of the age of Marcus Aurelius – of uncertain nature and effect but much less destructive than the bubonic plague of the reign of Justinian – the empire suffered few major calamities until the middle of the third century. Finally, the *pax Romana* encouraged a modest increase in population, which raised demand and stimulated a measure of economic expansion. A rising population was easily absorbed in relatively underpopulated territories such as north Africa, the Iberian peninsula and Gaul through immigration and colonization.

On the other side, one might question the potential of the economy for growth. We have seen that the economy was underdeveloped, and that most of the labour force was employed in agriculture and lived at subsistence level. The first century and, even more so, the second have been considered prosperous by observers ancient and modern, and for the rich few this was doubtless the case: they became richer. But for the vast majority of the population the situation was otherwise. To take agriculture, the basis of the economy, for subsistence farmers the margin of surplus production was narrow and was largely siphoned off by the imperial authorities and city-based landlords in taxes and rents. The workers on the larger estates, whether they were technically slave or free, did not share the profits and standard of living of the landowners. The rich, for their part, were consumers rather than investors of wealth. Technology – an important determinant of the economy as a whole – remained backward, preventing a major advance in the productivity of agriculture, and also standing in the way of an expansion of trade and manufacturing.[14] To take the factor of power: the Roman world remained largely dependent on animals and humans for its power. The windmill was unknown in the countryside until the eleventh century. The draught-horse was not employed for farm-work for lack of a satisfactory harness; the ox and mule were slower animals with less traction power. This had consequences also for land transport. It was expensive to haul heavy goods, among which must be counted wheat, overland, though one must not forget the vital importance of rivers navigable to small commercial boats. Sea transport was cheaper but insecure and largely restricted to the period from April to October. The primitiveness of commercial institutions and commercial law is consistent with this picture of a relatively small and underdeveloped 'trading sector'.[15] Industrial technology, if we except the Phoenician invention of glass-blowing in the first century BC, registered no major advance. Traditional techniques remained in use. Production was in small units, methods and tools were simple and overheads low. The poverty of the masses restricted demand.

The picture can be drawn too bleakly. A failure to pursue the goal of higher productivity in industry or agriculture through heavy capital investment and economies of scale was not peculiar to the Romans. For the same reason it is only of limited interest that the Romans lacked the full legal concept of agency, double-entry bookkeeping or sophisticated credit and banking institutions, and merely to observe these deficiencies does not help us to isolate the characteristic features of Roman underdevelopment. Our position is that the economy was capable of a measure of expansion, and is likely to have expanded, under the Principate. This is essentially a modest claim. Thus, for example, industry could achieve expanded output (not to be confused with higher productivity) merely through the multiplication of small producers working in isolation or in integrated enterprises. Where slaves were employed, as they characteristically were in firms larger than the family, for example in the Italian pottery industry, there is the likelihood that owners would seek higher returns through greater exploitation of the labour force in order to pay for the not inconsiderable investment that slaves represented. However, we would not claim that such growth as the economy experienced as a by-product of the injection of slave labour, or

---

[14] Finley (1981), ch.11; Landels (1978); White (1984).
[15] On ancient accounting, see de Ste. Croix (1956); Macve (1985).

in other other ways, was self-sustaining and resulted in structural change. The inherited framework of economic life remained largely intact.

The problem of documenting economic growth and gauging its significance is particularly acute in the area of trade. An ingenious attempt by Hopkins to demonstrate an expansion of trade (see p. 50) revolves around four propositions: first, the imposition of money taxes in the provinces by the Roman government greatly increased the volume of trade in the empire; secondly, levels of consumption were considerably higher in the Roman than pre-Roman period, at least in the West, 'illustrated but not I think proven' from artefact finds; thirdly, a greater incidence of shipwrecks shows more seaborne trade than ever before; fourthly, there was a growth of the supply of money such as to finance greater interregional trade. The arguments cumulatively make an impact, although singly they remain unsubstantiated, as is disarmingly admitted, or (as is the case with the second and fourth arguments), if anything, they establish that trade expanded in the late Republic rather than the early Empire.[16]

An alternative approach, which we favour, is to investigate the possibility of changes in the infrastructure of trade, in technology and commercial institutions, such as to point to increased activity in the trading sector. Here there was little significant development in the period of the Principate. For example, in the central matter of ship construction, the late Republic and late Empire are the main periods of innovation.[17] First, Mediterranean shipbuilders were already in the first century BC constructing large ships in the range of 250-400 tonnes for the bulk transport of food and other commodities. Secondly, throughout our period, and indeed until about AD 400, they appear to have built merchant ships outer-shell-first, a laborious and expensive method, instead of building them up from the internal frame, the skeleton method. This is particularly significant in view of the fact that skeleton construction was known and used in the Celtic provinces.

The several changes in the containers by which primary products were carried, wine in particular, have long intrigued archaeologists. A developmental model, according to which each change represented an improvement in the ratio of contents to container and can therefore be seen as a technical advance with commercial implications, is over-optimistic. The weight, solidity and capacity of amphorae were matters of more than academic interest to Romans (cf. Pliny, *HN* 35.161).[18] But one cannot be certain that technical and commercial considerations lay behind the abandonment over three or four decades at

[16] Hopkins (1980).
[17] Pomey and Tchernia (1978); Hopkins (1983b). On Celtic ships, Casson (1971), 338-9; Marsden (1977).
[18] Tchernia (1986b).

the end of the first century BC of one Graeco-Italian amphora (or clay jar) as a main carrier of wine (the so-called Dressel 1) in favour of another, lighter amphora, modelled on the amphorae of Cos (the so-called Dressel 2-4). Again, although the introduction of ships that transported wine in massive jars (*dolia*) anchored in the ship-centre, known from the Augustan period, may be seen as a technological innovation, it was one that was not persisted with after what seems to have been an experimental phase. Finally, it is too early to say whether the wooden barrel was making much of an impact, let alone replacing the jar, by the end of our period. As with the skeleton technique of ship construction, this was an innovation that might have come to the Mediterranean much earlier than it did, apparently the turn of the second century: the barrel was a standard carrier of wine and other agricultural products in the north-western provinces throughout the period in question.[19]

Adaptations in the law of partnerships and agency have implications for the history of commerce.[20] In the case of partnership, the key question is whether a principal who is one of a firm of partners (*societas*), in contracting with a third party, has the standing of an independent agent or whether he acts for his colleagues. In Roman, as opposed to English, law, he bound himself only; he could recover from his partners by the action on partnership, but the partnership would then automatically collapse. The inconvenience of these rules for commercial intercourse needs no special emphasis. Major adjustments were made in the late Republican period affecting two kinds of partnership – and reflecting their increased importance. An association of public contractors (*publicani*) was held to possess a quasi-corporate status; it had common property and a common fund at which a claim could be directed by a third party. Again, any member of a firm of bankers was liable to be sued over a contract entered into by one of their number. The Principate, however, saw only minor developments toward the generalization of the idea that a partner's contracts bind his co-partners (e.g. *Digest* 14.3.13.2, Ulpian).

In the matter of agency, the achievement of the imperial jurists is slightly more impressive. The institution of agency has a clear economic significance. There are gains in both the speed and volume of economic exchange where a class of professional middlemen exists to preside over commercial operations. But without legal rules that create contractual obligations between a principal and a third party such a class cannot arise. The strict civil law position was and remained that no acquisition was possible through another person who was not in one's power. But this rule contained an important qualification; it left open the possibility of

---

[19] See now, for these developments, and interpretation, Tchernia (1986a).

[20] For brief introductions, see e.g. Nicholas (1962), 185ff., 201ff.; Kaser (1971-5); Crook (1967a), 189ff., 229ff., 241ff. On commercial law in general, see Huvelin (1929) and, with relation to maritime commerce, Rougé (1966), pt.3.

the employment of quasi-agents in the shape of family dependants, in particular slaves and sons, who had no independent legal capacity. There is ample evidence in the juristic sources for the use of slaves in particular in business on behalf of their masters. But the range of commercial operations was widened by the introduction of additional remedies (*actiones adiecticiae qualitatis*) that made a principal liable for the debts of his business manager or ship's captain, where the representative was acting within the terms of his commission. The so-called 'institorial' and 'exercitorial' actions, covering land-based and maritime business respectively, were probably late Republican innovations, and may be added to the other indices of commercial expansion in that period. But imperial jurists extended the concept of 'indirect' agency, and therefore removed further restrictions on commercial operations, by broadening the category of people falling under 'institorial' actions (*Digest* 14.3.5.7, Labeo) and devising an action against a person who authorized a representative to carry out a particular transaction (*Digest* 14.3.19 pref; 19.1.13.25, Papinian).

Finally, the Principate saw no major developments in the Roman law of banking. The only sign that lawyers were shifting their position to take account of commercial realities is in the rather halting movements they made toward recognizing deposit banking as a specific institution. *Depositum* was traditionally gratuitous; the receiver held the object on trust and returned it on demand. But texts of Antonine and Severan jurists recognize an investment account at a bank as a category of *depositum* and admit the payment of interest to the depositor (*Digest* 16.3.28,24,26.11).

This brief investigation of some aspects of commercial law suggests that, first, Roman law was capable of making adjustments to rules that inhibited the operation of business and trade, but was not prepared to sacrifice any major principles; and secondly, that the more striking developments, such as they were, did not take place in the period of the Principate, which was rather a period in which earlier developments were absorbed, interpreted and modestly extended. The legal authorities were not under great pressure from the 'commercial world' to break established traditions of economic behaviour. These conclusions are compatible with the hypothesis that trade and commerce experienced modest but not startling growth under the Principate.

Agriculture deserves special attention as the creator of the bulk of the empire's wealth. A case for progress in agriculture would centre on developments in the West of the empire, such as the spread of vineyards in Gaul, the extension of olive groves in north Africa and of wheat production in north Gaul, south Britain and north Africa. New land was opened up, old land converted to new use, and particularly in wet-farming areas, improved techniques developed (in Gaul) or diffused (in Britain), notably in the labour-intensive operations of harvesting and ploughing. Agricultural slavery was introduced at least in pockets, creating the possibility of higher returns through a more complete exploitation of the work force. Foreign investment and immigration boosted the agrarian economy of the western provinces.

An additional stimulus – but also a crucial limiting factor – was provided by the tax demands of the central government. The interests and needs of the Roman government were few. Apart from war and diplomacy, its basic concern was to supply and finance the military, bureaucracy and court. Beyond feeding the plebs of the city of Rome, a standing obligation, the government committed itself to expenditure on public buildings and amenities for the capital city and the periodic furnishing of material aid to communities in times of crisis. It was the tax on agricultural land in all the provinces (but not Italy) which paid for the bulk of this expenditure. To the extent that this constituted a new demand, or surpassed the impositions of earlier authorities (Roman or pre-Roman), then the size of the surplus had to be increased in order to meet it. In addition, some change of land use was forced on farmers, insofar as they had to provide the army with supplies, or alternatively, in areas lacking a substantial military garrison, produce goods that they could sell to raise money-taxes. This was exploitation, and in aggregate exceeded anything witnessed previously in the Mediterranean world. The main countervailing factor was the opportunity for profit provided by the existence, and for some farmers and traders the accessibility, of those large and stable groups of consumers, the residents of Rome and the frontier legions. Of all the commodities needed by inhabitants of Rome, only grain was provided and distributed by the state for most of our period, and, what is more, in insufficient quantities to feed the total population of the city. Moreover, the frontier army was not entirely provided for by means of tax or requisitions, compulsory and unpaid for, exacted far away or close at hand.[21]

Urban populations throughout the empire formed additional, multiple, focal points of consumer demand. The period of the Principate saw urban growth, for example in the Spanish and African provinces, and this may be taken as an index of the economic development of the countryside. A large number of non-productive consumers were supported by increased food production. The city was the seat of social, legal and religious amenities, the centre for the processing of primary products and the production of craft goods, and the market centre for the sale and distribution of locally produced and imported commodities. These constructive functions of the city have to be set against its fundamentally exploitative role: it was the city which as the agent of central government supervised the taxation system, adding its own

[21] Hopkins (1980): tax stimulated production; cf. Whittaker (1978); Shaw (1983), 149ff.: tax might have depressed production.

burdens on the rural population in the form of financial demands and personal labour services. It was the city to which the flow of rural rents was directed, in its function as the base and consumption centre of the large landowners. There was no radical readjustment of the priorities of the urban elites away from the traditional goals of conspicuous consumption, social status and political honour toward profitable investment.[22]

The character and scale of the demands of central and local government, and the opportunities for production for and sale in a sizeable market, varied spatially and over time. The reactions of rural populations were similarly diverse. Intensification (through extension of the cultivated area, shortening of fallow, higher labour input) and specialization (in particular, higher investment in cash crops) were more widespread responses than technological innovation to external demands and market conditions. The Romans in north Africa built on indigenous farming techniques, even in the vital area of water conservation and utilization.[23] Britain under the Principate is now thought to have witnessed at worst stagnation, at best the diffusion of techniques that had already made an initial impact on agriculture.[24] The large granaries, mechanical mills and exotic plants that appeared in Britain in our period have implications for distribution and consumption rather than agricultural productivity, and they were received rather than developed indigenously in the province. Gaul presents a contrast, at least on the surface. Pliny associates with Gaul three innovations: a wheeled plough, an 'improved' Gallic scythe for haymaking and a harvesting machine for grain (known also from sculptured relief and a description in the late imperial writer Palladius).[25] It is tempting to associate these developments, the impact of which cannot be properly measured, with the administrative reorganization of the Gallic provinces by Augustus, the concentration of a very substantial legionary garrison in the North, and the expansion of urbanization. By the same token, the emergence of plough coulters and asymmetrical ploughshares in Britain in the third century might reflect Rome's use of the province from this period as a granary for the Rhine armies. It would be consistent with this analysis to attribute the comparatively sluggish development of British agriculture in the first two centuries of the empire to lower demands on cultivators in that province on the part of the resident army, the civil administration and the few and modest urban centres. But the prudent course, given the

---

[22] Finley (1981), 3-23; Hopkins (1978b).
[23] Shaw (1984a).
[24] Jones (1981) and (1982), mildly corrected by Fulford (1984), 137.
[25] Pliny, *HN* 18.172 (wheeled plough); 261 (scythe); 296, cf. Palladius 7.2.2-4 (mechanical reaper). All are ascribed to Gaul and the last two are said to be labour-saving. See Kolendo (1980); White (1967a) and (1984).

quality of the evidence, is to avoid exaggerating either the moribund state of British agriculture or the impact of technological innovation in Gaul.

It remains to consider the effect of the city of Rome itself on agricultural production. A city of one million people could only have grown so big, and remained so big, by drawing on the resources of the whole empire. It is customary, and accurate, to view the western provinces as the main suppliers of Rome (leaving aside grain-rich Egypt): African and Sicilian grain, Gallic wine, African oil, Spanish wine and, more particularly, oil were consumed in quantity in Rome. Spanish oil alone came in at the rate of about four million kg per annum in around 55,000 amphorae, as Monte Testaccio, a hill of broken pottery, bears witness. The western provinces were closer to Rome and had made greater advances in agricultural production than the eastern provinces, which were already more or less completely developed, were only lightly garrisoned and experienced no significant spread of cities.[26] Italy's contribution is usually overlooked, or played down. Worse still, Italy is commonly held to have fallen into gradual and inexorable decline, a victim of provincial competition. Yet one might have expected Italy to have prospered in the early empire, or at least those areas of Italy well placed to supply the capital city, once civil war and associated dislocations (notably the settling of large numbers of veterans) had ended, and the countryside could enjoy the benefits of freedom from the land tax, absence of an army to supply or man, and a reduced rural population. These expectations are to some extent realized, if one studies the performance of Italy, not so much in cereals – though as much as 10 per cent of Rome's grain may have come from Tuscany, Umbria, Campania and Apulia under the Principate – as in the products that Rome's inhabitants were able to buy with the money they did not have to spend on grain, because of the stability and generous dimensions of the grain distribution system.

Foremost among these products was wine. Rome under Augustus needed more wine than ever. Italian wine producers responded in two ways, by the development of popular wines, particularly in Campania and the north Adriatic region from Veneto to Piceno, and by the diversification of *grands crus*. The early empire was a period of modest innovations in agricultural technology, to judge from the rather patchy accounts of Columella and the elder Pliny, more particularly the latter. Thus Pliny refers to Greek-invented devices for raising water, such as the water wheel and pump, in his discussion of the irrigation of a market-garden; and he presents stages in the development of the lever press in some detail and with attention to chronology.[27] Columella's forte was arboriculture, especially viticulture. He himself introduced

[26] Jones (1940), ch. 4. On Monte Testaccio, Rodriguez-Almeida (1984).

[27] Pliny, *HN* 19.60; Columella 2.16, cf. 11.10; Pliny, *HN* 18.317; see also 18.97 (but the text is garbled).

refinements of technique (for example, an improved auger for bore-grafting) and as one of a new breed of provincial farmers who bought up farms in Italy (Iulius Graecinus, father of Agricola and composer of an agricultural treatise, was an earlier representative), was well informed about and perhaps personally involved in the importation and acclimatization of more productive foreign vines and other fruit-bearing trees.[28]

This picture is clearly at odds with the thesis of Italian decline, which dominates the modern literature and must be treated in some detail. The classic formulation is that of Rostovtzeff.[29] Provincial competition caused the collapse of medium-sized estates where the bulk of the production of wine and oil for the market was located. These estates (and the small freeholdings, the expropriation of which continued under the empire) were absorbed by a few wealthy proprietors who were satisfied to take in a safe though low rent, and turned away from direct exploitation through slaves under a bailiff to indirect management through tenancy, from the production of wine and oil by 'scientific' methods to corn-growing essentially by the methods of peasant agriculture. This impressive edifice is built upon a number of isolated texts, mainly literary, from the period Nero-Trajan: Columella's picture of a wine industry on the defensive or in the doldrums; Domitian's vine edict forbidding the planting of vines in Italy and ordering the destruction of all or some provincial vines; Pliny the younger's grumblings about the short supply of suitable tenants; the depressed condition of the Italian countryside as revealed by the alimentary scheme of Trajan.

None of this amounts to much. Around the Augustan period a change-around occurred as Italian wine producers unable to maintain their bulk exports to Gaul looked for other outlets. Columella's treatise, as we have seen, reflects these positive developments, as well as the standard, recurring criticisms of viticulture. As the most speculative branch of farming, viticulture had always been the object of hostile attention from the more cautious and conservative landowners. These traditional opponents were now perhaps joined by those farmers who had been unable to respond to changing conditions, who had perhaps persisted with old, unproductive vines when newer, more fertile provincial species were available. If provincial competition set back the Italian wine industry in this period, it was in this very limited way,

---

[28] The literature has focussed on Columella's pessimism and his accounting practices. For the latter, see Duncan-Jones (1982), ch.2; Carandini (1983); comment by Finley (1985a), 181-2.

[29] Rostovtzeff (1957), 19-22, 30-6, 54-75, 91-105, 165-75, 192-204; Sirago (1958), 250-74; Martin (1971), 257-310, 370-5. Our account leans on Tchernia (1986a). See the briefer, but useful critique by Purcell (1985), who talks of a 'boom' in Italian viticulture in the early imperial period. His coverage, however, does not extend beyond the reign of Trajan.

rather than by displacing Italian wine from the market of Rome, which was more or less insatiable.

Again, the edict of Domitian (or rather edicts, since a late author alludes to a second edict which prohibited the planting of vines within city boundaries) does not indicate a downturn in the fortunes of Italian viticulture.[30] Suetonius provides a context for Domitian's extraordinary attack on wine production: there was a shortfall in cereals that coincided with a bumper wine harvest. That is all that a first reading of the sources entitles us to infer, apart from the fact that the edict was discriminatory against provincial vine-growers; but this is what one might have predicted in view of the still privileged position of Italy in the empire. It is a quite different, and implausible, claim that the edict was a protectionist measure designed to support a flagging wine industry in Italy. A brilliant piece of deduction by the leading historian of Italian viticulture invites us to deepen the analysis. There was a short-lived crisis in the wine industry of central Tyrrhenian Italy in the last years of the first century. It was a crisis of overproduction following a period of underproduction. The eruption of Vesuvius on 24 August, 79, had wiped out at a stroke the vineyards extending from the foot of Vesuvius to Pompeii, Stabiae and Nuceria; but, as the amphorae remains have established, this branch of the Italian wine industry met a very significant proportion of Rome's needs, especially in the area of popular wine. The planting of new vines (in intramural areas of cities too, as Domitian knew or was to discover) was successful but uncontrolled; it was bad luck for the growers concerned that an excellent year for grapes coincided with a poor year for cereals. The edict represents the impulsive reaction of an emperor who knew from the experiences of each of his predecessors, if not yet from his own, the political dangers involved in permitting his subjects, in particular the plebs of Rome, to go hungry. But in addition to popular pressure, Domitian might have been offerred the not-disinterested advice of large landowners worried by the prospect of losing their share of urban markets to the new growers.

So far we have found no evidence of a structural crisis in the wine industry or in Italian agriculture in general. The missing pieces are not provided by the complaints of a landowner about his tenant-farmers (e.g. Pliny, *Ep.* 9.37), which might belong to any age, or by the scheme of the paternalistic emperor Trajan for feeding the children of country towns in Italy, not in itself evidence for worsening conditions in the countryside or for recent population decline.

The decline thesis has been restated, with great energy and power, and with new arguments, by a group of Italian scholars led by Carandini.[31] In

[handwritten marginalia: wheat + wine were basically the only things shipped around]

---

[30] Suetonius, *Dom.* 7.2, cf. 14.2; Statius, *Silv.* 4.3.11-12; Philostratus, *v. Ap.* 6.42; Eusebius, *Chron.* (ed. Fotheringham) p.273; Tchernia (1986a) IV,3; also, Levick (1982), 67ff.

[31] Carandini (1980) (1981), deriving from Staerman (1964) (1975); see comments of

this version it is a crisis thesis, involving the collapse of the 'slave mode of production', as practised above all in the setting of the large villas of central and southern Italy. Since wine production was the main specialist concern of these enterprises, the debate still revolves around the historical development of the Italian wine industry. But whereas the classic statement of the decline thesis is made in terms of mainly literary sources – and an earlier statement of the crisis thesis by the Russian scholar Staerman depends upon literary, juridical and epigraphic sources – now arguments drawn from archaeology are employed. One argument treats the sharp downturn in the Trajanic period of amphorae of types Dressel 2-4, the main carriers of Italian wine in the first century, as evidence for the collapse of Italian viticulture. Another finds confirmatory evidence in villa decay and abandonment in the area that was formerly the centre of speculative wine production and of the 'slave mode of production', central Italy from Etruria to Campania.

One problem is that the two phenomena are correlated in only a limited way. Only in maritime Etruria, in the area between Monte Argentario and Pyrgi, is there a chronological coincidence between the decadence of villas and the disappearance of Dressel 2-4. The dilemma is not resolved by a chronological extension of the period of crisis. Apart from throwing doubt on the appropriateness of the term 'crisis', this leads to confusion: did the crisis cover the century from the mid-second century to the mid-third (Staerman), or the second century from Trajan to Commodus (Carandini) or the whole period from Augustus to Severus (Carandini again)?

Again, the archaeological arguments raise doubts. The sudden reduction in the numbers of Dressel 2-4 might mean simply that these amphora types were replaced by other carriers yet to be identified, just as Dressel 2-4 had supplanted the heavier Dressel 1 in the last decades of the first century BC. This is not altogether an argument from silence. Some literary references indicate that the better quality Italian wines continued to sell well in Rome and elsewhere, and that they were still carried in (unidentified) amphorae. It is worth emphasizing that Italian products bypassing Ostia, because they came to Rome overland or by river, leave no archaeological record in any period. Secondly, villas did not decay at the same time or universally. (They continued, incidentally, in Spanish Tarraconensis, which apparently found a suitable replacement for Dressel 2-4 in the container Gallic 5.) In maritime southern Etruria the villas had decayed by the Antonine period, but further inland not till the early third century; similarly they were still in operation in third-century Latium near Rome, in the *ager Falernus*, along the Adriatic coast and in south Italy (where they survived, in small numbers

---

Rathbone (1983), Tchernia (1986a), ch. 5; cf. Tchernia (1980), on the end of Dressel 2-4 and the continuation of amphorae (and wine) production.

as ever, into the fourth century at least). The cycle of growth, prosperity and decay – which affected other types of agricultural exploitation as well as the medium-sized slave-staffed estate – was differently paced between and within regions.

The present state of the evidence means, therefore, that it is impossible to provide a firm chronological setting or a convincing socio-economic context for structural change of the kind that has been posited. The wine industry as far as we know was forced to make one major reorientation, and only one, between the inauguration of the first emperor and the middle of the third century, a period of prolonged political instability, constant civil and foreign warfare, and reduced markets. This was right at the beginning of the period, when the slave-staffed villas, which had flourished especially in central Tyrrhenian Italy on the remarkable export trade in wine to Gaul, had to find other outlets when that trade petered out. Rome, hardly neglected by Italian wine producers in the late Republic, a period of rapid population growth, was an even better customer at the beginning of the Principate.

Rome, as far as we know, remained a city of around one million people at least until the second half of the second century. Provincial products poured in. Agricultural writers led the chorus of ritual complaint, but it must have been obvious to all that Italy with Rome in its midst could not be self-sufficient in the main products, let alone the luxury items required by the elite. On the other hand, it is difficult to believe that Italian farmers, those with easy access to Rome by river, sea or land, ever lost their share of the huge market provided by the capital city, whatever the quality of their products. Rome must always have absorbed most of whatever surplus remained, whether of wine or of some other product, after local and regional needs had been satisfied.

The period of the Principate, then, saw in the first place the expansion of provincial agriculture especially in the West. To be sure, this was partly a consequence of public policies, and the fruits were tapped by successive Roman governments in the form of taxes and rents, and more directly through the extension of imperial landholdings outside Italy. Secondly, it saw a period of recovery followed by moderate prosperity in Italy, for example in the northern provinces from Lombardy to Histria, in the central areas of Umbria and inland Tuscany and in Campania and parts of Latium. Our sources for provincial agriculture are of course very limited, and archaeology does not and cannot fill the gaps in our knowledge left by literature. The treatise on agriculture that survives from the period, that of Columella, is Italy-centred, but by no means presents a full and accurate picture of the state of agriculture in Italy in the middle of the first century. The evidence that we have, however, is compatible with the hypothesis that in at least some areas of the agricultural economy of Italy and the provinces, step-by-step advances

but

in techniques and knowledge were made, better crop-combinations and seed selections were practised, more efficient units of exploitation were arrived at and labour was more effectively utilized. Such changes represented progress, but within limits: they are consistent with a rise in productivity, but one of only modest dimensions. From a comparative perspective, that is to say, set against historical periods that saw major technological breakthroughs, the period of the Principate deserves to be categorized as one of relative stagnation.

CHAPTER FOUR

The Land

The younger Pliny, a Roman senator originally from Como in north Italy, wrote to a friend that his investments were almost entirely in rural property (*Ep.* 3.19). Many or most senators would have been similarly placed, especially those who like Pliny were not among the most wealthy and who were not from Rome itself or its environs. Pliny is thought to have been worth about 20 million sesterces, but fortunes twenty times more substantial are known from the early Principate. Pliny's fortune was itself twenty times larger than the minimum property qualification for the Roman senate, one million sesterces. There must have been a considerable number of men in Italy and the provinces who had the basic census requirement for senatorial membership but never became senators.[1]

This chapter proceeds from the premiss that land was the basis of the personal fortunes of the rich and of the wealth of the empire to examine patterns of landholding, the spatial distribution of estates, their internal structure, management and labour strategies, the *mentalité* of large landowners, the existence and viability of subsistence farming and the productivity of agriculture. The discussion is Italy-centred because detailed evidence for provincial agriculture is lacking; trends such as the extension of arable and the wider diffusion of cereals, vines and olives are treated in another section (see Chapter Three).

Geographical distribution of property

We envisage three broad types of property disposition among the wealthy, which roughly correspond with the three categories of landowners outlined above:

1. Local gentry held their land more or less entirely in their region of origin.
2. Middle-ranking senators and equestrians of municipal background had, on top of their local estates, one or more additional centres of property.

[1] Duncan-Jones (1982), ch. 1; app. 7.

3. The richest members of the Roman elite possessed a complex of properties in Italy and abroad.

One could attain the basic senatorial census by building up holdings simply in the territory of one's place of origin, and many men of limited ambition did so. Two examples will suffice, one from the late Republic, the other from the early Empire. First, Sextus Roscius, whose son was a client of Cicero, owned land worth six million sesterces at Ameria in the Tiber valley in the time of Sulla. Secondly, the so-called alimentary inscription documenting the poor relief scheme provided by the emperor Trajan for Veleia, a town in the hills above Piacenza (Placentia) in Emilia, shows three estates falling within the city territory of about the minimum senatorial census.[2] There may have been others unrecorded of the same type, in addition to estates of the requisite value that flowed over into the territories of the adjacent cities of Piacenza, Parma and Luca. Veleia too, though merely an obscure hill town, attracted capital from the neighbouring rich, mainly from Piacenza, in particular because of its ample pasturage (*saltus*). Few of the local magnates concerned, if they were indeed only local magnates, would have owned property much further afield.[3]

In contrast, Pliny came into possession of a property worth perhaps 7 million sesterces a good way from Como, at Tifernum Tiberinum in Umbria. A letter (*Ep.* 3.19) shows him on the point of purchasing a farm probably adjoining that estate for 3 million sesterces (reduced from 5 million). This was all in addition to estates inherited from both parents and other properties at Como, and various non-productive properties, i.e. houses, on Lake Como, at Laurentium near Rome and at Rome itself on the Esquiline. Among men of equestrian standing from Como who acquired property elsewhere can be named the elder Pliny, uncle of the younger Pliny, if as seems likely it was he who acquired the Umbrian property and later transmitted it to his nephew and heir; and Calpurnius Fabatus, the father of Pliny's third wife, a landowner in Campania and Ameria as well as Como. The productive property of Pompeia Celerina, mother of Pliny's second wife, was divided among three towns on the via Flaminia (Ocriculum, Narnia, Carsulae) and Perusia further north, and may represent part of a more extensive senatorial estate with a nucleus somewhere in Tuscany or Umbria.[4]

The extension of the landed interests of former municipal magnates

---

[2] Cicero, *Rosc. Am.* 18-20; *CIL* XI 1147, *oblig.* 13,16,17. Other estates declared at over one million sesterces are formed only partly, or not at all, out of Veleian land. Bibliography includes de Pachtère (1920); Duncan-Jones (1982), ch.7, 211-15; de Neeve (1984), 224ff. See also the parallel inscription *CIL* IX 1455, from Ligures Baebiani, with Veyne (1957) and (1958); Champlin (1981).

[3] *CIL* XI 1147, e.g. *oblig.* 6,9,30,31.

[4] Duncan-Jones (1982), 324.

was a natural consequence of their social and political promotion. In this respect there was little difference between a man like Pliny from the backblocks of Italy, and someone of provincial origin who entered the Roman elite. Provincial senators inevitably acquired Italian land, in the first instance somewhere handy for the capital and on a relatively small scale. Trajan directed them to increase their stake in Italy to one third of their fortune, but half a century later this was reduced by Marcus Aurelius to one quarter.[5]

The wealth of Pliny and his circle, and of the average provincial senator, was relatively modest, and the geographical spread of their investments limited. Wealth of a different order, differently distributed, is revealed by the elder Pliny's reference to the six men who 'owned half of Africa', and whose estates, once confiscated by the emperor Nero, formed the basis of the vast imperial *saltus* in that area (*HN* 18.35); or by Seneca's characterization of the archetypal rich man (and as the owner of 300 million sesterces Seneca could write with authority) who, among other things, 'farms land in all the provinces' (*Ep*.87.7). The requisite information is not available, but one would expect senatorial provincial investment to have been centred on the western part of the empire, which fell easy prey to foreign capital under the early Principate, rather than the economically developed, urbanized and sophisticated East. There is none the less evidence of Roman senatorial property in the East, for example in Macedonia and Asia, in the estates of Q. Pompeius and Rubellius Plautus, respectively. The 'Romans' who are attested as payers of a land-tax in an inscription from Messene probably belonging to the early Empire may not have been of high status, even though their total payment was considerable. They are best seen as representatives of the quite substantial class of enterprising but relatively low-status Italians who had been economically active in the eastern (and western) provinces since the late Republic. Egypt was a special case, as the emperor's private domain to which Roman senators and other high officials were denied access. Members of the imperial family, and the closest associates of emperors (such as Maecenas, Pallas and Seneca) were granted the income of individual estates without, however, acquiring ownership.[6]

Property size

Seneca, Pliny and Columella deplore the existence of huge properties. The term *latifundium* appears in the literary sources precisely in their period, the mid-first century AD. There has been no conceptual

[5] Pliny, *Ep*. 3.19.4; cf. *SHA MA* 11.8.

[6] D. Rathbone (pers. comm.); Crawford (1976); *PIR*[1] P450; R85; *IG* V 1 1432-33 (Messene), dated to the imperial period by Giovannini (1978), app. II, 115-22; Hatzfeld (1919); Wilson (1966).

innovation: Varro wrote a century earlier of a great estate (*latus fundus*) owned by a rich man (1.16.4). His tone is neutral. In contrast, for the later writers *latifundia* symbolized the degeneracy of Italy or rich Romans. Their disapproval was moral. *Latifundia* are associated in their works with gangs of chained slaves, often with criminal records, and in Columella (though he does not use the term) with the downgrading of free citizens into a state of dependency akin to debt-bondage.[7]

But what was a *latifundium*? No definition or technical discussion survives. The agronomists proper avoided the term and even the phenomenon, outside the preface of Columella. The elder Pliny wrote that 1,300,000 sesterces would buy a *latifundium* (*HN* 13.92), but this is the most casual suggestion and only confuses the issue. By that criterion, the younger Pliny, not to mention the elder Pliny himself, the source of much of his nephew's property, become *latifondisti* several times over. It is hardly surprising, then, that modern accounts do not coincide. On the one hand, the 'ranch', on which livestock-raising on a large scale was carried on, and the extensive cereal farm (best-known from north Africa and Sicily, but also posited for Italy), are both termed *latifundia*; on the other hand, the term is sometimes used loosely for the conglomeration of scattered properties of more moderate size that are thought to have commonly constituted a senator's estate – roughly in the range of the 'model' farms of the agricultural writers (200 iugera or 50 hectares for an arable farm, 100 iugera or 25 hectares for a vineyard, 240 iugera or 60 hectares for an oliveyard), or larger.

If Seneca and Columella were attacking a real contemporary phenomenon, in however rhetorical and exaggerated a fashion, their criticism appears to have been directed chiefly at individuals who had in their hands vast tracts of arable, some of which had been allowed to degenerate into pasture land. It is hard to find convincing specimens among known landowners. Of two examples of extreme wealth cited by the elder Pliny, one is not apposite. L. Tarius Rufus, an admiral of Augustus, invested and lost 100 million sesterces in land in the region of Picenum (*HN* 18.37). We are not told the quantity and quality of the land purchased, but wine-jars bearing his name have been found. If most of the land was under vines, then Pliny's cautionary tale, otherwise obscure, becomes comprehensible. This was a case of someone who sank all his money in a risky investment in one corner of Italy, and suffered bad fortune predictably and deservedly in consequence. Pliny's other example is a more appropriate target of abuse from critics of huge estates. C. Caecilius Isidorus, a freedman who was probably an heir of the great Republican family the Metelli, owned or leased, among other things, a vast area of arable and pasturage. On his death in 8 BC, Isidorus

---

[7] Columella 1.3.12; Pliny, *HN* 18.35; Seneca, *Ben.* 7.10.5; White (1967b). On property size, Duncan-Jones (1976a) (1982), app.1.

bequeathed 3600 pairs of oxen, 257,000 other stock and 4116 slaves, plus 60 million sesterces in cash (*HN* 33.135).[8]

It is highly improbable that there were many *latifondisti* who specialized in animal husbandry on anything like the scale of Isidorus. Extensive livestock-raising in a Mediterranean setting required access to, though not necessarily ownership of, a large amount of grazing land and in contrasting climatic zones, broadly, mountain and plain. Long-range transhumant pastoralism, which is first directly attested in Varro, is likely to have 'taken off' in Italy, in particular on the Puglia-Abruzzi route, more than a century earlier, when victory in war and confiscations had given the Roman state control over the whole of central and southern Italy. Varro himself owned land at both ends of this transhumant route. Yet his own 800 sheep, and his failure to cite another, larger flock (he mentions one of 700), suggests that even long-range pastoralism was practised for the most part on a relatively modest scale in his period. There is an absence of data for the Principate, but any attempt to swell measurably the significance of the industry under the empire is likely to founder on the economic argument of limited demand for the products of pastoralism. The Aragonese Dogana of the medieval and early modern period, with its millions of sheep, drove-trails (*tratturi*) of up to 111 metres in width, handsome revenues for the government and large export market, operated in a different world.[9]

We are left with the supposition that the property of most wealthy men was not concentrated into vast estates, but made up of a number of scattered properties of smaller size. But how much smaller? It is time we questioned the assumption that we are dealing with properties, vast or modest in size, that were made up of single units and farmed as such. Tarius Rufus is likely to have farmed not one integrated *latifundium* but a configuration of property in the same general area, especially if he specialized in viticulture: vineyards were generally of modest dimensions. The father of Cicero's client Roscius had 6 million sesterces invested in not one, but thirteen farms, all in one region but not necessarily contiguous.

In the case of Pliny's estates, we may distinguish between a stable nucleus comprising the ancestral properties and, circulating around it, a mobile band of property, consisting of major inheritances, smaller legacies – for example, 5/12 of an estate (*Ep*.7.11) – purchases, sales and gifts, including a small property (*agellus*) worth 100,000 sesterces made over to his nurse. This is the lowest rated property attested in Pliny's possession. It is also the only property clearly represented as one single farm (*Ep*.6.3). Pliny regularly writes of a plurality of tenants (*coloni*,

---

[8] Brunt (1975c). Leasing is a possibility, since Pliny does not specify land.
[9] Garnsey (1986b). The standard work is by Pasquinucci (1979).

often called simply *rustici*) when referring to both his Transpadane and Umbrian properties, and this makes one suspect that the operational units were multiple.

The core of Pliny's properties, and the original basis of his wealth, were those inherited from his father and mother. Pliny tells us nothing about the structure of these properties, but we do hear that they were deliberately exempted from dismemberment during his lifetime (*Ep.*7.11). This means that unless they were subjected to large-scale internal reorganization, of which there is no hint in the *Letters*, they retained essentially the shape they had had before the family became senatorial. Our hypothesis is that these estates consisted of numerous farms which were operated, if not managed, separately, and which, in terms of their individual areas, covered a wide spectrum, extending both well above and well below the optimum range recommended by the agricultural writers. This case is based on an excellent source for the size and distribution of properties among the most prominent members of a local landowning class, the alimentary inscription from Veleia. *bout la*

The Veleia inscription prompts six observations. First, property at Veleia was extremely fragmented. The three sets of proprietors who declared Veleian land worth around the senatorial census, Mommeius Persicus, Coelius Verus and the brothers Annii, had 35, 26 and 13 properties respectively.[10]

Secondly, the bulk of the properties were of small or modest size. Persicus owned 34 farms in the range of 8,000-85,000 sesterces.

Thirdly, there was commonly one substantial property that overshadowed the rest. The brothers Annii were unusual in having had three properties valued in the range 100,000-178,000 sesterces in addition to pasture land (*saltus*) worth 350,000. The only single substantial properties owned by Coelius Verus and Mommeius Persicus were, respectively, a *saltus* worth 350,000 sesterces (formerly integrated with that of the brothers Annii and a portion in the hands of the city of Luca), and the farm (*fundus*) called *Carbardiacus vetus* worth 210,000 sesterces.

Fourthly, when we look at the way small farms relate to large, we find that the element of random scattering is minimal.[11] Mommeius Persicus was largely in Ambitrebius, the parish covering the hill country on both sides of the lower Trebbia valley before it reaches the plain. He was the owner of more than 60 per cent of the property declared in the parish, and despite the evident existence of a number of landowners who appear on

[10] Some were grouped together for the purpose of evaluation for reasons that are not transparent, e.g. *oblig.* 13,16,17.

[11] De Pachtère's reconstruction of the disposition of *pagi* is conjectural; cf. Petracco Sicardi (1969). But the rough location of Ambitrebius is not in doubt. The fragmentary character of Veleian property disposition is well brought out by de Neeve (1984), 224ff.

the inscription only as neighbours, was patently the largest single proprietor in the parish. Much of his land must have been held in a bloc or blocs. The distribution of the holdings of the Annii and of Coelius Verus was less concentrated but still far from chaotic. Their holdings in *saltus* in the upland zone where Veleia confronts Luca were together worth almost one million sesterces. Linked with the *saltus* were several farms (11 between them) overlapping several parishes (as did the *saltus*), which brought their holdings in the area to 800,000 and 600,000 sesterces respectively, or around 4/5 and 3/5 of the total value of their holdings.

Fifthly, over time, landowners had acted not only to limit the geographical distribution of their properties, but also to reduce the number of units of management and operation. Three factors invite this inference: the declaration and evaluation of single units of *fundi* (farms) rather than the more normal *fundus*, a phenomenon especially pronounced in the declaration of the Annii; the contiguity that is demonstrable or that can be plausibly inferred between individual holdings, notably within the estate of Mommeius Persicus; and perhaps also the multiple names of very many farms.

Sixthly, we note the contrasting phenomenon of the splitting up of property – Mommeius Persicus declared no fewer than nine properties that are identified as fractions (usually half) of farms. The estates of the rich were both swelled and reduced by this process of fragmentation, a product of inheritance and marriage customs and the operation of economic forces. With each succeeding generation the battle between the contrary tendencies toward integration and disintegration was joined anew.

Among the other estates declared at Veleia, the others worth at least 200,000 sesterces (the qualification for jury service at Rome, twice the qualification for the local council, half that for equestrian status) reveal essentially the same pattern.[12] The estates are characteristically made up of many holdings, they are small or modest in size, and one (lying in the range 94,000-150,000 sesterces) is considerably more substantial than the rest. Again, it is common to find a number of close-knit estates built around one consolidated farm in a single parish: thus, Cn. Antonius Priscus in Domitius, Virius Nepos and Dellius Proculus in Iunonius, C. Calidius Proculus in Albensis. The estate of M. Antonius Priscus is different in an interesting way: he has 14 properties of aggregate value 233,080 sesterces but no single one is worth more than 35,000. The bulk of the ancestral properties of the Antonii are in the hands of another member of the family, Antonia Vera (as dowry?), and of an outsider Q. Accaeus Aebutius Saturninus, and his own share of a divided inheritance consists of a series of small parcels of land. Yet his scraps of land are almost all in the parish of Albensis, and are commonly contiguous or

---

[12] In order of mention, *oblig.* 28, 2, 15, 21, 5 (cf. 20), 25, 41.

nearly so. His is an extreme case of the concentration that can underlie fragmentation. In short, the holdings of the moderately rich and the 'millionaires' at Veleia conform broadly to the same pattern. What distinguishes the latter is their control of pasture and also their capacity to acquire land, considerable in aggregate, away from the area where their property is concentrated, and indeed outside Veleian territory altogether. Coelius Verus had land in Parma and Placentia, Mommeius Persicus in Placentia. In this they evoke comparison with a number of rich declarants at Veleia who appear to have held much or most of their property elsewhere and were probably based in Placentia or another town; predictably, they were interested especially, and sometimes only, in Veleian pasture land.[13]

What relevance has the pattern of property-holding in the territory of an ordinary Italian town among a group of 'middling' landowners to the estates of other local elites and of the Roman elite itself? The configuration of property at Veleia about the turn of the first century was a product of the accidents of inheritance and marriage and the chance operation of economic forces over an extended period of time. It was not precisely reproducible elsewhere. Differences in terrain, climate, accessibility from major centres and transport routes, and population density ensured that city-territories would project contrasting images. However, the same forces for property accumulation and division were active in other Italian and non-Italian towns and their territories. Senatorial and equestrian property was not immune. The higher status, greater wealth and wider horizons of their owners need not have made any significant difference. The property of the rich was far more fragmented than has been imagined, if we are thinking in terms of units of management and labour.

Management and labour

In no area of ancient economic history are the sources more conspicuously inadequate and the truth more difficult to grasp than in the comparative historical development of tenancy and slavery. What do we gain by measuring Columella's coverage of tenancy against that of Varro or Cato, or the younger Pliny's against Cicero's; by juxtaposing verses of Horace and Martial indicating the coexistence of slavery and tenancy; or by charting the growth and decline of a handful of villas?

In matters of management and labour the propertied class had several options. One was the 'slave estate', wherein slaves made up both the permanent labour force and management, and temporary labour, free or slave, was brought in at times of peak activity, in particular, for the

[13] *Oblig.* 6, 9, 30, 31.

harvest. If the landowner did not administer his estate 'directly' through a slave bailiff (*vilicus*), then he leased his land (by *locatio-conductio*). Tenancy was not a monochrome institution. A tenant (*colonus*) might in principle supervise slave-workers (cf. Columella 1.7.3; Pliny, *Ep.* 9.37), provided by either himself or the landlord, on a property of considerable size. Such tenants included men of some status and means, like Verus, graciously thanked for taking on the farm that was Pliny's gift to his nurse (*Ep.* 6.3), or Rufus, the friend of the son of Calpurnius Fabatus and a possible manager for his country estate in Campania (*Ep.* 6.30). On the other hand, a tenant might work a rather smaller farm himself with the aid of his family. The numerous farms at Veleia that were given a low capital value probably included a number that were worked as single economic units by small men on tenancies. Apart from obvious differences in length of tenancy and level of rent, tenancies also varied in the way rent was exacted, as a fixed payment or an agreed proportion of the harvest (*métayage*, introduced by Pliny in place of a fixed money rent on one of several of his properties, *Ep.*9.37).[14]

Agricultural slavery was at its peak in the last two centuries of the Republic, at least in central and southern Italy. Tenancy was an accepted way of running rural estates in Italy of the late Republic, and was always dominant in some shape or form in the empire at large. The question is whether it is necessary to believe in a decisive swing of the pendulum away from slavery and toward tenancy in the heartlands of agricultural slavery in the early Principate.[15]

The reduction in the numbers of slaves in agriculture, assuming that there was one, was a much longer and slower process than has often been imagined. Theories that entail a speeded-up and shortened process of change fail to establish their point. It used to be thought that agricultural slavery collapsed with the end of the era of expansion marked by the reign of the first emperor, Augustus. As the slave supply diminished, so slave prices rose and slave labour became unprofitable. But the supply of slaves did not fall off drastically after the reign of Augustus. Wars continued, though on a reduced scale. The slave trade, which was well-organized and crossed the frontiers freely, was always an important source of slaves. There were other significant sources, including breeding, and the exposure or sale of unwanted children. The argument for decline from rising slave prices is not impressive. Jones' calculation on which it rests, that 'a slave in the second century cost eight to ten times his annual keep as against a year or a year and a quarter's keep in fourth-century Athens', is based on inadequate and misleading data. In any case, if all the available literary evidence is

---

[14] On tenancy see Johne, Köhn and Weber (1983); de Neeve (1984). The interdependence of the slave estate and the peasant system of production is a theme of Garnsey (1980a). See also Rathbone (1981).

[15] Contrasting views in Finley (1980), ch.4; de Ste. Croix (1981), 226-59.

marshalled, then the case for the survival of slaves in numbers throughout the period of the Principate seems established. The implication of the legal sources that slavery was important in Italian agriculture in the second and early third centuries is worth stressing. There is no sign that slaves could only be afforded by the very rich.[16]

It has been proposed that there was a crisis in agricultural (and industrial) slavery at some point in the second century, to be explained in terms of a structural defect in the 'slave mode of production'.[17] This is presented as a problem of supervision, brought on or aggravated by a supposed transformation of medium-sized properties into *latifundia* on which larger slave staffs were employed. The problem was solved by the widespread division of the large estates into tenancies controlled by freedmen and promoted slaves (the so-called *quasi-coloni* of the juristic texts). This reconstruction founders on the evidence for the survival of slaves in the Italian countryside in and beyond the 'period of crisis'. Even supposing it were agreed that the 'slave estate' disintegrated, and that the specialist wine production that was its hallmark came to a halt in this period (both assertions might be contested), then slaves must have been redeployed without change of status into other forms of rural production. This is not at all problematic. Leaving aside the traditional use of slaves in familial farming units, slaves were employed in enterprises devoted to livestock-raising and cereal production by rich Italians before the 'Catonian' slave estate evolved. As to the solution that is proposed to the 'crisis', we should think twice before accepting, without evidence, that large-scale parcelling of property took place in the second half of our period, whether because of a crisis in the supply or management of slaves or for some other reason.

Finally, we may briefly mention the theory that changing economic attitudes among landowners produced a swing toward tenancy in the early Principate. This argument rests on the ephemeral basis of two assumptions, that landowners were less interested in their estates under the Principate than under the Republic, and that the less interested a landowner was in his estate the more likely he was to turn to tenancy. But at least the thesis raises questions that we have not yet considered about the attitudes of landowners to their rural investments.[18]

Attitudes

What, if anything, can be divined about the economic attitudes of men of property from the way their estates were structured, managed and

---

[16] Harris (1980); Jones (1956), 194, reprinted in Finley (1968); and last note.

[17] Carandini (1981). See the comments of Rathbone (1983), Tchernia (1986a), ch. 5 and above pp.60-2. For pre-Catonian forms of slave exploitation see Frederiksen (1981).

[18] Brockmeyer (1968).

worked? The normal view, powerfully advocated by Finley above all, is that the social and political value placed on land investment hampered the development of economic concepts and institutions in antiquity. Landowners had a strictly limited notion of profit and how to seek it, and a gravely defective method of calculating it (as illustrated by Columella's attempt to demonstrate the profitability of viticulture). In general, they were held in bondage by a value system that emphasized consumption rather than productive investment.[19]

The case of Pliny, recorded in the act of purchasing property, is pertinent, since the property in question adjoined his existing estate in Tifernum Tiberinum (*Ep*.3.19). Pliny displays some proto-economic thinking. He is aware of the vulnerability of a large property in a single climatic zone, and he knows and can appreciate the savings that will accrue from employing one bailiff/manager rather than two, and having to keep up only one farmhouse to the standard required of a senatorial proprietor. Even if certain economies in the use of farm equipment and farm labour follow more or less automatically from a unified management of the two properties, one is left with the impression that Pliny was not much exercised over these matters, and that more non-economic factors, including aesthetic considerations, dictated his decision.

When Pliny bought the property, he was an established senator, his financial situation was stable, his political position secure. It does not follow that all landowners at all times shared his casual approach to economic matters. His uncle was of conservative inclinations, to judge from his distrust of viticulture and his fondness for Catonian paradoxes such as 'nothing could be less advantageous than running your estate as well as possible' (*HN* 18.37). But he has several anecdotes illustrating the speculative pursuit of profit, and only one of them has an unhappy ending: Tarius Rufus and his disastrous investment in Piceno, the freedmen who bought a run-down vineyard near Rome, improved it and quickly sold out at a handsome profit, and Seneca who bought the same property for four times the previous price (*HN* 14.48-52). Attitudes to profit-seeking in agriculture differed, even among the aristocracy. Yet profit-seeking is not the same as profit maximization, and a value system that put a premium on wealth-consumption could not at the same time promote productive reinvestment.

In the same way, the grouping of properties at Veleia does not demonstrate the systematic pursuit of economies of scale. There were farms formed by the amalgamation of several smaller units, but many others that were evaluated singly for the purposes of the Trajanic scheme, and by implication were worked as independent economic units.

[19] Finley (1985a), ch.4.

Some belonging to the same proprietor were contiguous, but others were not. The full point of the distribution of properties escapes us, since we cannot map the farms onto the terrain and read off their likely products. The desirability of linking arable and pasture was clearly appreciated, but in general the benefits of contiguity would have been realized only imperfectly. In any case those benefits were often outweighed in the minds of proprietors by the advantages of dispersal of property through diverse ecological zones, a traditional risk-reducing peasant strategy.

The reality is likely to have been complex. Landowners were flexible; they had to be, since the best-laid plans were likely to be disrupted by deaths – or births. They did not follow any unitary strategy, but in structuring and administering their properties used a wide variety of options. In making decisions, they were guided by essentially practical considerations, to do with the lie of the land, the products of the farm, and the availability of suitable management and labour, and without the benefit of a conceptual apparatus that was created by the agricultural revolution of the eighteenth century.

Peasant farming

At Veleia, no proprietor declared an estate of value lower than 50,000 sesterces. In the corresponding and roughly contemporaneous (but less informative) inscription from Ligures Baebiani, a small town near Benevento in the south of Italy, one landowner owned and declared property worth only 14,000 sesterces. This points to a threshold of 10,000 sesterces below which landowners were not permitted or not persuaded to participate in Trajan's scheme.[20]

In theory, then, we would expect a class of small independent farmers operating at or near subsistence level to have existed in both places. Their children might even have been among the beneficiaries of the scheme, those who received the payments made by the declaring landowners as interest on the loans they were given by the government.

Small peasant proprietors – that is, owner-occupiers operating on or near subsistence level – keep a low profile in the period of the Principate. Their omission from the inscriptions of Veleia and Ligures Baebiani – unless they are some of the many landowners named only as neighbours – is symptomatic. Literature, the product of the social and cultural elite, does not notice the independent peasantry as a class, except for soldiers turned peasants, and then only momentarily. It is uninterested in status demarcations among the rural population. Thus, the poverty of Simulus, the farmer of the pseudo-Virgilian *Moretum* is securely established, but

[20] Veyne (1957) (1958); Champlin (1981).

we are left in doubt whether he was a slave tenant (*quasi-colonus*), a freedman tenant (*colonus*) or an owner-occupier, freed or freeborn. Archaeological evidence shares this deficiency. Field-survey can show the survival of small-unit farming, as in Tuscany and the Molise, but it cannot distinguish an owner-occupier from a tenant. To make matters worse, peasants do not leave monuments. Their farmsteads, built of perishable materials, have not survived. The normal 'small site' of the archaeological field-survey turns out to have a relatively elaborate construction inappropriate to a basic peasant cottage. Its owner might have controlled perhaps 50 to 80 iugera or $12\frac{1}{2}$ to 20 hectares and produced cash crops for the local market.[21]

The small owner-declarants at Ligures Baebiani fit into this sub-class of peasants operating at above subsistence level. One might say that 14,000 sesterces, the value of the cheapest property declared there, would have bought 56 iugera or 14 hectares of arable at 250 sesterces per iugerum, a quarter of the price Columella plucked out of the air for land suitable for development as a vineyard (3.3.8).

The collapse of the independent peasantry is a cliché of Roman agrarian history. The problem of their invisibility can be solved at a stroke by denying their existence at any significant level. The argument might run as follows. Exploitation by the state in the form of prolonged, mass recruitment into the army, the disruption of civil wars and economic pressure from the rich, had drastically undermined the position of the free peasantry of the middle and late Republic. Italy under the Principate was no longer in turmoil, and army recruiters, unless they were raising an entirely new legion, looked to the provinces for legionaries and auxiliaries. Yet the decline of the peasant proprietor continued inexorably. Aristocrats accumulated landholdings at their expense and brought them increasingly into service as tenant-farmers.

Plausible though it sounds, this view reveals misunderstandings of the make-up and way of life of the rural population and the nature of its relationships with the large landowners. Owner-occupiers, tenant-farmers and farm labourers working for a wage were three overlapping categories; thus owner-occupiers were a major recruiting ground for tenants.[22] Certainly, large landowners drew their tenants and seasonal labourers from a wider group, including landowners of moderate means and urban residents engaged in non-agricultural pursuits (Columella disapproved of the tenant of urban base or origin, *colonus urbanus*, 1.7.3). Nevertheless they preferred men with roots in the neighbourhood, (cf. Columella 1.7.4; Pliny, *Ep*.6.30). If poor peasants were in demand, it is also the case that they were tempted or forced to seek ways of increasing their meagre incomes. This has the consequence that an

[21] Kenney (1984), e.g. Introd. il-l; Potter (1979); Barker et al. (1978).
[22] Garnsey (1980a), 37-8.

increase in the number of tenancies, if this was achieved through the transformation of the conventional 'slave estate' into one or several tenancies, might actually mean more employment for (a similar number of) peasant proprietors.

But of course additional tenancies could be created in another way that would have depleted the numbers of owner-occupiers, namely, by the simple conversion of impoverished proprietors into tenant farmers working the same or other land. This is certainly a possible scenario. Whether large landholders customarily added to their landholdings in this way is another matter. Owners of moderate-sized properties were also vulnerable, because of their exposure to market fluctuation and competition. Peasants, insofar as they produced for subsistence, were not in competition with the wealthy producers.

There is the additional point that large landowners who used free men as labourers and managers were actually sustaining the peasantry by offering additional sources of income. This was calculation, not charity; we cannot even be sure that the numerous landowners who participated in Trajan's alimentary scheme did so voluntarily and with humanitarian motives.[23] There were landowners in all periods who exploited peasants ruthlessly, whether within or outside a patronage relationship. But a large-scale or systematic expropriation of the peasantry would have increased the mobility of this section of the rural population, and undermined the economic position of the large landowner himself. Meanwhile the army with its policy of distributing land to soldiers on discharge was available as a mechanism for the regular replenishing of the stock of peasant proprietors.

Productivity

At the basis of most discussions of the fate of the independent peasantry lies the assumption that peasant farming was not economically viable, essentially because of primitive farming methods and low productivity.

First, there are some misconceptions to be identified and dealt with. There is an assumption, often left unspoken, that farming to be successful must be capital-intensive. This is linked with the further supposition that technological progress necessarily leads to higher productivity. A sophisticated technology is not in fact required to work much of the land in the Mediterranean basin. Heavy machinery is unnecessary and sometimes harmful in semi-arid and arid zones, as is being painfully discovered at the present time in regions as far apart as south Italy, Portugal and the Middle East. On a tiny property a hoe or mattock may be sufficient for the purpose in hand, namely, to break up the soil and

[23] Garnsey (1968a); *contra*, Duncan-Jones (1982), 298ff.

control surface weeds; on a slightly larger estate, the animal-drawn ard plough is sufficient for the same purpose. The heavier mould-board plough that turns the soil over is unnecessary, while deep ploughing with the aid of a caterpillar tractor causes all kinds of ecological damage.

Next, misguided historical comparison has played a part in producing a warped view of the predicament of the farmer of antiquity. The medieval-ancient comparison is suspect, especially where the comparison being attempted is between very different agricultural systems and physical environments. It is futile to suggest that as English agriculture leapt ahead with the introduction of the heavy plough, among other developments, so Italian agriculture stayed in a depressed state for lack of it. Again, on the subject of yields: medieval yields[24] in northern Europe (particularly in England, which remained caught in the two- to four-fold range, that is to say, a return of twice- to four-times seed was achieved) are no kind of marker for ancient Mediterranean agriculture, not least because Mediterranean farmers had the benefit of light, warm soils which enhance germination, as opposed to the cold, heavy germination-retarding soils of the North. In general, we should be wary of the naive evolutionist assumption that ancient agriculture was necessarily less productive than that which followed because it was chronologically prior, as if we are compelled to believe in a linear movement from antiquity to the modern period, with yields and efficiency in general progressing in a continuous upward curve.

The ancient-modern comparison, often implicit at least in the literature, is particularly pointless. It has limited interest in itself and is singularly uninformative on the subject of ancient farming standards. Little is achieved by a statement of the obvious, that the ancients lacked high-yielding crops such as maize and potatoes, or for that matter the improved strains of wheat now available to farmers; or again, that they lacked modern methods of land improvement, notably chemical fertilizers and advanced irrigation techniques, not to mention the heavy machinery alluded to above. What counts is the extent to which the food needs of a society are met by the existing economy, and in particular by the prevailing agricultural system. The efficiency and productivity of ancient agriculture is to be judged with reference to its ability to maintain ancient societies over time.

On yields, it hardly needs saying – the agronomists all make this obvious observation – that there must have been enormous variation from one area and terrain to another in the Mediterrenean region. This is easily illustrated for large units and for the modern world from contemporary data.[25] Average wheat yields in the third decade of this century in kilograms per hectare (kg/ha) at a sowing rate (e.g.) of 135

[24] Slicher van Bath (1963) lists no Italian yield figures from the medieval period.
[25] Hopkins (1983b), 91.

kg/ha range from 1710 or a little less than thirteen-fold in Egypt to 269 or two-fold in Cyrenaica. Elsewhere in north Africa, Tunisia registered 400 and Algeria 540, or three-fold and four-fold respectively. Italy including Sicily had an average yield of 1200, a little under nine-fold, and Greece 620, or about four-and-a-half-fold. This should warn us against generalizing from the whole of the Mediterranean (with or without Egypt, which practised irrigation agriculture) or the whole of the Roman empire. But generalizing about yields for Italy or Greece or the north African provinces is just as dubious a practice. The contrast visible in the modern data between the extraordinarily high yields reported from the wadi-valleys and alluvial fans of the interior of Tripolitania or southern Numidia and the modest returns from the dry-farming belt in north Africa would be mirrored in the ancient sources, if we had a full complement of evidence; as it is we have no yield figures from antiquity with which to contrast a number of notices of yields evidently achieved through flood-zone practices, which both ancient writers and modern commentators have found incredible.[26]

Leaving aside this data from north Africa, the ancient literary sources do contribute a few scraps relevant to Italy and Sicily. There are three main texts. Varro (*Rust*. 1.44.1), commenting on the diversity of yields from one district and soil to another, says that one place might yield ten-fold and another fifteen-fold from the same seed, as in some parts of Etruria. Columella states (3.3.4) that at least in the greater part of Italy, a four-fold yield in cereals (*frumenta*, not, we note, in wheat, *triticum*) was rare, implying that the yield usually fell below this level. Cicero in the *Verrines* (2.3.112) gives for the territory of Leontini in Sicily the sowing rate of six *modii* per iugerum, or a little over 160 kg/ha, a wheat yield in a good year of eight-fold, a little over 1300 kg/ha; and another yield in an excellent year of ten-fold, or about 1625 kg/ha.

The comments of Varro and Columella are both very brief. Varro is treating legumes and cereals together in a chapter dealing with sowing. He gives specific sowing rates for beans, wheat, barley and emmer (*far*), adding the caveat that they should be varied according to locality and richness of soil. Then follows the illustration from Etruria. This reads like an authentic piece of information drawn from a good source, and it suggests that relatively high yields were a fact of life in Etruria. It is significant that the lower of the two yields cited is still high, when a more striking contrast would have strengthened Varro's point. Moreover, there is no hint of tendentiousness about the passage, in contrast with that of Columella. Columella is set on conveying an unfavourable impression of the productivity and profitability of cereals – in a mere throw-away sentence, moreover – as part of his detailed, elaborate apologia for viticulture. There is the additional suspicion in Columella's case that the

[26] Shaw (1984a).

yield figure has been plucked out of the air rather than arrived at following anything that could be called systematic research. The notion that he has given a genuine maximum, or average, yield figure for Italy as a whole is insupportable; and, as we saw, his figure refers to cereals in general.

Cicero's figures are worthy of close attention, and not only because he is the only source writing unambiguously about wheat. He supplies two seed: crop ratios, a sowing rate, a figure for land registered as under cultivation (30,000 iugera or 7,500 hectares), two rival bids for the tithe (36,000 *medimnoi* or 216,000 *modii*, and 41,000 *medimnoi* or 246,000 *modii*), as well as other circumstantial details. He was of course an attorney with a brief to exaggerate the crimes of the governor Verres and his henchmen, in this case Apronius. Thus it is possible that he deliberately understated the wheat yield of the territory of Leontini in order to exaggerate the slice of the total harvest exacted from the farmers by Apronius. On the surface his seed:crop ratios, as they apply to good or excellent not average years, point to a mean ratio of less than 1:8. Yet the bids for the tithe imply an expected return from the land of twelve-fold or 1950 kg/ha and 13.66-fold, about 2225 kg/ha, for the year in question. Cicero regards the bids as high and that of Apronius as artificially high, since he had no intention of exacting merely a tithe. But he might have been less prepared to impute the same evil intentions to Minucius, the higher but unsuccessful bidder. The claim that a ten-fold return in the territory of the Leontini was 'very rare' begins to look a little shaky. A mean yield of eight-fold for this land looks like a reasonable conjecture.

The land of Leontini was hailed by Cicero as prime cereal land and the people of Leontini as leading cereal producers (*Verr*.2.3.47,109), though it turns out that they did not own their land. It was farmed by managers, typically men from Centuripa, for absentee landlords, among whom we may suppose were a considerable number of rich Italians. In view of their interest in Sicilian grain, not to mention the interest of the Roman state, it is likely that the territory of Leontini was as productive as the existing state of agricultural technology allowed. There was, however, other good cereal-producing land in Sicily. Such data as survive from the seventeenth and eighteenth centuries show average yields of seven- to ten-fold from large estates in the environs of Palermo, Agrigento and Enna, all in the western sector of the island.[27] The average yield for Sicily as a whole, insofar as this concept has any meaning or practical utility, might not have been significantly lower. Six-fold was a common average yield from nineteenth-century Sicily, at least until the last quarter of the century, which witnessed an agricultural crisis caused by external competition. This led among other things to the conversion of a significant amount of good cereal land to other use and to a reduction in average yield.

None of the evidence on yield thus far considered relates to the

[27] Aymard (1973).

independent peasantry or to small-unit farming in general. Cicero was talking of sizeable estates. Referring to Verres' third year as governor, he revealed that the average farmer in the territory of Leontini put under seed more than 930 iugera, over 230 hectares. The comments of Varro and Columella, insofar as they are based on personal contacts and observation, were surely based on the experience of their social peers. Thus the recent attempt of Evans to arrive at a rough yield figure which is relevant to the smallholder takes on added significance.[28] Proceeding from the stipulation of Caesar's Campanian law of 59 BC that colonists drawn from families with at least three children would each receive ten iugera (two and a half hectares) of land in Campania, and from a basic subsistence figure of 230-275 kg wheat equivalent per person per year,[29] Evans arrives at a minimum annual yield figure in wheat for the land in question of approximately four-and-one-half- to five-fold (4.4–5.1:1). Since Campanian land was of particularly high quality, this yield figure is taken as support for Columella, and for 'perilously low' average yields in wheat and other cereals in Italy, Sicily and other parts of the empire.

The argument is flawed. It turns out that the yield figure is meant to apply if the whole of the allotment of $2\frac{1}{2}$ hectares is under wheat and in every year. But, first, the calculation works only if small farmers practised monoculture in grain. This is quite uncharacteristic of, if not actually incompatible with, subsistence farming. In these circumstances, it is quite improper to ask what level of productivity in wheat will provide for the subsistence needs of a family expressed in wheat equivalent. Wheat equivalent is a term applied by agricultural economists for subsistence needs, including essential non-food items (housing, clothing, etc.) as well as food, in terms of the staple crop rather than money; this is appropriate with respect to a society where producers consumed the greater part of the crop and often or usually paid taxes and rents in kind. The term is properly used in this way, rather than as a term for production, where the implication is that the total subsistence requirement of the household would be met from the wheat harvest. In passing, we may note that wheat is a low-yield crop, and that naked wheats, on which the calculations of the agricultural economists are based, are unlikely to have been the dominant crop of the subsistence peasant in Campania or elsewhere in Italy and the empire at large. Peasants engaged in producing food essentially for their own consumption grew a wide variety of cereals and other crops. The net result is that the yield figure thought by Evans to have been necessary for the survival of an ex-soldier peasant family in Campania is unrealistically high. Secondly, since Evans believes in more or less universal biennial fallow, which means that half the land is rested each

[28] Evans (1980) and (1981). Earlier discussions include Barbagallo (1904), White (1963), Ampolo (1980).
[29] Clark and Haswell (1970), 64ff.

year, his calculations imply a return on seed sown of roughly nine- to ten-fold (8.8-10.2:1). This is by no means a low yield, and in fact recalls the returns cited by Cicero from Leontini.

In short, returns on seed sown seem relatively high, whether in Sicily following Cicero, or in Etruria following Varro, or on Evans' own figures, in Campania under a biennial fallow regime. Columella is the odd man out, and the various attempts to save him – by urging that he must have been referring to intercultivated grain, that he deliberately omitted Etruria and Campania, that he was furnishing not a crop yield but 'the productive capacity of a given property' – only emphasize the shakiness of his testimony. There is nothing we can do about Columella except distrust him.

The upshot is that the ancient evidence, such as it is, does not support an argument for 'perilously low' average yields in wheat or other cereals in Italy, Sicily or any other part of the empire. Even in the case of the smallholder, it is improper to deduce or simply assume that he necessarily expected and received a low return. A re-evaluation of the peasant economy of the Roman period of classical antiquity is overdue, one which escapes the stifling effect of the initial premise that it laboured under a chronic weakness which guaranteed its collapse, except insofar as the farmer could supplement his income and food resources off the estate. One might start by exploring the implications of the fact, already appreciated by prehistoric archaeologists and beginning to influence the writing of ancient history, that smallholders, especially where settlement was dispersed and farmers lived and worked on or near their properties, were in a position to obtain good returns from their crops by intensive methods of production.[30]

[30] Halstead (1981); Jameson (1977-8).

CHAPTER FIVE

Supplying the Roman Empire

Under the Principate, the Roman government was in a position to exploit the whole of the Mediterranean basin, north-western and central Europe and the Balkans. The existence of this massive empire had implications for distribution and consumption in Rome, Italy and the empire at large. Under the heading of distribution, one might ask: How did the city of Rome, the central government and the Roman army secure the consumption items they needed? How far was the government involved in the supply of essential foodstuffs? On consumption, the key questions include: What claims were made by Roman imperial governments on the food resources of the provinces, and with what consequences for the subsistence and survival chances of groups and communities, small and large?

Rome

Augustan Rome was a city of around one million residents, and there may have been more. Recipients of Augustus' handouts of cash or grain numbered at various times 320,000, 250,000 and 200,000, by his own reckoning (*Res Gestae* 15). These were exclusively male citizens. The middle figure of 250,000 recipients, if eligibility began at the age of ten, implies a population affected by the grain dole of around 670,000. A slave population of 30 per cent, a reasonable estimate, brings us not far short of one million inhabitants, without counting in, on the one hand, resident free foreigners, and, on the other hand, citizens of both high and low status not involved in the grain dole.[1]

One million people is a large number of consumers. No city in the western world grew so big again until London topped the one million mark in the eighteenth century. Rome could only grow so big, and remain so big, by drawing heavily on the resources of the whole empire.

Let us try to quantify the requirements of Rome under Augustus.

---

[1] On the grain supply of Rome see Rickman (1980); more briefly, Garnsey (1983a). On the population of Rome, see Hopkins (1978a), 98-9. On the age of eligibility: the lower limit might have been not 10, cf. Brunt (1971), 382 (Suetonius, *Aug.* 41.2 says 11, *sc.* in error), but 14, cf. *Oxy.Pap.* x1 13 (J. Rea), or even, as Keith Hopkins suggests (pers. comm.), 17, the age for military service; but the higher the age of qualification, the larger the population.

Needless to say, almost all numbers are rough estimates and represent only orders of magnitude. There are five headings:

1. Rome's subsistence requirement (food only) in wheat equivalent: 200,000 tonnes p.a.
2. Rome's subsistence requirement in wheat alone: 150,000 tonnes p.a., around 22.5 million *modii*, assuming wheat made up 75 per cent of total food energy requirements.
3. The requirement for the grain dole (*frumentatio*) in wheat: 80,000 tonnes, or 12 million *modii*, for 200,000 recipients, at 5 *modii* per person/month. (Or, 100,000 tonnes, 15 million *modii*, for 250,000 recipients.)
4. Actual consumption rate of wheat: around 200,000 tonnes, or 30 million *modii*, p.a.
5. Total wheat imports: variable, in the range of 200,000-400,000 tonnes, or 30-60 million *modii*, p.a.

The first figure is the total subsistence requirement, food only (housing, clothing, etc., excluded), measured in terms of the prime staple, wheat. The assumption is that around 1700 calories are needed per person/day. At the ratio of approximately 3000 calories to 1 kg wheat, 200 kg minimum are required per person/year, thus 200 million kg or 200,000 tonnes for one million people. For completeness, it would be necessary to furnish estimates of how much food was consumed and imported, both in terms of wheat equivalent.

The remaining estimates are in terms of wheat, the main staple. The peculiar significance of wheat in dietary and political terms is implied in the special treatment it received in imperial Rome, as in classical Athens. Grain alone was distributed in Rome until the turn of the second century AD.

The second estimate is the wheat required by Rome's inhabitants for subsistence: this amounts to three quarters of the previous figure, or 150,000 tonnes. One might make a case for a lower percentage figure for wheat, to reflect the relatively favourable position of Roman consumers. Modern evidence shows that the percentage of cereals in the diet decreases as prosperity increases. But did the majority of Roman consumers become more prosperous, and how far were alternative sources of food energy available, meat in particular, at prices they could afford? Prices were high in Rome. Salaries were also high, but then unemployment and underemployment were rife, as in third-world cities today.

The third figure, 80,000 tonnes or 12 million *modii*, the amount of wheat needed for the hand-out, needs no further explanation.

The fourth figure, 200,000 tonnes or 30 million *modii*, represents annual wheat consumption. Some favour a much higher figure, as much as 400,000 tonnes, or double our estimate.[2] That figure is a product of the juxtaposition of two isolated literary texts, both unreliable, one dating to the mid-fourth century, the other to the mid-first. The former (*Caes*. 1.6) gives a figure of 20 million *modii* for Egyptian wheat exported to Rome under Augustus (perhaps twice the true figure), and the latter (Josephus, *BJ* 2.383,386) a ratio of 2:1 for north African and Egyptian wheat exported to Rome. Neither passage can bear much weight, and to combine the two is a quite unacceptable procedure. We place no more credence in the figure of 75,000 *modii* per day that occurs in a third source (*SHA Sept. Sev.* 23 cf. 8), although, as a rate of actual consumption (which is not how the author presents it), it gives a figure of approximately the right order, about 27.5 million *modii*, over 180,000 tonnes, for the reign of Septimius Severus.

Finally, the actual amount of wheat imported fluctuated within the range of around 200,000-400,000 tonnes, 30 to 60 million *modii*, enough to keep alive $1\frac{1}{3}$-$2\frac{2}{3}$ million people, before deductions for grain lost or spoiled. The interest of the government and the initiative of private traders combined to ensure that much more grain would come into Rome than that which was earmarked for the distributions, which fell far short of the requirements of the population at large. The government appreciated that there was a shortfall, even if it was not equipped to calculate its size, and was interested in making it up. The consumption needs of the court, administration and resident soldiers (around 21,000 men) had to be catered for. Then, families of three or more on the list of grain receivers, unless represented by more than one person, had to supplement from other sources a dole sufficient only for two people. Augustus showed an awareness of this when he issued double rations during the shortage that began in AD 6 (Cassius Dio 55.26ff.). The lowering of the age of eligibility was a more permanent strategy, followed by Trajan and possibly one or more of his predecessors.[3] Finally, no emperor could disregard the rest of the population altogether. The political risks were too great. The whole Roman plebs was a privileged category.

Roman governments did not operate with the figures cited above, with the exception of the grain for the dole. They might, however, have had rough import targets. Perhaps not Augustus. His record suggests a lack of system and a dangerous degree of improvisation. Crises were resolved,

[2] Casson (1980); Rickman (1971), app. 3, corrected in Rickman (1980), 231ff. (40 million *modii*, around 270,000 tonnes); cf. Garnsey (1983a). For d'Escurac (1976), 174, 30 million *modii* (200,000 tonnes) is the subsistence requirement, not the consumption rate.

[3] Pliny, *Pan.* 26-8 says that Trajan introduced 5,000 new infant grain recipients. The number is small, and if authentic, suggests that the age of eligibility had been reduced at some point between Augustus and Trajan (as Andrew Wallace-Hadrill has suggested, pers. comm.). It is difficult to accept both a reduction of the minimum age and a paring down of the list of grain recipients to 150,000; cf. Rickman (1980), 181.

not always very fast, rather than averted (cf. Cassius Dio 55.33ff.; *Res Gestae* 15). It looks as if he did not always have adequate reserve stocks available, but was able to produce grain in emergencies by putting pressure on private grain holders and distributors. He did, however, bequeath to his successors a permanent office headed by a prefect of the grain supply (*praefectus annonae*).[4] There are signs that the more responsible post-Augustan emperors were interested in introducing more order and regularity into the supply system than Augustus was able to achieve. Tiberius on one occasion dismissed contemptuously talk of crisis, pronouncing himself satisfied that he had succeeded in increasing the flow of grain from the provinces (Tacitus, *Ann.* 6.13). In Tacitus' report of the incident Tiberius does not say how this was achieved, but it is likely that in his measures he was anticipating Claudius' panicky drive to add to the number of regular, bulk suppliers. This policy, extended no doubt by later emperors, and combined with an increase in the amount of tax- and rent-grain, brought stability to the system of supply, and ensured that Rome would avoid dangerous shortages except in conditions of civil war. It is in this context that we can begin to talk of government import targets.

At what levels would such targets have been set? Emperors and prefects of the grain supply appreciated that the amount of grain flowing into Rome varied from year to year in accordance with fluctuations in harvest levels in surplus-producing areas and the vagaries of the weather at sea. To be sure of building up adequate reserve stocks in all years, and to allow for damage to grain in transit or storage, the government had to set high targets, higher than estimates of real consumption, whatever rough-and-ready estimates existed.

Import targets or no, the consequence is the same. Rome imported much more grain than it needed.

We come now to the mechanisms of supply and the extent of government involvement. A preliminary point is that the state was not concerned with the import of items of consumption apart from grain for most of our period. Septimius Severus (193-212) is said to have added rations of oil (*SHA Sept. Sev.* 18.3), and Aurelian (270-275) free pork and cheap wine (*SHA Aurel.* 35.2, 48.1). It was once brought home to Augustus that wine was expensive and in short supply. His answer was that it was enough that water was a 'free good' in Rome: 'My son-in-law Agrippa has taken good care, by building several aqueducts, that people shall not go thirsty.' But Augustus was also hostile to the grain dole in principle. He is said to have toyed with the idea of scrapping it altogether, but knew that for political reasons he could not (Suetonius, *Aug.* 42.1,3). He did, however, substantially reduce the number of recipients. Less secure or more indulgent emperors gradually extended

---

[4] D'Escurac (1976).

the range of goods in which the government was interested. Prefects of
the grain supply are commemorated at Rome by oil traders from both
Africa and Spain in the first half of the second century (*CIL* VI
1620,1625b). We may speculate that these officials had been authorized
to buy olive oil and wine on a regular basis from bulk suppliers. This
practice, coupled with the transport under contract of the same products,
more especially oil, originating on imperial estates, would have made for
an easy transition when the government eventually undertook the
obligation to supply and hand out these commodities to the people of
Rome.

The government did not exercise direct control over the grain supply
system at all stages. The production, storage and processing of the grain
can be dealt with briefly; collection and transport are more problematic.
The bulk of the grain that reached Rome was grown on private property.
It was exacted (as tax or requisition) or bought by the government or
sold in the market. The contribution of rent-grain from public and
imperial estates (unattested but probable) is likely to have been much
less significant. On the other hand, it is also likely to have increased, as
confiscations and legacies brought more good-quality arable into
imperial possession. In the matter of storage, too, one can envisage a
steady extension of state ownership and control at the expense of private,
so that whereas state grain overflowed into private granaries in the age of
Augustus, state granaries were holding stocks of private suppliers in the
age of Septimius Severus. Finally, once the grain earmarked for
distribution was taken out of storage and handed out by officials of the
government, the profitable business of converting the distributed grain
and other unmilled grain into flour and then bread was in the hands of
independent millers and bakers. Some of these were very prosperous, as
the impressive private tomb of the baker Eurysaces at the Porta
Maggiore in Rome bears witness. Trajan tried to encourage more men of
means to go into the baking business, or existing bakers to expand their
enterprises; but unless the lawyer of a generation later, Gaius,
misrepresents his ruling, his overtures were aimed exclusively at people
of Latin rights (of intermediate status, neither Roman nor alien), who
were offered citizenship for turning 100 *modii* into bread for each of ten
years.[5]

The bulk of the grain imported for the distributions, as we saw, had the
status of tax in kind. In the late Republic, tax- and rent-grain had been
collected by associations of tax-farmers (*publicani*) awarded state
contracts for the purpose. This system of tax collection was gradually
phased out under the Principate, and was in any case never adopted in
Egypt, one of the main grain-exporting provinces. But the state

[5] Rickman (1971), 164ff. (granaries). For bakers, see *CIL* VI 1958 (Eurysaces); Gaius,
Inst. 1.34, cf. *CIL* VI 1002 (dedication by association of bakers to Antoninus Pius, AD 144).

authorities did not increase the extent of their active involvement in the assembling of tax-grain. This was left to local officials in each province to be performed as an unpaid public service under the general supervision of the provincial governor. Next, there was no state merchant fleet to carry the tax- and rent-grain to its destination. This function was performed by private shipowners paid by the government. This was a profit-making enterprise made more attractive by the favourable terms provided by the state; Claudius, for example, gave shipowners engaged in transporting state wheat to Rome exemption from the *lex Papia Poppaea* (an Augustan law that penalized the unmarried and childless), Roman citizenship and concessions normally awarded for parents of three children. Later emperors added and confirmed the valuable privilege of exemption from compulsory public services.[6]

How extensive was the government contract system? Grain imports were not in their entirety underpinned by such a system. The government would not have exchanged contracts with those very numerous suppliers who were either small and casual or who needed no incentive to contribute grain to the market – including high-status Romans and Italians whose households could not consume or usefully store all the surplus grain they produced on their estates. Claudius offered privileges only to shipowners who agreed to transport 10,000 *modii* of wheat, a little under 70 tonnes, for six years. Within a little more than a century, the threshold had been raised to 50,000 *modii* or around 350 tonnes, carried in one or more ships (*Digest* 50.5.3). Emperors and prefects of the grain supply did not give privileges indiscriminately. They were interested, or especially interested, in bulk suppliers. But bulk suppliers were not necessarily contracted to the government, especially in the formative stages of the development of the imperial supply system. In the long term, governments intent on securing a stable and regular food supply would try to increase the number of suppliers operating within a contract system, with its attendant attractions and constraints.

The army

The Roman army grew from a low at the death of Augustus of around 300,000 legionaries and auxiliaries to a high at the death of Septimius Severus of around 400,000.[7] As a body of consumers, it was divided, unlike the city of Rome. Numerous provinces had permanent contingents of either legionary or auxiliary standing. This dispersal prevented the

[6] Suetonius, *Claud*.18.3-4,19; Gaius, *Inst*.1.32c; *Digest* 3.6 (Claudius), cf. 50.5.3;50.6.6.5.

[7] Army size: various estimates in MacMullen (1980); add Campbell (1984), 4-5. Military supply: briefly, Watson (1969), 102ff.; Wierschowski (1984), 151-73. Among case studies, see Lesquier (1898), Cagnat (1913), Gren (1941), 135-55; Le Roux (1977); and for Britain and the Rhineland, following notes. See also Whittaker (1986).

creation of an integrated system of army supply. Strategies were arrived at that were appropriate to particular localities and sufficiently flexible to cope with changing circumstances, including military movements and fluctuations in the size of the resident garrisons. On the other hand, it is axiomatic that Roman officials, the emperor and his military and civilian subordinates, would take responsibility for organizing a system of supply, and that it would be a comprehensive system and subjected to a high degree of control. The army was the backbone of the imperial order. The necessity of preserving its military effectiveness as well as loyalty to the political authorities explains the attention paid by emperors to its requirements. In contrast, the government supplied the people of Rome grudgingly and only partially, with the end of preserving its political passivity, or, at most, general support for the regime.

Quantifying the needs of the army is a formidable undertaking. To be comprehensive, it would have to take in, among other things, raw materials such as iron (a store of about a million nails, weighing around ten tons, was found at the temporary Flavian fortress of Inchtuthil in Scotland), timber (at Inchtuthil, around 5,000 cubic metres of sawn wood were used for about 28 km of barrack-walling alone), other building materials, animals for cavalry, transport, meat and leather (around 54,000 calf-hides were required merely to equip a legion with tents), products of the clothing industry, such as cloaks, tunics and blankets, other equipment and weaponry, before we come to basic food rations.[8]

The content of normal rations will have varied with the region, but soldiers received at least grain, vin piqué or vinegar consumed with water as *posca*, and, normally, meat.[9] In round figures, 300,000 soldiers would have consumed about 100,000 tonnes of wheat per year, or 15 million *modii*, at one kg of grain per person/day. As the army grew over two and a half centuries by a third, so did its cereal consumption, reaching around 150,000 tonnes, or $22\frac{1}{2}$ million *modii*, under the Severans. These estimates might be judged either much too low or a little too high. They are the former if cavalry received twice as much wheat as infantry, as they did in the second century BC according to Polybius (except that citizen cavalry received three times as much as infantry) (6.39.13).[10]

The figure of 100,000 (or 150,000) tonnes will be too high if the estimated daily grain ration of one kg is too high. This figure for consumption (there is no other from the imperial period) is derived from late Egyptian papyri which show soldiers receiving bread rations at three Roman lbs or around one kg per day. The same soldiers were given two Roman lbs of meat, two pints of wine and $\frac{1}{8}$ of a pint of oil. Jones' word

[8] Richmond and McIntyre (1934); Pitts and St. Joseph (1986), 45ff.; 289ff.

[9] On diet, see Davies (1971); Tchernia (1986), (wine/*posca*).

[10] Animal feed (barley or hay) must be included in any comprehensive account of the food requirements of the army. There may have been as many as a thousand animals attached to each legion. See Pitts, St. Joseph (1986), 181, citing Mócsy (1972).

for this diet was 'positively gargantuan'. In fact, the figure for cereal consumption, taken in isolation, is only marginally higher than Polybius' $\frac{2}{3}$ *medimnos* of wheat per month, equal to 4 *modii*, or about 27 kg, for Roman and allied infantry in the second century BC. This is in turn approximately the same as what had been termed a standard Greek military ration of one *choenix* of wheat per day in the classical period. The chained slaves of Cato's second-century-BC treatise *On Agriculture* ate much more, 4 or 5 lbs of bread per day, but they consumed little else (*de agr.* 56).[11]

One hundred thousand tonnes of grain will do as a rough estimate of the cereal consumption of the army under Augustus, rising to 150,000 tonnes under Septimius Severus.

State organization of military supply has consequences for the geographical range over which supplies were sought, the status of the goods that found their way to the camp and the methods by which they were brought.

Most supplies were local in origin. That is, the military provinces and the areas adjacent to them took the lion's share of the burden of army supply. Commodities judged essential or in considerable demand were sought from further afield only insofar as they could not be obtained, or not in sufficient quantity, near the army base. In this category should be placed the Spanish olive oil that found its way to the Rhineland and Britain. In general, long-distance transport was expensive and inefficient. Even if governments had been prepared to pay the cost, they would have been intolerant of the inefficiency involved, when keeping army regiments contented and on a war footing was at issue.

Living off the zone or region of occupation was not always a practical proposition. Strategic rather than economic considerations were sometimes paramount in the choice of site for an army base, as is obvious from the way in which the army was deployed in Syria, north Africa or Britain. Again, the army demand for food, raw materials and a wide variety of manufactured goods simply could not always be met locally, especially in the early days of conquest and pacification, even if the tribes and communities involved had been hospitable to a sizeable occupying force – an argument more applicable to the northern frontier regions than to the more developed East. As pacification gave way to peaceful coexistence with the local population, the presence of a settled garrison frequently stimulated the growth of an 'army' of local producers and suppliers. This was not always a spontaneous development. The village structure of first- and second-century Dobrogea in the province of Lower Moesia was the product of a series of enforced colonizations of conquered tribesmen, which had the specific object of supporting the lower Danubian frontier with supplies and manpower. Moreover, it is

[11] Jones (1964), 629, 1261-2; Foxhall and Forbes (1982), Table 3 and *passim*.

significant that elsewhere in Lower Moesia the Roman occupation had very little effect on local settlement patterns. Similarly, British archaeologists have noticed that the proximity of the army did not stimulate agriculture in the highland zone or in Wales; and that for that matter it did not provoke the appearance of a new, indigenous northern pottery industry on a scale to compete with or replace imported pottery. The situation in the south-west of England was different: here it seems that the locality, within a radius of about 30 miles, played an important part in the supply of the garrison at Gloucester. But to return to the North, where the bulk of the army was stationed: it was the South that shouldered the main burden of supplying the army of Britain. To put it in another way, the category of middle-distance supply was important in Britain.[12]

The British army also received goods from Gaul or further afield. In the period from the invasion to the end of the first century, a very significant level of imports was sustained in artefacts. Not only in artefacts: pottery and other small manufactures typically travelled pick-a-back, in the gaps left by a primary cargo, and can therefore be taken as proxy for the bulk movement of raw materials and perishables. The latter items are invisible, and their identity and relative importance can only be guessed at: in the British case perhaps iron, cloth, hides and some foodstuffs. Should we include cereals in the list of long-distance imports? The discovery by archaeologists of grain pests such as *Sitophilus granarius* on British sites, unattested in earlier periods and therefore foreign, can tell us nothing whatever about the regularity of grain imports or the quantities involved. It is still therefore in principle open to advocates of British self-sufficiency to argue that the province paid its own way in respect of the most important staple of all. The case is stronger for the second century, if the fall-off in the import of (visible) manufactures and (invisible) primary products can be correlated with increased agricultural production in Britain. A partial correlation can be admitted. Another factor, perhaps the primary factor, in the decline of imports was the reduction in the size of the military establishment in the province in the second and third centuries.[13]

The British case illustrates the difficulty of gauging the relative importance of neighbourhood, regional and long-distance supply in any particular instance, especially as the balance between the various categories was likely to alter over time. But the supposition still stands that an army by preference supported itself from the locality and region where it was stationed. If necessary, goods were ordered in bulk from long-distance suppliers, and the order might well have been substantial in the early period of military occupation. But the balance tilted away

[12] Poulter (1980), 735-8; Sommer (1984), 36-9; G.B.D. Jones (1984), 868-9; Davies (1984); Hurst (1985), 123-5 (on Gloucester).

[13] For the above argument, see Fulford (1984).

from long-distance imports as suppliers closer to hand grew in number and capacity, and as the state authorities grew more interested in and more expert at exploiting them. The significance of this last factor, not touched upon thus far, will emerge when we come to discuss the means by which supplies were extracted from the civilian population.

The status of the goods supplied to the army and the methods by which they were introduced are a second index of the degree of state involvement in army supply.

The army to some extent supplied itself.[14] This was a matter of practical necessity, in as much as the environment was unfriendly, the resources of the civilian population insufficient, and imports inadequate. Thus, for example, in the Rhineland, it was standard for military personnel to make cooking pots, *mortaria* and other pottery, iron articles and implements, leather goods and certain weapons, and for that matter, to graze animals on land attached to the legion. We are a long way from the more organized state production system of Diocletian, but self-supply was not a negligible factor in earlier times, and would have reduced the army's dependence on and interaction with the local economy.

The goods it could not produce, or not in sufficient quantity – grain, fodder, meat, a wide variety of processed foods (beverages, milk products, salt and so on), clothing, armour and weaponry – had to be acquired in other ways. Almost from the first in the history of Rome's relationship with a frontier area, food and equipment came in as tax, tribute or contributions under some other name from defeated enemies and other peoples who acknowledged Roman supremacy.[15] Collection and transport might be supervised by soldiers or civilian officials. In more settled times and environments, these exactions characteristically took the form of obligations imposed on the civilian population through the agency of city officials.

To tax should be added requisitions. Where requisitioned goods were paid for rather than merely seized, as in times and places where good relations with civilians were accorded some value, the price was presumably fixed by the buyer and therefore usually below the market rate. Compulsory purchase may be supposed to have been a fundamental source of supplies everywhere, as it can be shown to have been in Egypt. This is not surprising, for the following reason. The return of taxes in kind, if levelled as a percentage of the harvest, was unpredictable, while goods travelling from a distance might be held up or lost. While in the

[14] E.g. von Petrikovits (1974a); Darling (1977); Pitts and St. Joseph (1986), 105ff., 114-15 (citing Vegetius 2.11; *Digest* 50.6.7). For the products of agriculture and animal husbandry, see Mócsy (1967); Le Roux (1977), 350ff.

[15] The importance of tax in kind is conceded by Gren (1941), 138ff.; Brunt (1981), 161-2 (over-cautious); Wierschowski (1984), 152 (whose discussion none the less concentrates on government purchase).

matter of vital staples, in particular grain, the authorities stockpiled supplies (British military granaries were built to hold one to two years' supply of grain), the precise needs of a garrison in other items might have been underestimated. Topping up must have been a common necessity; in which case, it was better diplomacy to buy than to impose a supplementary tax. This is what the detachments of soldiers from Stobi on the lower Danube and from Dura-Europus on the northern Euphrates were doing when they went in search of grain for men and animals, or clothing, or horses. Distances covered were usually short (but an expedition set out from Stobi for Gaul for clothing and perhaps wheat). The more important point is that these missions have all the appearance of regularity. Requisitioning was routine.[16]

Goods brought in from a distance fell into the same general categories as those acquired locally: taxes in kind, rents in kind (from imperial estates), purchases. Insofar as goods were transported in bulk over distance, this was in the hands of private traders. The same traders also carried goods on their own account for sale en route and in the camp. Such foreign imports did not necessarily lose out in any competition with local products. Their transport was in effect subsidized by the state; they were a 'freeloading' secondary cargo riding on the back of bulk goods carried, typically, under government contract.

In addition, local and regional traders, and camp-followers from the organized communities that grew up in the vicinity of the camps (*canabae* and *vici*), sold to soldiers. There was money left from pay after deductions for food, clothing and equipment for supplementary purchases (though some of this, together with occasional special payments, was credited to the soldier's account). Still, this kind of commercial operation was essentially a peripheral activity, though no doubt profitable to the traders and producers concerned. It involved the sale of luxuries or at least 'optional extras', quality tableware, good wine and other food items not provided as standard rations, whereas, as we have seen, the basic provisioning and equipment of a regiment was handled by Roman supply officials in other ways. Our impression is that as little as possible of the task of supplying the army was left to the initiative of independent traders or to 'market forces'.

When an army was on the move, requisitions or compulsory purchases bulked larger. The impact on Rome's subjects was greatest when a major campaign was in preparation. In that event the zone of supply was broadened and more systematic, and comprehensive requisitioning was imposed by government representatives under the overall control of a special official usually of senior equestrian rank (*praepositus annonae*). Already in the reign of the first emperor, a systematic

[16] Lesquier (1898), 354-6, 363-8, with Carrié (1977); Gilliam (1950), 180,243ff.; Fink (1971), 217ff. (Stobi, Dura Europos). On British military granaries, Gentry (1976), 28.

attempt had been made to work out the extent of the obligations of urban residents and country dwellers alike to mobile state employees, military or civilian, in respect of food, equipment, transported facilities and hospitality. In a recently published inscription, the second emperor, Tiberius, apparently confirmed earlier measures and attempted to curb their abuse on behalf of provincials in Pisidia.[17]

Emperors received many complaints in the centuries that followed, and sometimes responded sympathetically. Yet the arrival of an emperor with his entourage could spell disaster for communities that lay in his path. Honorific inscriptions from the imperial period that praise a benefactor for both rescuing the city in time of food shortage and providing for an imperial visitor imply an association between the two: 'The city celebrates Manios Salarios Sabinos, gymnasiarch and benefactor, who very often in times of shortage sold grain much more cheaply than the current price, and when the emperor's army was passing through provided for the annona 400 *medimnoi* of wheat, 100 of barley and 60 of beans, plus 1000 *metretae* of wine at a much cheaper rate than the current price.' The city was Lete in Macedonia and the emperor Hadrian, whose two visits to Sparta brought two subsistence crises on that city. On the other side, some fortunate host-cities benefited from imperial largesse.[18]

The third century, when warfare was more frequent, and in the middle decades constant, is usually represented as a period of fundamental change in the method of military supply. First, extraordinary exactions became more common and played a more vital part in the supply of the army than previously. Furthermore, as civic order and military discipline degenerated, authorized limits were bypassed and payment became desultory or vanished altogether. Secondly, the range of foods that were dispensed as normal rations expanded to include oil and wine, while grain was no longer deducted from pay. These developments (for which the evidence is very thin) may have been introduced by the Severan emperors as part of their policy of improving the material conditions of the army, but they gained an additional raison d'être by the middle of the third century, as inflation gathered pace and the value of military pay plummeted. In earlier periods soldiers had been able to supplement their basic rations by purchase; this was no longer possible. The question is, whether these developments justify talk of a new military tax, instituted by Septimius Severus and later formalized and systematized by Diocletian. This is the *annona militaris*, defined in the literature as

---

[17] Mitchell (1976). On the *praepositus annonae*, Bérard (1984). For a city's response to an extraordinary annona demand, see Bean and Mitford, *Journeys in Rough Cilicia 1964-68* (1970), nos. 19, 20, 21a (Side, E. Pamphylia, Severus Alexander, AD 233).

[18] *Ann.Brit.Sch.Ath.* 23 (1918-19) no.7, pp. 72ff.; *SEG* XI 492, with *Ann.Brit.Sch.Ath.* 27 (1925-26), 227ff. (Hadrian on the move); Cassius Dio 69.16.2; Ziegler (1977) (1978) (Severan emperors to the rescue).

the pay of the soldiers raised as tax and distributed to them in kind.[19]

Soldiers had always received rations and equipment as stoppages of their pay, which was calculated in money. Under Diocletian, and *a fortiori* under Septimius Severus, they were still paid their annual *stipendium* in three instalments in the traditional way.[20] The difference was that inflation had reduced the value of money and left the soldiers with nothing after the standard deductions had been made. Any 'profit' came to the soldier in the form of donatives and extraordinary exactions from the civilian population. Both were frequent in the third century, were administered or connived at by the Roman authorities, and constituted a practical alternative to a new tax.

Distribution of the burden

At the risk of oversimplification, we propose a broad three-fold division of provinces by function. The three functions are: the provision of wheat for the city of Rome; the provision of wheat and other necessities for the army; the provision of cash for soldiers and officials. The hypothesis is that there was not a province that did not play one of these roles. The category of dual-function province is not excluded – Egypt is an obvious candidate.

First, providers of wheat for Rome. These were the main surplus-producing areas of the West, namely, north Africa, Sicily and Sardinia, plus, in the East, Egypt. A passage of Pliny shows that grain also came to Rome from Gaul, the Chersonese, Cyprus and Spain. Pliny was not presenting a list, and if he had been, it is not complete. But in any case, the burden was shared unevenly among this latter group and the main suppliers.[21]

The unevenness of the division becomes clear if we inquire into the status of the grain coming to Rome. The group of main suppliers provided the tax-grain (plus the bulk of the grain that came in through supplementary tax, requisitioning and compulsory purchase), the single most important category. The same group provided most of the rent-grain from public or imperial estates. With a third category, rent-grain from the estates of the Roman elite brought in for their private consumption and for distribution in or outside the market, we move to some extent outside the band of main suppliers, to wherever upper-class

[19] Van Berchem (1937) (1977); cf. Tchernia (1986a), 13ff.; Corbier (1978), 295; Jones (1964), 623ff.

[20] Jones (1964), 623,1257-8.

[21] Pliny, *HN* 18.66. Italy provided grain, Moesia on the lower Danube rarely (cf. *ILS* 986). In general, Rickman (1980), 94-119, but he excludes Sicilian tax-grain, 104-6, as does Neesen (1980), Gabba (1986), 77ff., with unsatisfactory arguments. *Contra*, Brunt (1981), 162; Garnsey (1983a), 120-1. On Sardinian grain, Rowland (1984).

Romans had estates at no great travelling distance from Rome: in addition to Sicily and north Africa, Spain, the old Gallic province, and, importantly, Italy.[22] Finally, grain purchased from private suppliers, some under contract to the government, could have come from anywhere, wherever the shippers involved had contacts. We know that 'the five colleges of marine shippers of Arles' worked for the Roman supply system (*annona*), though there is no proof that their cargoes inevitably originated in Gaul.[23] The task of supplying Rome was spread somewhat beyond the main surplus-producing provinces through the agency of such companies.

Next, provinces that supplied the army. The bulk of army supplies were local in origin. This means that the main burden fell on the northern and north-western provinces. Taking as our yardstick the disposition of the legions around AD 150, almost two-thirds of the army was concentrated in this sector of the empire. The Danube-Balkan region by itself supported ten legions of about 55,000 men and about 140 auxiliary units of about 80,000, more than half of them cavalry – in short, not much less than two-fifths of the total army of the mid-second century, and requiring almost 50,000 tonnes of wheat alone each year. The north-west also had a substantial military presence, about 50,000 and 45,000 legionaries and auxiliaries in Britain and Germany, respectively. North Gaul was a major supplier of the Rhine armies; Britain and to some extent Gaul provided for the British army; while the Danubian legions drew deeply on the resources of the Balkan provinces.[24]

No major grain exporter to Rome had to put up with a large garrison as well. Egypt in the mid-second century had two legions and perhaps 17 auxiliary units, about 20,000 men in all, and Africa Proconsularis with Numidia about half as many in the same period.

The third category of province comprises those contributing money-taxes, about half of which, very approximately, 400 million sesterces, went to the army as pay, donatives and discharge payments.[25] Such provinces were either without garrisons or only lightly garrisoned, and with the addition of Italy, which did not pay the land tax, they furnished much of the political and cultural leadership of the empire: in particular, the Iberian peninsula, the south of France, and western Asia Minor.[26]

---

[22] The assumption is that the considerable *familiae* of the rich (the urban prefect Pedanius Secundus had 400 household slaves; Tacitus, *Ann*. 14.43) would not have been fed entirely from market-purchased goods. Cf. Whittaker (1985).

[23] *CIL* III 14165,8; XII 672, on which Pflaum (1960), no. 186, p.507 is unconvincing.

[24] For estimates of unit numbers we are indebted to Dr Roxan.

[25] The figures are from Hopkins (1980), 116ff., cf. 124-5; see also Campbell (1984), 161ff.

[26] Egypt and Gaul (Caesar's Gaul) are cited as significant contributors of cash-taxes in Velleius Paterculus 2.39 (cf. Suetonius, *Iul*. 25).

The upshot is that the burden of supporting the Roman government with food, other supplies and cash was distributed over the whole empire. Rome was engaged in tapping the resources of every corner of the Roman world.

Subjects as consumers

It is easy to slip into the language of gloom and doom when discussing the subsistence problems of Rome's subjects. The beginning of *On the wholesome and unwholesome properties of foodstuffs*, a treatise of Galen, the mid-second century physician and philosopher, is commonly quoted, but unfortunately without the prolegomenon that provides the context:[27]

> The famines occurring in unbroken succession over a number of years among many of the peoples subject to the Romans have demonstrated clearly, to anyone not completely devoid of intelligence, the important part played in the genesis of diseases by the consumption of unhealthy foods. For among many of the peoples who are subject to the Romans, the city-dwellers, as it was their practice to collect and store enough grain for all the next year immediately after the harvest, left what remained to the country people, that is, pulses of various kinds, and they took a good deal of these too to the city. The country people finished the pulses during the winter, and so had to fall back on unhealthy foods during the spring; they ate twigs and shoots of trees and bushes, and bulbs and roots of indigestible plants; they filled themselves with wild herbs, and cooked fresh grass. (VI 749ff.)

The passage cannot be taken as a description of normal conditions, as it is regularly presented, for two reasons. The first emerges from the passage itself, unless it is quoted selectively. Galen is picturing the behaviour of city-dwellers and rustics in the throes of a severe famine. The treatment is rhetorical. Galen shows in a number of colourful anecdotes that he was familiar with the cunning and resource demonstrated by country folk in the face of natural and human constraints. Secondly, famine itself, and the urban-rural confrontation that it engendered, were not everyday occurrences. If Galen had thought he was describing the norm, he contradicted himself many times in the course of his ample descriptions of peasant diets, in his *On the properties of foodstuffs*, and elsewhere, and in vignettes like the following, embodying a youthful memory:

> But I myself, when travelling as a young man into the countryside some

[27] As in MacMullen (1974), 33. For introducing us to the delights of Galen as a source for social history, we have to thank Vivian Nutton.

distance from Pergamum with two companions of the same age, came upon
some peasants who had already eaten their supper, and the women among
them were just going to make bread – for they had run out of it. One of
them straightaway threw some wheat into a pot and boiled it, and after
adding a little salt, gave it to us to eat. We naturally had to eat it, since we
were hungry from our long journey. For this reason, too, we made a good
meal of it, though it felt as heavy as mud in our stomachs. And the whole of
the next day we had bad indigestion, and could take no food at all, having
no appetite and being full of wind. We also had blackouts before the eyes,
for nothing of what we had eaten could be evacuated. But that is the only
way by which indigestion can be relieved. (VI 498-9)

Galen's hosts may well have enjoyed the discomfort of their guests, but
it would be perverse not to read the passage as an illustration of
harmonious relations between peasants and city-folk, at least on an
individual and non-official level, and as evidence of the availability of
wholesome food in peasant households.

Subsistence or near-subsistence peasants were certainly vulnerable,
especially tenants burdened by both rent and tax, but also
owner-occupiers forced to raise cash-crops in order to pay tax, in the
process undermining their subsistence base and exposing themselves to
the instability of market forces. But peasants were also resilient, and
they operated effective, traditional strategies for survival. We should also
allow for the role of rural patronage in blunting the sharp edges of
confrontation between rich and poor, and the access enjoyed by rural
labourers with an urban base to whatever supply systems evolved in the
cities.[28]

We turn now to cities, and start with a concrete problem. Casson
raised the question of the effect of the annexation of Egypt in 30 BC on
the communities of the eastern Mediterranean. The East, he says, would
have starved, had it not been the case that Rome was already drawing
regularly on Egyptian grain stocks in the last century of the Republic.
Unfortunately for this argument, there is a complete lack of evidence
from the late Republic for the import of grain from Egypt. The silence of
Cicero is particularly puzzling, notably in the *De imperio Cn. Pompeii*,
where Rome's three sources of support are identified as Sicily, Sardinia
and Africa. Starvation in the East (and glut in the West) therefore
remains a possibility.[29]

The following considerations may be adduced.

First, Rome may have reserved the lion's share of the exportable
surplus of Egypt, but it did not want or take the whole of it. There is
scattered evidence from Greece, Asia Minor and Judaea for the relief of

---

[28] In Garnsey (1979) it is argued that Italian farmers were partly city-based and partly
country-based.

[29] Casson (1954); against, Meiggs (1973), 472-3.

food shortage with Egyptian grain, covering the whole period from the first decade of the Augustan Principate to the early third century. The principle, as laid down in a second-century inscription from Ephesos, is that the city of Rome heads the queue. An unidentifiable emperor writes to the Ephesians:

> It is clear that you will make prudent use of this agreement, bearing in mind the necessity that first the imperial city should have a bounteous supply of wheat procured and assembled for its market, and then the other cities may also receive provisions in plenty. If, as we pray, the Nile provides us with a flood of the customary level, and a bountiful harvest of wheat is produced among the Egyptians, then you will be among the first after the homeland.[30]

It is specifically implied that in a normal year there was plenty of grain to go around, once Rome's needs had been satisfied.

Secondly, Egypt under the Principate had more grain to export, in comparison with the last phase of independence, when the country experienced considerable disruption and unrest. Improvements in distribution are likely to have been achieved already under the first emperor, perhaps too a better agricultural performance.

Thirdly, the eastern Mediterranean had been the theatre of regular and destructive civil and foreign wars in the last century of the Republic. Many communities had suffered not only war damage, but also recurrent requisitions and direct punitive action. The region gained more, it might be suggested, from the cessation of these wars than it lost through the annexation of Egypt.

Fourthly, there was some shift in population East to West in the early empire, and therefore a reduction in the number of consumers in the East. The population of the city of Rome picked up significantly under Augustus, making up the losses of the previous two decades, and possibly rising above the levels of the 60s and 50s. Under the Republic, Rome's gain in manpower had been Italy's loss, if the conventional picture is accepted, though the slaves who poured into the city were for the most part provincial in origin. Under the Principate, mortality rates and conditions of life in the capital necessitated a continuous high level of immigration simply to maintain the population of Rome at its Augustan levels.[31] It is arguable that under Augustus and his successors proportionately more provincials came to Rome and fewer Italians than under the Republic. The capital city now attracted more 'betterment' than 'subsistence' immigrants. In other words, by comparison with the period of accelerated demographic expansion, fewer free men were driven

---

[30] Wörrle (1971); cf. *CIG* 2927,2938; Josephus, *AJ* 15.299ff., esp. 305ff.

[31] For population growth and replacement in London, see Wrightson (1982), 127-8 with nn. and bibl.

into the city by economic necessity, and more migrated more or less freely from a relatively prosperous background in search of self-enrichment. To the extent that the East, specifically eastern cities, contributed to that demographic movement, and their contribution was probably significant, then there was a fall in the aggregate demand for staple foodstuffs in the East.

Fifthly, it had happened before. Over an extended period of time, Rome had conquered and absorbed one by one the most fertile and productive areas in the Mediterranean region. The annexation of Campania, Sicily, north Africa or Egypt are punctuations and turning-points, ushering in short periods of accelerated change. Each advance caused perturbations in the region immediately concerned and in economically linked areas. States were forced to adjust their supply systems, political loyalties and land use. Some held their own, others suffered short-term or permanent decline. In the long term, the vulnerability of the majority of cities in the region concerned was not significantly increased, their survival chances not seriously undermined, by Rome's latest advance.

So much for the specific matter raised by Casson, whether the annexation of Egypt threatened the East with starvation. To take further the associated, broader issue, whether the Roman imperial government prejudiced the future of subject communities by cornering the surplus of the richest agrarian provinces, we turn to a consideration of the local evidence for food supply and food shortage. The documentation is of necessity drawn from the cities of the Greek East. It would be convenient if the evidence were spread evenly around the provinces of the empire, and between urban and rural environments, but this is not the case.

We present first three indicators of continuity with the past, that is, with the Hellenistic period, and then two of change.

First, there were periodic food shortages, when prices rose and supplies of essential foodstuffs were deficient. This was nothing new. Food crises were endemic in the Mediterranean region.

Secondly, local institutions for 'famine relief' remained essentially the same. Every city had developed over time rudimentary mechanisms and practices designed to keep it supplied with necessities, especially grain, at reasonable prices. The post of grain commissioner (*sitones, sitophylax, curator annonae*) is widely attested and has the appearance of a standard public service, at any rate in the East.[32] The Roman period shows little institutional change and little significant development in the scope or range of local government responses to crisis. The lack of public monies in the form of permanent funds for the purchase of goods in short supply is particularly conspicuous.

This statement does not require modification in view of Egyptian grain

[32] In general, Garnsey (1986a); for *sitonai* etc. in the East, see Jones (1940), 217-18.

distributions (attested at Oxyrhynchos, Alexandria and Hermopolis in the 260s and 270s, and at Hermopolis in AD 62) or lists of 'receivers of distributed grain' in some Lycian cities. The Egyptian distributions were temporary and isolated phenomena; we cannot even say that distributions were regular in Lycia. No regular distributions in other provinces are hinted at in the documents. If local governments were intended to follow Trajan's Italian example of funding poor relief schemes, they failed to do so. For that matter, permanent funds financing regular distributions were a rarity in the Hellenistic age. There is another point: in Lycia, the distributions were funded by private benefactors, acting in rotation. In one inscription, a man from Oenoanda claims to have been the first to do so twice. Thus something less than a permanent grain fund operated here. Samos at the turn of the third century BC had done better, with its grain fund financed by private donations.[33]

Thirdly, euergetism, the public display of generosity by individuals, remained the key factor in the response of local governments to shortage – as indeed the Oenoanda inscription suggests. Graeco-Roman euergetism was essentially the same as its Hellenistic predecessor. Its ideology was civic, not humanitarian – very few euergetists would have described what they were doing as poor relief.[34] The attitude of its exponents, the rich, was (still) ambivalent: they were producers and occasionally traders as well as benefactors.

Two indicators of change can be taken together. The rich, as just stated, were in a position to indulge in profiteering as well as benefaction, and this gives the food supply system, such as it was, a fragile look. Our impression is that speculation in essential goods was less under the control of local government in the Roman than in the Hellenistic world. It is not coincidental that subsistence crises were frequently resolved from the outside, typically by the intervention of Roman officials. A provincial governor was praised at Aelium Coela in the Thracian Chersonese for having 'looked after the interests of everybody with zeal during a very severe shortage of foodstuffs'. At Pisidian Antioch in the province of Cappadocia, the governor Antistius Rusticus was called in by the local magistrates and councillors to relieve a grain crisis in AD 92-3. He issued an edict compelling those with grain stocks to release that which was surplus to their own subsistence needs at a price of one denarius, presumably well below the market rate. A second-century

---

[33] *Oxy.Pap.* xl (J. Rea); Eusebius, *HE* 7.21.9; Wilcken, *Chrest.* 425; Kraut (1984) (Egypt); *ZPE* 24 (1977), 265ff. no.1 (Tlos); *TAM* II.2. 578 (Tlos); Balland, *Fouilles de Xanthos* 7 (1981), 185ff.; and some unpublished inscriptions from Oenoanda (by courtesy Dr Alan Hall); cf. *Syll.*³ 976 (Samos). A few private poor relief schemes are attested, e.g. Pliny, *Ep.*7.18; Balland (above); and see Duncan-Jones (1982), 341.

[34] For the social class of recipients, *Oxy.Pap.* xl 8 (J. Rea); critique by Rowland (1976); cf. Finley (1985a), 201. The classic treatment of euergetism is by Veyne (1976).

proconsul of Asia exerted his authority over bakers, whose failure to supply bread had led to civil disturbances in Ephesos. The emperor Hadrian promulgated a law at Athens designed to prevent local traders from causing artificial shortages of olive oil by sending it abroad.[35]

Civic councils in these instances were powerless to resolve crises and unable to control profiteers, who might have included some of their own members. However, the intervention of Roman officials in such circumstances, though it brought short-term benefits, had long-term negative consequences. The morale, initiative and authority of local government was undermined, and the tendency to dysfunctioning aggravated. On the other side, the imperial power may be credited with having made possible and even inspired the extraordinary outburst of civic munificence that marked the second and early third centuries all over the empire. But there can be no doubt that of the two phenomena, the spirit of euergetism, and the sapping of local initiative and authority, the latter would be the more enduring.

Conclusion

The cities of the Roman world were apparently able to cope with the periodic food shortages that they suffered, although there was a tendency, perhaps a growing tendency, to lean on the authority and charity of the imperial power. This was an ominous development.

This general conclusion must be qualified. The evidence is thin. Few cities are visible, and when they come into focus, we are given only a partial glimpse of their condition. The inscriptions that inform us about individual food shortages are honorific. Their function was to advertise the generosity of men who by their benefactions had averted crisis. They issued from communities that were not in serious disarray or slow decline. The latter did not expose their weaknesses through the medium of epigraphy.

The problem recedes once it is recognized that the central government had a firm stake in the survival and welfare of cities in general, less so in those of individual cities, with some exceptions. Cities were needed to perform a narrow range of essential administrative duties, and for this their economic viability and demographic base had to be preserved. But this general commitment to cities did not extend to the preservation of any individual community at a given level of prosperity. So the territories of cities and their revenues were increased or diminished; some were demoted and became subservient to others, some were promoted or created out of nothing, for a variety of reasons, often trivial. The

[35] *Forsch. Eph.* III no.48; McCrum and Woodhead, *Documents of the Reigns of the Flavian Emperors* 464; Buckler (1923), 30-3; *SEG* xv 108 = Oliver, *Ruling Power* 960ff.

continually changing pattern of urbanization in the empire is not to be mistaken for an endemic weakness in the administrative infrastructure of the empire.

A conclusion relating to the peasantry follows similar lines. The ebb and flow in the countryside, as peasant households collapsed, survived, migrated and prospered, should not be confused with the issue of the survival of the peasantry as a class. If there was no group survival of the farming population, then the cities, dependent upon the agricultural resources of the countryside, would certainly have been in a state of collapse. As a fourth-century prefect of the city of Rome put it to the Roman senate in time of famine in Italy: 'If so many cultivators are starved, and so many farmers die, our corn supply will be ruined for good. We are excluding those who normally supply our daily bread' (Ambrose, *off.* 3.45ff.).

It remains to bring these conclusions to bear on the issues raised earlier, the demands of the government and the way they were distributed.

Taxation, tribute, impositions under some other name, were not a new phenomenon in the regions that made up the Roman empire. What occurred as a result of imperial conquest and the imposition of empire-wide censuses was that tax was raised somewhat more efficiently and from a wider area than ever before. Tax rates remained relatively low, at least outside Egypt, and Vespasian is the only emperor known to have raised them. A high level of taxation was unnecessary. The requirements of the government were very limited, because its concerns were few.

Thus, the demands of the central government were not such as to threaten the future of Rome's subjects. Moreover, although those demands were greater in aggregate than those made by any previous imperial state in the Mediterranean region, they were also distributed throughout the empire, and the empire was big enough to absorb them.

Rome - suppling it
Army - supplying it
3 types of provinces
Egypt + relief feed zone

PART III

CHAPTER SIX

The Social Hierarchy

The Principate of Augustus was preceded by two decades of civil war, in which armies of a size not previously seen in Roman history fought for the supremacy of their generals. The confusion of traditional social distinctions that accompanied the collapse of Republican political institutions is illustrated by two anecdotes relating to the first of the civil-war victors, Julius Caesar. Caesar was said to have admitted to the Roman senate 'men of foreign birth, including semi-civilized Gauls who had been granted Roman citizenship', and who now discarded trousers for togas. A stage performance before Caesar won for the actor Decimus Laberius equestrian rank, which he had lost because of his lowly profession, 'so that he could walk straight from stage to orchestra, where fourteen rows of seats were reserved for his order'.[1]

The social disruption penetrated to the household and family. Appian claimed that the pressure of the triumviral proscriptions, supervised by the second of the civil-war victors, Caesar's heir Octavian (later Augustus), caused men to fear betrayal even by their wives, children, freedmen and slaves. The result was 'a shocking change in the condition of senators, consulars, praetors, tribunes ... who threw themselves with lamentations at the feet of their own slaves, giving to the servant the character of saviour and master. But the most lamentable thing was that even after this humiliation, they did not win pity' (BC 4.13).

Against this background of social turmoil, Augustus established his military supremacy and restored peace and constitutional government. Augustus' policy went beyond simple social conservatism: the pattern of social inequality and differentiation continued from the Republic, but innovations now gave distinctions of rank sharper definition. The social order that he established was stable and enduring. Under the Principate as a whole, the divisions and tensions deriving from the unequal distribution of wealth, rank and status were counterbalanced by forces of cohesion such as family and household, structured vertical and horizontal relationships between individuals and households, and the ideological apparatus of the state.

[1] Suetonius, *Iul.* 76, 80, 39.2; cf. Cassius Dio 52.42.1 on the second triumvirate.

Sources

The evidence for imperial society is limited in quantity and quality. While these deficiencies should not be allowed to determine what historical questions are asked, they do circumscribe the field of questions to which convincing answers can be given.

For the social historian, the two principal types of evidence for the Roman empire (outside Egypt) are literature and inscriptions. Many kinds of evidence on which historians of other periods rely never existed under the Principate or have not survived. No systematic, self-conscious description or analysis of imperial society and its constituent elements was written. Though Romans did use written documents to establish legal relationships and obligations, these have not survived in quantity; nor has reliable statistical evidence, such as population figures.[2]

The period did produce a substantial corpus of literary works in many genres, ranging from history and biography to letters, legal treatises, satirical poetry and prose fiction laced with fantasy. The diversity offers some safeguard against generalizations based on any one genre. For all the variety, however, the literature was written by a tiny fraction of the population; the authors were uniformly men of the leisured elite, and their works convey the perceptions of the upper strata of society.

The hundreds of thousands of inscriptions form the largest body of evidence from the Principate. But only a handful are long enough to provide much insight into social relations, and the great majority are brief, formulaic funerary or career inscriptions. They do not constitute a genuine sample of the millions originally erected, nor did those millions evenly represent the populations of the empire over space, time or social group.[3] This is partly because the standard epitaphs and honorific, career inscriptions are essentially an artefact of Romanization, which did not affect all areas of the empire equally. Nevertheless, the epigraphic evidence broadens the historian's vision insofar as it issued from groups outside the imperial elite. Most dedications were set up for modest people who did not enjoy privileged rank. The poor, of course, are not represented even in this record.

Finally, the literary and epigraphic sources share the limitation of being highly sporadic in nature. The lack of a series of comparable literary works, or of a representative sample of inscriptions whose distribution over time can be taken as significant, makes the identification and explanation of trends in Roman society very difficult.

[2] Finley (1985b), ch. 3.
[3] MacMullen (1982); Saller and Shaw (1984a).

Class analysis

In recent years, the problem of analysing persisting social inequalities has been presented in terms of the need to characterize or label the divisions in Roman society. Should these divisions be identified as status distinctions in the manner of Weber? Or as class distinctions following Marx?[4] In our view, this is not a helpful approach to the analysis of social inequality and social structure in the ancient world. Class analysis has suffered from the assumption of many supporters and critics alike that it consists essentially in the identification of given social entities with a specific membership. Even in the analysis of contemporary society this approach has created difficulties. Class membership is open to conflicting interpretations, if only because class boundaries are inevitably in a state of flux.[5] The problems are compounded when this aspect of Marx's mode of analysis, derived from eighteenth- and nineteenth-century society, is imported into the ancient world. Did slaves and peasants constitute classes? If so, did they make up one heterogeneous class or two classes? This kind of problem gives rise to endless and often fruitless debate.

There is a way of proceeding that does not discard the useful insights that Marx's analysis can undoubtedly provide.[6] Marx employed specific class categories – bourgeoisie, proletariat, and so on – developed in the context of nineteenth-century industrial society, and not transferable to ancient Rome. But he also developed conceptual tools for identifying the fundamental processes producing and reproducing inequalities in society over time. We can make fruitful use of this aspect of Marx's class analysis without committing ourselves to imposing modern categories on Roman social divisions.

In brief: instead of focusing in the first instance on the membership of social groupings, we can begin by examining the processes giving rise to and preserving inequalities, and then use this analysis to throw light on the structure of the social hierarchies found in our period.

Among the processes maintaining inequality, we can follow Marx in emphasizing those entailed by (1) the property system, (2) the legal system and (3) the occupational system (or division of labour). The position of the ruling groups depended on their control over productive property (the means of production), as the ultimate source of their wealth and power. Their domination of the legal system legitimized their control over property through ownership rights and the use of sanctions, including coercion, to enforce and safeguard the distribution of property in their favour. The division of labour followed from and further reinforced the social hierarchy, since occupational position gave

---

[4] Finley (1985a), 49-51; de Ste. Croix (1981), 84-96.
[5] Poulantzas (1975)
[6] What follows is a development of E. Garnsey in Giddens and Held (1982), at 427,631.

individuals and groups access to (or excluded them from) control of property and the means of production. The operation of these interacting processes entailed exploitation. It is through exploitation that surplus value is extracted and property becomes productive.

The system of acquisition and transmission of property was the basis of the Roman framework of social and economic inequality. This was an agrarian society, in which wealth was essentially in land and acquired by inheritance through the family. In the main, only where the family had died out and there were no adopted heirs, were outsiders able to gain control over valued resources. It was a peculiarity of the Roman system that the outsiders who benefited were characteristically select lower-class dependants (freedman, slaves) who had won the confidence or affection of their master. Augustus did not block off this avenue of social mobility, although he did seek to reduce the scale of slave manumission, and to restrict the capacity of freedmen to pass down property within the family.[7]

In general, emperors did not, and could not, closely monitor entry into the propertied class. But they did introduce one new way of gaining admission, duties in the service of the regime and the empire. Soldiers were rewarded for their role in preserving the social order with adequate, and in the case of officers, generous, pay and a substantial remuneration on retirement, which put veterans in a position to establish themselves as prosperous members of local communities.[8] Moreover, insofar as veterans did become members of the provincial upper classes, they benefited from the official favour shown to this group as a whole. In return for cooperating with the central government in the areas of administration, jurisdiction, and law and order, the urban elites of the provinces were able to consolidate their local social and economic power.

Inequalities, deriving from uneven property distribution that was confirmed or even accentuated by imperial policies, were underpinned by Roman law. In effect, the decisions of emperors (constitutions, rescripts), supplemented by interpretations of authorized jurists, were the fount of law under the Principate, and held validity wherever Roman officials exercised jurisdiction. In practice, the shortage of functionaries made the imposition of a unified legal system across the empire unfeasible, even had this been an aim of the imperial government.[9] Where local law and juridical procedures were well established, as in most parts of the East, they were permitted to continue in operation, with Roman courts offering appellate, and in the case of Roman citizens, first-order, jurisdiction. In the underdeveloped West, however, the introduction of Roman courts, procedures and remedies was actively pursued. This, like other aspects of

[7] Briefly, Treggiari (1969), 15ff., 30, 73ff.; Brunt (1971), 558-66.

[8] Campbell (1984), 181ff.; MacMullen (1963), ch. 5.

[9] Jolowicz and Nicholas (1972), chs. 21-3; Schulz (1946), pt. 3; on the limitations, Galsterer (1986).

Romanization, worked in favour of the Rome-backed local elite. It was they who benefited from the extension of Roman law with its highly developed property rights, from the entitlements attached to Roman citizenship in general, and from the legal privileges associated with social status when these gained official recognition in decisions of emperors from the time of Hadrian.

The other aspect of those imperial enactments was their confirmation of the subservient position of the mass of the population, the *humiliores* as opposed to the *honestiores.*

The direct exploitation of labour by rich proprietors was a central feature of Roman imperial society. Enrichment in the Roman world did not take the form of the accumulation of profit through the activity of companies employing wage-labourers. Wealth was generated for members of the propertied class to a large extent by the labour of their personal dependants.[10]

Most of the working masses laboured in agriculture: low productivity ensured that a relatively small proportion of the population could be spared from the production of essential foodstuffs. Slaves had made up a large part of the work-force of the wealthy in Italy and Sicily ever since the period of overseas expansion began at the end of the third century BC. The evidence for the status of labour in the provinces is less satisfactory. Agricultural slavery certainly existed in pockets of the empire, as in Tripolitania, where Apuleius' wife Pudentilla gave her sons 400 slaves, together with other property. Elsewhere in Africa, the agricultural work-force was largely free, as it was in Egypt, the other main grain-producing province of the empire. Dependent non-slave labour systems of one kind or another existed in Gaul and Asia. There seems little doubt that across the empire humble free men constituted the majority of farm-workers, but the scanty evidence frustrates generalizations concerning their legal and customary position in the relations of production.[11]

The brutal efficiency of slavery as a form of exploitation needs no special emphasis,[12] though as we shall see shortly, some slaves fared better than others. The situation of non-slave labour ranged very widely, from debt-bondage on the one hand, to relative independence on the other. Debt-bondage persisted, even after the abolition of one of its forms, *nexum*, in the early Republic. The 'many' *obaerarii* associated by Varro with Asia, Egypt and Illyricum (*Rust.* 1.17.2), and the *nexi* of citizen status who, together with slaves, worked the vast holdings of the rich (presumably in Italy), according to Columella (1.3.12), were certainly bondsmen.[13]

[10] De Ste. Croix (1981), 49-69, 179-204; see Brunt (1980), 90-1, on wage labour.

[11] Apuleius, *Apol.* 93, cf. 17, with Garnsey (1978), 236-8; Whittaker (1980); bibliography for the East in Finley (1985a), 222 n. 17, 245, n. 11.

[12] Patterson (1982); Finley (1980), ch. 3.

[13] De Ste. Croix (1981), 165-8.

Other labourers were 'free' tenants, but many were unable to escape intense exploitation on account of their economic circumstances or lack of power. Pliny described the condition of tenants on an estate he intended to buy: 'The previous owner quite often sold off the tenants' pledges for their debts; and while he reduced the debt of the tenants (*coloni*) for a time, he depleted their resources for the future, on account of the loss of which they began to run up their debts again' (*Ep.* 3.19.6). Though juridically free, these tenants were apparently unable to break away from their grasping landlord and their debts to him, and to overcome their impoverishment by establishing themselves on economically viable farms. On an imperial estate in north Africa (*saltus Burunitanus*), the emperor's procurator provided force to maintain the exploitation of the subtenants at the hands of the wealthy lessees. When the humble subtenants protested that more than the agreed rent and days of labour were being demanded of them, the procurator sent in soldiers, 'ordering some of us to be seized and tortured, others fettered, and some, including even Roman citizens, beaten with rods and cudgels'.[14] Clearly, freedom and citizenship did not always protect tenants against oppressive landlords.

Peasants who owned their land had a better chance of establishing their independence. There were various pressures pushing them toward dependence on richer, more powerful neighbours: the need for loans, for protection and for temporary jobs to supplement their income. The government burdened them with demands for taxes, army service and corvée labour. Nevertheless, comparative studies suggest that peasants can be surprisingly resilient, and the conditions of the Principate – prolonged peace and relatively light taxation in many regions – were not wholly adverse to them. The heavy taxation and demands for services that made rural patronage so prominent in the later empire and gave rise to the tied colonate had yet to arrive.

Orders

Orders are those social categories defined by the state through statutory or customary rules. Augustus restored the Republican system of orders (*ordo*, rank), but with sharper definition.[15] The senatorial order remained the most prestigious, a small circle of several hundred families perceived to be worthy by the traditional standards of birth, wealth and moral excellence. Augustus set out to rebuild the senate and revive its shattered morale by purging it of members of dubious standing who had infiltrated

[14] *CIL* VIII. 10570+14464, translated in Lewis and Reinhold (1955), 183-4, with Rostovtzeff (1910), 370. On rural violence, MacMullen (1974), 5-12.

[15] Demougin (1982); Nicolet (1977) on the Republic and (1984); Cohen (1975). On the imperial hierarchy of orders more generally, Alföldy (1985), ch. 5.

the order during the civil wars – a series of revisions brought the senate down from about 1,200 to 600 – and by accentuating the difference between senators and those of lower rank. During the late Republic, senators had had to meet a census requirement of 400,000 sesterces, which was no different from that set for equestrians. Augustus fixed a substantially higher qualification for senators, one million sesterces.[16] In addition, the wearing of the toga with the broad purple stripe (*latus clavus*) was restricted to senators and their sons and to equestrians who had been given permission to stand for office.[17] The recruitment of new senatorial families now lay with the emperor. Moreover, prohibitions on unworthy behaviour were formally legislated and not left to the whim of censors as in the past. Augustus disallowed legitimate marriage between senators and freedwomen. A later senatorial decree of AD 19 banned senators and their families (and equestrians) from disgracing themselves by performing in public spectacles.[18]

The senatorial order was emphatically not a hereditary aristocracy. Yet the prestige ascribed to high birth led Augustus to promote the hereditary principle in order to raise the senate's stature. Thus, sons of senators were encouraged to follow in their father's footsteps, not only by wearing the *latus clavus*, but also by attending meetings of the senate with their fathers (Suetonius, *Aug.* 38). Furthermore, senatorial distinction was recognized as extending to descendants of senators for three generations (*Digest* 23.2.44 pref.), and the order was offered incentives to reproduce itself.[19]

[handwritten marginal note: Senatorial Rank is somewhat hereditary.]

The second, equestrian, order was also characterized by an aristocratic, not a professional, ethos. In the view of the historian Cassius Dio (52.19.4), the equestrian order resembled the senatorial in possessing similar criteria for membership – high birth, excellence and wealth – but in the second degree. In terms of wealth, the Republican census requirement of 400,000 sesterces remained in force. To that was added in the reign of Tiberius a requirement of two previous generations of free birth – another effort to increase the social distance between the privileged orders and those of servile origin (Pliny, *HN* 33.32). Like senators, equestrians were the subject of attempts to legislate moral respectability, as in the *senatus consultum* mentioned above banning members of the two leading orders from performing in public spectacles.

The equestrian order was much larger than the senatorial order, numbering in the thousands, and was correspondingly more amorphous. Historians differ on precisely what constituted membership in the order – property at the required level and free birth, or possession of the 'public

[16] Cassius Dio 56.41.3; *Res Gestae* 8; Jones (1960), ch. 2; Nicolet (1976); Millar (1977), 290-300.

[17] Chastagnol (1971) and (1973).

[18] *Digest* 23.2.4 pref., with Treggiari (1969), 82ff. For the decree, Levick (1983).

[19] Hopkins (1983c), ch. 3; on the marriage laws, p.143.

horse' by imperial grant.[20] The decree of AD 19 identified the order
vaguely as 'those who have the right of sitting in equestrian places' at
public spectacles. According to Pliny the elder (*HN* 33.32), Tiberius
later brought the order 'into unity', but nothing is said of the
administrative procedures introduced to accomplish this.

The 'unity' did not preclude diversity. Under the Republic, some
equestrians had had only modest fortunes and no political ambitions
beyond their home towns, while others, particularly the leading public
contractors (*publicani*) referred to by Cicero as the 'flower of the order',
had enjoyed wealth and political influence comparable to senators'
(Cicero, *Planc*. 23). Under the Principate, the emperors began to give
administrative as well as military responsibilities to equestrians; as the
number of equestrian offices increased and their hierarchy developed, the
office-holding minority of the order came to resemble senators insofar as
they derived honour from the rank of their office.[21] By the end of the
Principate, the leading equestrian, the praetorian prefect, actually took
precedence in court protocol over senators. The rank-conscious Romans
would not allow the vast social gap between the greatest and humblest
equestrian to go unmarked, and so by the late second century a new
hierarchy of epithets was invented to designate the office-holding
equestrians (*egregius* or 'excellent' for procurators, *perfectissimus* or
'most accomplished' for senior prefects, and *eminentissimus* or 'most
renowned' for praetorian prefects).[22] These several hundred specially
distinguished equestrians were the minority of the order belonging to the
imperial elite centred in Rome; the majority were essentially local
notables, marked out by a golden ring and a narrow purple stripe on the
toga (*angustus clavus*).

The decurions or councillors of the towns across the empire constituted
the third of the aristocratic orders – 'aristocratic' insofar as decurions,
like senators and equestrians, were expected to possess respectable birth,
wealth and moral worth. The definition of respectable birth was less
stringent for decurions than equestrians; sons of freedmen – not,
ordinarily, freedmen themselves – were admitted to town councils. Just as
the size of towns varied, so did the wealth of its leading citizens; in the
major cities the wealth of some decurions exceeded that required of
senators. The census qualification of the unexceptional town of Comum
in northern Italy was set at 100,000 sesterces, or a quarter of the
equestrian census (Pliny, *Ep*. 1.19). Moral excellence was more difficult
to guarantee, but at least men with a criminal past and those in

[20] Demougin (1982), 77; Alföldy (1985); Stein (1927); Wiseman (1970); for the broader
view of membership, Millar (1977), 280, but note the change in epigraphic usage from
exornatus equo publico to *eques Romanus* pointed out by Duncan-Jones (1967), 149f.
[21] Sherwin-White (1940); Pflaum (1950); Brunt (1983) and (1969) on equestrians in the
Republic.
[22] Millar (1964), 21 and (1983a); Pflaum (1970b).

demeaning occupations, such as auctioneers and undertakers, were excluded.[23]

These requirements were designed to ensure that local councils were composed of men of property, whose social standing was not in question. Sometimes, however, people were admitted who were not highly approved in the Roman value system. The third-century jurist Callistratus wrote that, although traders should not be barred absolutely from the local council, 'yet I believe it to be dishonourable for persons of this sort, who have been subject to the whippings [of aediles in the marketplace], to be received into the order, and especially in those cities that have an abundance of honourable men (*honesti viri*). On the other hand, a needful shortage of the latter men requires even the former for municipal office, if they have the resources' (*Digest* 50.2.12). Wealth was permitted to override other criteria of social acceptability for strictly practical reasons. Not only were councillors and magistrates unpaid; they were actually required to contribute fees to the public treasury on entry into the council or into an office or priesthood. Their wealth was used in addition for other, voluntary expenditures to justify their privileged status in the community, and was the ultimate surety for the tax payments due to the imperial treasury.[24]

The three elite orders comprised only a tiny fraction of the population of the empire. Below them in the official hierarchy came the great mass of the humble free, and at the bottom of the heap, the slaves. Within the former category the principal legal divisions lay between freeborn and freed, and between citizen and non-citizen. The formal legal disabilities of being a freedman were not in practice very inhibiting: a slave properly manumitted by a citizen became a citizen, but was barred from the elite orders, from service in the legions and from legitimate marriage to senators.[25]

The citizen/non-citizen distinction lost much of its significance in the course of the Principate. At first Roman citizens, at any rate those residing in the city of Rome, remained in possession of at least the vestiges of the rights they had enjoyed under the Republic, and the benefits that accrued from empire. Gradually the exclusivity on which privileges were based was lost, as the citizen body grew to incorporate provincials, a development culminating in Caracalla's grant of citizenship to virtually all free inhabitants of the empire in AD 212. As the distinction between victor and conquered disappeared, the legal divisions within the population tended to be overshadowed by social divisions based on the elite system of values. The result was the emergence by the reign of Hadrian of the formal distinction between the

[23] Duthoy (1974), 147-48; Lex Iulia municipalis 94, 108-23, with Crook (1967a), 65-7.

[24] On decurions, Garnsey (1970), 242-5; Gagé (1964), ch. 5; on their obligations, Millar (1983a).

[25] Duff (1928); Buckland (1963), 87-90; Crook (1967a), 50-5.

elite and the humble masses (*honestiores* and *humiliores*).[26] The privileged *honestiores* included the three aristocratic orders and veterans, rewarded for their service in protecting the social order. The remainder of the free population fell into the category of *humiliores*, the legal disadvantages of which will be considered shortly.

In applying this rough, binary classification to the free population, we run the risk of oversimplifying and thus distorting the social reality. In particular, a sizeable heterogeneous group of men of free birth can be distinguished from both the elite orders and the humble masses. The *apparitores*, that is, the lictors, scribes and other staff of Roman magistrates to whom attention has recently been drawn, are but a small segment of this group. However, the *apparitores* actually serve to confirm the essential dichotomy, insofar as their rank derived from their position as appendages to the ruling aristocrats. There was no genuine 'middle class' in the sense of an intermediate group with independent economic resources or social standing.[27]

Finally, slaves. In Roman law, slaves were classified as chattel, not persons, as a 'speaking tool' (*instrumentum vocale*) that could be bought and sold or punished at the will of the masters. Some imperial rulings gave limited recognition to their humanity. For instance, Claudius decided that masters who abandoned sick slaves to avoid the costs of caring for them could not reclaim them if they recovered health. By the reign of Hadrian, *ergastula* (the private prisons on estates where slaves were kept in chains) were prohibited by imperial law, the punitive sale of slaves was regulated, and the master's right of life and death over his slaves was taken away. Such laws may have suppressed some of the worst abuses, but they did not alter the slave's fundamental lack of power and honour vis-à-vis his master. The psychological oppression associated with lack of freedom, the threat of the whip, of the break-up of slave families and of sexual abuse, continued unabated.[28]

In a culture so sensitive to rank, how was the hierarchy of rank made known and reinforced across culturally diverse communities? Rank was asserted in the clothing that people wore. For senators and their sons Augustus reserved the toga with the broad purple stripe. Equestrians were marked out by the gold rings on their fingers and the narrow purple stripes on their togas. So strong was the association of rank with apparel that some unworthies at the beginning of the Principate usurped equestrian privileges simply by wearing a gold ring, prompting Tiberius' regulations to restrict the rank to the deserving (Pliny, *HN* 33.32). Similarly, Claudius threatened punishment against non-citizens who called themselves by the *tria nomina*, the three names that, along with

[26] Garnsey (1970), ch. 11 and, more briefly, (1974); de Ste. Croix (1981), 455-62.

[27] Purcell (1983); Gérard (1976), ch. 6.

[28] Buckland (1908) remains standard on the legal position of the slave; Finley (1980), ch. 3; Bradley (1984).

the toga, indicated possession of Roman citizenship.[29]

Romans paraded their rank whenever they appeared in public, and nowhere more conspicuously than at public spectacles in theatre, amphitheatre and circus. In Rome, Augustus confirmed and extended late Republican arrangements that allocated special seats or rows of seats to senators, equestrians and citizens:

> He issued special regulations to prevent the disorderly and haphazard system by which spectators secured seats for these shows, having been outraged by the insult to a senator who, on entering the crowded theatre at Puteoli, was not offered a seat by a single member of the audience. The consequent *senatus consultum* provided that at every performance, wherever held, the front row of stalls must be reserved for senators ... Other rules of his included the separation of soldiers from civilians; the assignment of special seats to married commoners, to boys not yet come of age, and, close by, to their tutors; and a ban on the wearing of dark clothes, except in the back rows.[30]

Rank was very important and was shown at all times by clothes.

In the municipalities, the seating was arranged to give spatial definition to the distinction between the curial order and ordinary citizens. Caesar's law for the colony of Urso in Spain had already specified detailed regulations for seating in the amphitheatre and theatre, and laid down enormous fines for violations – an indication that something more was at stake than getting a good seat to watch the show.[31]

Putting everyone in his proper place was a visual affirmation of the dominance of the imperial social structure, and one calculated to impress the bulk of the population of the empire. There were other displays of rank, such as the annual parade in Rome for equestrians, which Augustus renewed (Suetonius, *Aug.* 38.3; Cassius Dio 55.31.2), and the public banquets and distributions in the municipalities, at which the quantity of food or money was handed out in proportion to rank, not need.[32] The impoverished may have resented this principle, even as public event after public event imprinted it in the communal consciousness.

If the advantages of high rank were conspicuous and real, so also were the disadvantages of falling outside the circle of privilege. Under the Republic, citizens had won legal protection against flogging, torture and execution, and in general, against the arbitrary use of force by magistrates. In the imperial age, these rights survived for a time; as is well known, they were asserted by St. Paul on more than one occasion.

[29] Reinhold (1971); Brunt (1961), esp. p. 76; Crook (1967a), 46-9, on documentation of citizen status.

[30] Suetonius, *Aug.* 44; cf. Dio 60.7; Suetonius, *Claud.* 21; Tacitus, *Ann.* 15.32.

[31] Riccobono, *FIRA* no. 21 (Lex col. Gen. Iul. Urs.) 125-7, specifying a fine of 5,000 sesterces; cf. no. 13 (Lex Iul. mun.) 138-9.

[32] Duncan-Jones (1982), 184-8.

However, as the *honestiores/humiliores* distinction came to supersede that between citizens and non-citizens, the privilege of exemption from corporal punishment came to be reserved for *honestiores*, and in a parallel development, cruel penalties associated with slaves were extended to the humble free. The dual-penalty system, together with a differential evaluation of legal testimony in accordance with rank, were formally enunciated in law by the end of the second century, but must have long been practised by judges, for they were deeply rooted in traditional, aristocratic values. Some decades before the earliest reference in the extant legal sources to a formal *honestiores/humiliores* distinction, the younger Pliny advised a provincial governor in Spain to preserve 'the distinction of orders and dignity' in legal hearings, because 'if these distinctions are confused, nothing is more unequal than equality itself' (*Ep.* 9.5).[33]

Status

A Roman's status was based on the social estimation of his honour, the perception of those around him as to his prestige. Since statuses reflect values and outlook rather than legal regulations, distinctions are less precise than in the case of orders. The principal ingredients of rank – birth and wealth – were not always in step with each other; a few of the very wealthiest came from very humble backgrounds, and some with the best pedigrees fell into poverty. Other factors, such as power, education and perceived moral stature, lent prestige to their holders and were not the exclusive possession of men of high rank. Contradictions between status and rank gave rise to tensions, which sometimes rose to the surface, as in the resentment felt among senators at the immense power exercised by Sejanus, Tiberius' praetorian prefect and a man of the second rank.[34]

Each order accommodated fine gradations of status. Within the senatorial order, which experienced a high turnover of families, those who could boast of consular ancestors, *nobiles*, stood out from the mass of newcomers.[35] The minority of equestrians appointed to high office in the emperor's service were described as belonging to the 'equestrian nobility' (*equestris nobilitas*) long before the hierarchy of formal epithets emerged (Tacitus, *Agr.* 4.1). The wealthiest and most powerful of the decurions came to be known as the 'first men' (*primores viri*).[36] This internal stratification generally caused little difficulty.

The freeborn outside the elite orders constituted by far the largest

[33] Garnsey (1970); Millar (1984) on hard labour and corporal punishment.
[34] Hopkins (1974), 108-11.
[35] On the disputed definition of *nobilitas*, Hill (1969), Barnes (1974).
[36] *Digest* 50.14.6 pref., 50.7.5.5; Garnsey, (1974), 232.

single group in the hierarchy of ranks, and varied much in status according to occupation and resources. The lack of detailed information, however, makes it difficult to penetrate the complexity of what has been called the 'finely stratified sequence of status between eques and slave' for the empire outside Egypt.[37] One major division, however, is clear: that between urban and rural workers. Roman civilization was an urban phenomenon, built on the agricultural surplus from the countryside. Not only did the cities exploit the countryside to feed and clothe their residents, but the urban dwellers, a small minority of the whole population, were also contemptuous of the masses as 'rustics', who were unacquainted with the sophisticated culture of urban life and often literally spoke a different language.[38]

Even at the bottom of the hierarchy of ranks, there was a wide range of conditions. The lot of many slaves condemned to manual labour in harsh conditions, in particular, in the mines, was wretched. Apuleius offers a vivid glimpse of the condition of slaves working in a flour mill in his novel, *The Golden Ass*:

> Their skins were seamed all over with the marks of old floggings, as you could see through the holes in their ragged shirts that shaded rather than covered their scarred backs; but some wore only loin-cloths. They had letters marked on their foreheads, and half-shaved heads and irons on their legs.[39]

In contrast, urban household slaves generally lived in incomparably better physical conditions and often were allowed a *de facto* family life.[40] Slaves who ran workshops or commercial operations for the profit of their masters were permitted considerable freedom of action. The disabilities imposed by their legal position as chattel were circumvented by the device of *peculium*, a fund allotted to slaves against which they could contract obligations. The *peculium* might comprise not only working capital, but also property – and slaves.[41] Even within the category of slaves, wealth could confer power over others. Responsibility within the master's household also conferred power, which varied with the size and status of the household. The top slaves of the imperial household were able to exercise considerable influence and accumulate impressive wealth, as is attested not only by literary anecdotes, but also by inscriptions. Musicus Scurranus, Tiberius' slave cashier for the imperial treasury in a Gallic province, received a dedication from his own household slaves, sixteen in number (*ILS* 1514). One other important

---

[37] Purcell (1983), 127.
[38] MacMullen (1974), ch. 2; de Ste. Croix (1981), 9-19; Rostovtzeff (1957), ch. 11.
[39] *Met*. 9.12, with Millar (1981), 65.
[40] Treggiari (1975a); Flory (1978).
[41] Crook (1967a), 188-9; Buckland (1908), chs. 8-9.

element in the relatively high status of domestic and urban slaves was the likely prospect of manumission, a possibility denied their counterparts in the countryside and mines.

For all these status differences, the ultimate legal dependence of all slaves made them less difficult to accommodate in the Roman hierarchy than freedmen. Freedmen – as free, Roman citizens, able to accumulate great wealth in theory, and sometimes in practice, and yet tainted by their servile background – encapsulate the contradictions between rank and status that Roman society had to accommodate.

Most freedmen were humble men, married women of the same rank, often remained dependent on their former masters, and consequently presented no awkward contradiction between rank and status.[42] Some, however, rose to a status not commensurate with their inferior rank. The conservative aristocrats who urged the Roman senate in AD 56 to decree that disrespectful freedmen should be re-enslaved, were reacting against the phenomenon of successful freedmen, not simply against the way they humiliated their former masters (Tacitus, *Ann.* 13.26-7).

Imperial freedmen were capable of reaching the summit of the propertied class – they contribute four of the ten richest men known from the Principate – and were courted for their immense influence even by members of the elite orders. Unlike other freedmen, they generally married freeborn women.[43] Nevertheless, their servile origins were not forgotten, and generally prevented their rising into the aristocratic orders. Even the 'right of freebirth', a legal fiction by which an emperor certified a freedman as being of free birth and eligible for equestrian rank, could not wipe away the stain of servility in the eyes of the elite.[44] The intensity of the hostility directed against these men, whose position rested entirely on their proximity to and influence over emperors, can be sensed in the abusive language employed by the normally mild-mannered Pliny, as he described his reaction to an inscription honouring Claudius' freedman Pallas with free birth and the insignia of the second most senior magistrate, the praetor: 'Personally I have never thought much of these honours whose distribution depends on chance rather than on a reasoned decision, but this inscription more than anything makes me realize what a ridiculous farce it is when they can be thrown away on such dirt and filth, and that rascal could presume to accept and refuse them' (*Ep.* 7.29).

Aristocrats tried to justify their sense of outrage on some grounds other than the accident of servile birth. Freedom, citizenship and wealth, it was claimed, could not change the uncultured, servile spirit of a former slave. Petronius' portrayal of Trimalchio is the classic expression of this

[42] Rawson (1966); Weaver (1974), 126ff.
[43] Duncan-Jones (1982), 343-44; Weaver (1974), 126-9.
[44] Duff (1928), 85f.

stereotype of the boorish freedman.[45] Seneca described a real-life counterpart: 'Within our own time there was a certain rich man named Calvisius Sabinus; he had the wealth and spirit of a freedman. I never saw a man whose good fortune was a greater offence against propriety' (*Ep.* 27.5). Sabinus, we are told, paid great sums for slaves who had memorized all the works of Homer and Hesiod. At dinner parties he bored guests by repeating half-forgotten lines learned from these slaves. To judge by the tirade of Hermeros, one of Trimalchio's fellow ex-slaves in the *Satyricon* (57-8), successful freedmen were sensitive to the insults implicit in this elitist ideology and responded by emphasizing their personal accomplishments in buying their freedom and accumulating wealth.

The ideological conflict provoked by the careers of successful freedmen was never fully resolved, but an institutional compromise was developed in the cities of Italy and the western provinces from the reign of Augustus. Freedmen were barred from the local council, but could be honoured with the office of Augustalis. Like decurions and local magistrates, Augustales during their term of office enjoyed special seats at public events and the symbols of authority, such as attendants (*lictores*), rods (*fasces*) and distinctive clothing (the *toga praetexta*). In return, they paid a fee in respect of their office, and were exposed to the same pressure as decurions to provide voluntary, public benefactions. Thus the college of Augustales served the dual purpose of recognizing the superiority of these wealthy freedmen over the mass of the plebs and at the same time maintaining the most basic criterion of status, birth.[46] Their existence can be taken as evidence that no group of free men in Roman society was excluded from honours. It is, however, an exaggeration to compare their position as a 'second order' in the cities to that of equestrians in Rome. Unlike equestrians, they could move no higher. Freedmen's sons were the true *arrivistes*, not the freedmen themselves, since their servile birth ensured they would never 'arrive'.

Like rank, status was advertised in standard ways. Since status was linked with wealth, it could be demonstrated through conspicuous consumption. Apuleius' miser who wished to keep the size of his fortune secret by living in a small house with only one servant was an exception (*Met.* 1.21). For Seneca, a fine mansion and numerous beautiful slaves were among the foremost symbols commonly associated with wealth and status (*Ep.* 41.7). A century later Apuleius also took this for granted in his defence of the philosopher Crates against suspicions that the latter held the anti-social views associated with philosophers; the orator pointed out that Crates subscribed to the dominant social values, as demonstrated by his wealth, his large retinue of slaves, and his house

[45] The classic statement is by Veyne (1961); cf. Garnsey (1981); D'Arms (1981), ch. 5.
[46] Duthoy (1974) and (1978).

endowed with a superbly decorated vestibule (*Flor*. 22). The size of slave staffs in the households of the wealthy became extravagantly large in the pursuit of status. To save money by using a slave to perform more than one duty was regarded as déclassé. Consequently, the differentiation of labour on these staffs, made up of hundreds of servants, became very fine, with slaves devoted to such specialties as hairdressing or folding specific types of clothing.[47]

Laws were passed prohibiting conspicuous consumption, and moral philosophers like Seneca preached against measuring a man's worth by his ostentatious display of wealth. But the emperors themselves despaired of enforcing sumptuary legislation against such ardent status-seekers, and Seneca himself was accused of accumulating incredible wealth, extravagantly displayed in luxuries like 500 identical citrus wood tables with ivory legs, on which he served banquets.[48]

If rank was displayed predominantly on the public stage in the political and religious life of the city and in community events such as spectacles and banquets, the focal point of the parade of status was the private house. This was the scene of the *salutatio*, according to which clients and lesser friends of the great and powerful congregated at the doors of their patrons in the early morning to pay their respects in return for food, money, clothing and other favours. From the late second century BC, these morning callers were classified and received according to their status. The *salutatio* offered a visual demonstration of the social hierarchy in two ways. Clients were classed with reference to their place in the queue, and the patron in terms of the quality and number of his callers. The 'crowded house' was a barometer of and a metaphor for power and prestige.[49] In addition, private dinners within the house allowed for the display of distinctions of status. Just as the seating at public banquets was arranged according to rank, at private dinners seats, and sometimes the quality of food and drink, were chosen to correspond to each guest's status (Martial, *Epig.* 4.68, 6.11; Pliny, *Ep.* 2.6.2).

The high visibility of these displays of rank and status made contradictions between them embarrassingly obvious. When Sejanus began to fear that his enormous power and status, excessive in comparison with his second-order rank, would throw suspicion on him in the eyes of Tiberius, he moved out of Rome to avoid the crowded *salutationes* that made his position so apparent (Tacitus, *Ann.* 4.41). Again, the presence of the former senatorial master of the imperial freedman Callistus among his morning callers, and worse, the rejection of his greeting, were a patent and repugnant inversion of normal

[47] Tacitus, *Ann.* 14.42-5; Treggiari (1975b), (1979a), (1982).

[48] Gellius, *NA* 2.24.14 (Augustus' legislation); Tacitus, *Ann.* 3.52-5 (Tiberius' inability to enforce it); Cassius Dio 61.10.3 (Seneca's hypocrisy); on the house as a status symbol, Saller (1984a).

[49] Saller (1984a), 352; (1982), 127-9; Mohler (1931).

master-slave relationships (Seneca, *Ep.* 47.9). Such incidents showed aristocrats to be no better than 'slaves of slaves' (Arrian, *Epict. Diss.* 4.1.148, 3.7.31, 4.7.19). One criterion of a 'good' emperor, in the view of the aristocracy, was his firmness in keeping his freedmen 'in their place', so preserving the proper social order (Pliny, *Pan.* 88.1-2).

Social mobility

The oppressiveness of the social hierarchy depended in part on the limitations in opportunities for individual and group mobility. Several factors influenced the degree of mobility, including the chances of enrichment offered by the economy, and demographic trends that could leave open to newcomers more or fewer places in the higher orders from generation to generation. It has been suggested that for a traditional, pre-industrial society imperial Rome allowed upward movement to an unusual degree. Such a generalization needs to be qualified: mobility in certain sectors of the population may have been common, while for others the prospects were virtually hopeless.

The scale of movement among the elite orders of the Roman empire was remarkable. For reasons that are not clear senatorial families disappeared at an average rate of 75 per cent per generation – a rate of turnover well beyond that experienced by European aristocracies of the early modern period. Among patricians, an exclusive circle of families within the senate, of the 39 families known between AD 70 and 117, 22 left no trace in the reign of Hadrian, and most of the other 17 families disappeared in the Antonine era. The turnover of the great majority of senatorial families from one generation to the next must have diluted the value of lineage in claims to rank and status, as few imperial senators (unlike their Republican predecessors) could profit from the collective memory of their ancestors' achievements. The failure of senatorial families to have their sons fill their places left hundreds of openings in each generation for the wealthiest and most prominent members of the local elites to move into the senate. The new members increasingly came from outside Italy, so that the proportion of provincial senators rose from a tiny fraction under Augustus to perhaps a quarter during the Flavian era to well over half by the early third century.[50]

Access to equestrian rank and honours was even more open than to the senate. Simple membership in the equestrian order was not limited in numbers nor especially competitive among those with the necessary wealth, birth and citizenship. Equestrian offices, on the other hand, were relatively few and available to only a minority of equestrians. But they came open to new families in each generation, since very few sons of

[50] Hopkins (1983c), ch.3; Hammond (1957).

procurators followed their fathers into equestrian office. Demographic factors aside, they were prime candidates for promotion into the senate.

Social mobility among local elites has yet to be systematically studied. These groups, who provided the pool of recruits for the two highest orders, are likely to have been more stable.[51] The relatively few curial families who entered the imperial aristocracy already resembled senatorial and equestrian families in their wealth and values, facilitating their change of geographical focus. Movement into the local elites, in contrast, implied an increase in wealth, and wealth was usually passed on within families. Nevertheless, the smooth transmission of patrimony and rank could be disrupted for demographic and other reasons, leaving open many places for new men in the curial order.

What was the social origin of the new recruits into the urban aristocracies? Two upwardly mobile groups are visible in the sources: soldiers and a category of slaves. The success of a freeborn rural labourer, the harvester from Maktar in Numidia who rose to the status of a councillor and magistrate of his city, was highly exceptional.[52]

Each year a few tens of thousands were recruited into the army, receiving citizenship if it was lacking, on entry in the case of legionaries, and on discharge in the case of auxiliaries. Those who survived their term of service received ample discharge payment, which allowed them to set themselves up as landowners and to qualify for the local council in an urban community near the frontier. For the fortunate few who formed the officer class, the army provided the means for more spectacular climbs in the hierarchy. Some centurions were recruited directly from the propertied class, but most were promoted from the ranks. With the centurionate came authority and an income on a par with that of decurions. The minority of centurions who then reached the rank of *primuspilus* received equestrian status and income, and the opportunity for appointment to high equestrian procuratorships and even (for perhaps one in a decade) to the great prefectures.[53]

In the cities, slaves and ex-slaves had better prospects, paradoxically, than the humble freeborn. Insofar as profits could be made in commerce and manufacture, the more enterprising members of this group were well placed to make them, their masters having given them the incentive, the degree of independence, the initial capital and frequently the training that was required. Moreover, the position of favoured slaves in wealthy households opened up the possibility that they would be the beneficiaries not merely of working capital, but also of substantial legacies. Manumission, as well as inheritance by birth, adoption and legacy among those of the same social background, played a part in the wealth-transferring process. Epigraphic evidence, supplemented by

[51] Champlin (1981).
[52] *ILS* 7457, with Rostovtzeff (1957), 331.
[53] Dobson (1974a) and (1974b).

(hostile) literary sources, leaves no doubt that local councils in the western provinces were regularly replenished from the newly founded families of successful freedmen.[54]

The possibility that such a group existed in the cities of the Greek East cannot be ruled out because of lack of evidence. A letter of Marcus Aurelius preserved in an inscription shows that both Athenian councils (the Areopagus and the Council of 500) depended upon freedmen to fill up their ranks.[55] This is a revelation for which the corpus of honorific and funerary inscriptions from Athens (and all other Greek cities) left us totally unprepared. Greek names in the East are 'status neutral', whereas in the Latin inscriptions of the West, they frequently indicate servile origin.[56] Whatever the social background of the upwardly mobile group we are envisaging, it may be assumed that they were patronized by the men of property who constituted the urban aristocracies in the East, as in the West. The controlled entry of new members into the propertied class was a crucial element in the stability of the Roman system of inequality.

Property was a way to keep classes - employ slaves + tenants
3 upper orders + lower class - shown by clothes
Status - by use of wealth - rich could have low status
social mobility is high in 2 upper classes - soldiers move in

[54] Garnsey (1975) and (1981), 369ff.; Gordon (1931).
[55] Oliver (1970).
[56] Garnsey (1975).

CHAPTER SEVEN

Family and Household

Introduction

When Romans of the Augustan age compared their own times with their idealized past, they lamented, among other things, the decline in family morality. In early Rome discipline in the family was hard and standards of virtue high: in paradigmatic *exempla* fathers executed adult sons for disobedience in battle, and virtuous women esteemed their chastity more highly than their lives. Augustus clearly considered family *mores* to be of considerable importance, devoting much of his reforming legislation to marriage and child-bearing.[1]

The first emperor was right about the importance of the family in society, though unduly optimistic about his ability to produce effective reform. The family was the basic social unit through which wealth and status were transmitted. As such, the perpetuation of the aristocracy, the possibilities for social mobility, the distribution of landed wealth, and other matters depended fundamentally on patterns of family behaviour. Beyond the social realities of the time, the image of the Roman family has had a continuing influence on western legal, political and social thought. Following the reintroduction of Roman law in late medieval Europe, political thinkers used the nearly absolute legal power of the father in the family as a model for the power ascribed by nature to the absolute sovereign in the state. Again, nineteenth-century theorists concerned with the evolution of society, generalizing from the Roman family, proposed a universal stage in human history characterized by patriarchy.[2]

There is good reason to believe that this image of stark patriarchy is not an accurate reflection of family life in the Roman imperial era, but the image persists, in part because modern social historians have devoted little of their attention to the subject.[3] The family does not so much as appear in the index of the standard social histories of Rome written in the past decades. Research on the family has been left to Roman legal

---

[1] Brunt (1971), app. 9; Csillag (1976). Our discussion relates to Rome, Italy and the West. For *patria potestas* (or its absence) in Egypt, see Taubenschlag (1955), 130-49; Lewis (1970); *P. Oxy.* 3197, 3289 (references supplied by D. Rathbone).

[2] Saller (1986).

[3] A recent, welcome exception is Rawson (1986), with an excellent introduction and extensive annotated bibliography by the editor.

historians, with the result that much of the current image of the family is based on the law, in which 'the Romans ... pushed things to the limit of logic' so that the principles stand out 'in sociologically misleading clarity'.[4]

It is important to be clear about the limits of the evidence. Roman private law, the largest body of evidence for the family, is obviously indispensible, but legal rules are not a direct reflection of current practice: they could be modified through written agreements or disregarded. Though written documents were regularly used by the propertied class, too few have survived to give the social historian a sense of what was typical. The literary sources provide a corrective with statements revealing common expectations regarding family behaviour, but they are brief and written exclusively by upper-class males. The elite bias can be overcome, to a limited degree, by surveying the tens of thousands of funerary inscriptions of more modest Romans, which offer some important information about demographic variables and patterns of marriage.

Definitions

An understanding of the Roman family should begin with the linguistic categories of the Romans. The obvious Latin words for 'family' are *familia* and *domus* ('household'), but neither has the semantic range or emphasis of 'family' as it is used today with a standard meaning of 'father, mother and children'.[5] The jurist Ulpian (*Digest* 50.16.195) described the various meanings of *familia*, beginning with the distinction between *familia* as *res* and as persons. When used for persons, *familia* could indicate (1) all those under the father's power (*patria potestas*) including the wife (in a *manus* marriage), children, the sons' children, and adopted children; or, more broadly (2) all agnates (that is, those related through *male* blood who derive from the same house, including brothers, their children and their unmarried sisters, but not the sisters' children); (3) all related through males to a common ancestor (in other words, the *gens* or clan, which shared a common *nomen*); (4) the slave staff of a house, farm or other organization.

The first definition and the legal content of *patria potestas* have been largely responsible for the traditional image of the Roman family: a patriarchal household ruled by the *paterfamilias* (the oldest living male ascendant) and including his wife, his sons and unmarried daughters, and his sons' children. For a number of reasons, it will be suggested below, this image does not correspond to the reality very well, and, indeed, this

---

[4] Crook (1967b), 114.
[5] For what follows see Saller (1984a).

conclusion is supported by linguistic usage: *familia* in Ulpian's first sense simply does not appear in the literature of the late Republic and early empire. When Cicero in *On Duties*, for instance, discussed family obligations, he referred to wife, children and household (*domus*), but never to *familia* defined in this way. Under this definition most wives of the classical period were not in their husband's *familia* because they were not married in a fashion to bring them under the authority (*manus*) of their husbands, and a young boy whose father had died could possess power in his own one-man *familia*. A definition that excludes the wife not only illustrates how different *familia* in this legal sense is from our modern conception, but also how misleading it is as a basis for analysing the Roman family as a functioning social unit. Ulpian's other definitions can conveniently be considered with similar meanings of *domus*.

Domus in the sense of household was used by Romans more commonly than *familia* in references to the family. Though often defined as 'family', *domus* covered a larger group than is usually associated with the family today, encompassing husband, wife, children, slaves and others living in the house (not unlike the meaning of 'family' in early modern England where servants as well as blood relatives were included).[6] The difference between Roman and contemporary definitions, as well as Ulpian's fourth sense of *familia*, underlines a cardinal fact about the Roman family: it must be understood in the context of a slave household staff, at least for the prosperous classes. The pervasive presence of slaves must have had important results for paternal authoritarianism, child-bearing and patterns of sexual behaviour.[7]

Both *domus* and *familia* could be used to refer to kin outside the household, and, in particular, to descent groups. Since heavy emphasis is placed on descent in some cultures, influencing strategies of inheritance and marriage, some consideration ought to be given to the rather different notions of descent embodied in the two words.[8] Ulpian's third definition of *familia* – 'all related through males to a common ancestor' – refers to an agnatic descent group from which a daughter's children or a mother's blood kin are excluded. *Domus*, on the other hand, is a much larger group, precisely because it includes relatives linked through women. To judge from linguistic usage in letters and orations, the stress in thinking about descent among the Roman elite changed from *familia* in the Republic to *domus* in the early empire. In Cicero's references to the family background of his friends or clients in court, he consistently mentioned their *familia, nomen* (name) and *genus* (clan), all agnatic notions. In contrast, Pliny never used *familia* in such contexts, but always discussed the man's *domus*, with as much concern for maternal

---

[6] Flandrin (1979), 4-10.

[7] Saller (1987b); on authoritarianism in the late antique family, see Shaw (forthcoming, a).

[8] Saller (1984a), 348-9.

relatives as paternal. This development coincided with the rapid turnover of membership in the Roman aristocracy under the emperors: since most Roman aristocrats could no longer lay claim to an agnatic lineage going back generations that would be recognized by their peers from other regions of the empire, the emphasis shifted to the respectability of the new man's circle of relatives, paternal, maternal or by marriage.

The nuclear family

The evolutionary view of family history, popular in the nineteenth century and still repeated today, has been subjected to convincing criticism in recent decades by historians who have shown that people of past times did not, as a general rule, live in large, extended family units.[9] The literary and epigraphic evidence from Rome, limited though it is, certainly gives no support to the traditional belief that the Roman household usually included several nuclear families dominated by an authoritarian, elderly patriarch. Classical authors assumed that it was exceptional for adult sons to live with their fathers and for adult brothers to share a common household in a *consortium*.[10] A survey of funerary inscriptions indicates that the validity of this conclusion is not limited to the elite: not only are relatives such as grandfathers and uncles rare as commemorators in comparison with members of the immediate family, but also in comparison with friends and servile dependants. We would expect that if paternal grandfathers, uncles and cousins had regularly lived together in extended households, they would have formed sufficiently close ties to have been relied upon often for funerary arrangements in preference to unrelated friends. And yet the paternal grandfather and uncle are almost entirely absent from the thousands of commemorations.[11]

In the belief that for most Romans relationships within the nuclear family were of the greatest importance, most of the remainder of this chapter will be devoted to consideration of the legal, demographic, economic and affective aspects of the husband-wife and parent-child bonds.

[9] Emphasized by Laslett (1972) and Sieder and Mitterauer (1982), among others.

[10] On separate residences for adult sons, see below p.140. Crook (1967b), 117, notes that in the handful of literary passages about brothers in a *consortium*, the families tend to be poor and so have special incentive to avoid splitting the family estate. Plutarch, *Aem. Paul.* 5.5, says explicitly that the Aelii Tuberones displayed antique virtue in living on a single, undivided estate, that brothers in his day made every effort to separate their property clearly to avoid conflict.

[11] Saller and Shaw (1984a), 136-7 with n. 49.

Husbands and wives

In early Roman law a woman entering a marriage under her husband's authority (*cum manu*, presumably then the most common form) left her father's *potestas* and household to join her husband. The marriage could not be broken off without serious cause and heavy financial loss to the party in the wrong. While the husband lived, the wife's dowry and any property accruing to her went into the husband's full ownership. Upon the husband's death, according to the rules of intestate succession, the wife was entitled to an equal share of the patrimony as a primary intestate heir along with her children.[12]

From this rather tight husband-wife bond the law developed in the late Republic to the very loose relationship characteristic of the classical period. The form of marriage in which the wife did not transfer to her husband's authority (*sine manu*) was common in the late Republic and almost completely replaced the old form by the time the jurist Gaius (*Inst.* 1.111) wrote in the mid-second century after Christ.[13] In this type of marriage the woman remained in her father's *familia* and legal power, and participated in her natal family's property regime, not that of her husband and children. Thus, while the woman's dowry went to the husband for the duration of the marriage, the woman was a primary heir of her father and upon his death became an independent property owner. The separation of the wife's property from her husband's was reinforced early in the Principate by the extension of a prohibition on gifts between husband and wife to a ban on the wife standing as surety for her husband.[14] The woman's independence in managing her property was also strengthened during this time through the weakening of guardianship (*tutela*) over women, first by Augustus, who exempted women who had borne three children from the need of a guardian, and then by Claudius, who abolished altogether agnatic guardianship, the only type with any force (Gaius, *Inst.* 1.145, 171). In law, then, the conjugal couple was not one financial entity but two, with the wife enjoying complete legal independence in the ownership of property after her father's death.

The looseness of the classical conjugal bond is also apparent in other aspects of the law. The husband had no legal authority during the marriage over his wife who was in her father's power, but also had no general obligation of maintenance.[15] The financial penalties for breaking off the marriage largely disappeared in the late Republic, and from that time a divorce required no more than a notice of intent to dissolve the

[12] Corbett (1930), chs. 3-4; Watson (1975), chs. 1-3; (1967), ch. 3; Crook (1986a).

[13] On the legal implications of marriage *sine manu* see Crook (1967a), 99-107 and Corbett (1930), ch. 3.

[14] Crook (1986a) (1986b).

[15] Corbett (1930), ch. 5.

marriage by either husband or wife. Augustus' requirement of witnesses to the notice of intent was prompted by a need to make the end of the marriage a matter of public knowledge and hence adultery clearly distinguishable, but it cannot have served as an obstacle to divorce.

In sum, Roman women enjoyed a legal independence in marriage that is quite remarkable by comparison with the position of women in many other traditional agrarian societies. A striking indication of this can be seen in the changes introduced by the jurists in late medieval Italy. When Roman law was reintroduced, the classical principles of marriage in which the woman did not transfer from her father's to her husband's legal power were generally accepted. But the complete lack of authority of the husband over his wife was unacceptable, and so the law was modified: the wife's position in regard to her husband was assimilated to the Roman freedwoman's subordination to her ex-master, to whom respect and duties were owed, and the husband often exercised guardianship over his wife after her father's death (something not usual in classical Roman law).[16]

This notable legal independence of the woman in marriage was no doubt restricted by various social customs. The conventional difference in ages at marriage for men and women must have encouraged a psychological subordination of wife to husband. A survey of Latin funerary dedications suggests that men in the Latin-speaking West typically married for the first time in their late twenties or early thirties. It was for men who died at these ages that wives appear for the first time as a significant proportion of commemorators in place of parents; the most plausible explanation for the almost complete absence of wives among the scores of commemorators for men under twenty-five is that men were not generally marrying in their teens or early twenties. In contrast, husbands decisively replace parents as commemorators for women in their late teens or early twenties. This evidence points to a pattern of late male/early female marriage found widely in later Mediterranean societies. Literary and legal sources suggest that senatorial men and women probably married several years younger, but still with the characteristic age gap between husband and wife.[17]

Of course, not every wife was younger than her husband, nor were the consequences of the husband's usual seniority the same in all cases. Nevertheless, a passage from Pliny's *Letters* about his third wife illustrates the results the age difference will often have had. Pliny, in his forties, wrote to the aunt of his wife Calpurnia, still in her teens (*Ep.* 4.19): 'I do not doubt that it will be a source of great joy to you to know that [Calpurnia] has turned out to be worthy of her father, worthy of you and worthy of her grandfather. Her shrewdness and frugality are of the

[16] Kuehn (1981).
[17] Saller (1987a); on the Mediterranean type see Hajnal (1983) and Laslett (1983).

highest order. She loves me – a sign of her purity. To these virtues is added an interest in literature, which she has taken up out of fondness for me. She has, repeatedly reads, and even learns by heart my works. What anxiety she feels when I am about to speak in court! What joy when I have finished! She arranges for messengers to tell her of the approval and applause I win as well as of the outcome of the case.' In a sense this could be labelled a 'companionate marriage' in which Calpurnia shared the interests of her husband, and yet the young girl was clearly not on an equal footing with her consular husband, to whose interests and public achievement she subordinated herself.

Pliny's praise of Calpurnia offers some insight into the conventional values of marriage, at least from the aristocratic male viewpoint. First, reference to Calpurnia's shrewdness and frugality derives from the traditional ideal that husband and wife cooperate in running their house and estate, with the wife taking responsibility for managing the home while the husband deals with external affairs.[18] Columella in his work on estate management discusses the traditional role of the Roman matron in running the household, and then uses his idealization of the past to condemn the present, in which domestic tasks and management are left to slaves (12.pr.8-10). Pliny may have praised his wife for the traditional virtues of household management, but in fact slaves in aristocratic households relieved the wife of the necessity of housework for the joint benefit of the family. This may provide part of the explanation for the difference in usual age at marriage for women of the upper and lower classes: in humble families without slaves the inexperience of a twelve or thirteen-year-old wife would have been seriously detrimental to the household economy, while in wealthy households it was inconsequential.[19] In any case, as part of his scheme to prod the aristocracy into returning to the ancient virtues, Augustus advertised the fact that the women of his *domus* performed traditional domestic tasks, an attempt to set an example that was no more effective than Augustus' other attempts to turn back the clock.

The second virtue ascribed to Calpurnia, *amor* (love and devotion) for her husband, is connected with the ideal of the *univira*, the woman who devoted herself exclusively to one husband.[20] Love and devotion are not easy to isolate and identify, and are impossible to measure, leaving historians latitude to come to radically different conclusions about the quality of marital devotion and affection in this era.[21] Carcopino believed

---

[18] Pearce (1974).

[19] Treggiari (1976) (1979a); Saller (1987b). The different expectations of aristocratic and working class women are reflected in the iconography accompanying dedications as pointed out by Kampen (1981).

[20] Humbert (1972), 31ff.; Lightman and Feisel (1977).

[21] The methodological difficulties of writing a history of familial affection are perceptively discussed by Anderson (1980), ch. 3.

that marriage had degenerated to the point that it had 'become merely a legalized form of adultery'. In complete contrast, Veyne has recently suggested that the early imperial senatorial order invented and disseminated a proto-Christian ideal of the affectionate marriage.[22] Both views are suspect. The notion of degeneracy depends heavily on accepting the Romans' idealization of their past and the statements of moralists about the pervasiveness of contemporary vices, motifs that are suspect as history. The evidence for the instability of marriage and high rates of divorce among the elites of classical Rome, however, is convincing. A famous epitaph of the Augustan age boasted of a long marriage 'ended by death, not broken up by divorce' as something 'rare'.[23] Many elite Romans had more than one spouse in the course of their lives, and some went through a series of remarriages after divorce or the death of spouses.[24]

The case for the 'invention' of the affectionate marriage by the aristocracy of the Principate is even less compelling. Pliny is sometimes held up as the prototype of a loving husband who openly expressed a new sentiment, a longing and concern for his wife. But a century and a half earlier Cicero wrote to his wife from exile about his desire to embrace her and his concern for her well-being during his crisis (*Fam.* 14.1.3, 14.4.1). More generally, Lucretius in the late Republic gave poetic expression to what can only be described as powerful family affection. Asking what a man most fears he will miss after death, Lucretius answered: his home, his excellent wife, and his children who race to welcome him home and to secure the first kiss, 'touching his heart with sweetness' (3.896). The affectionate family obviously did not have to be invented during the Principate. The search for the origins of conjugal affection by Roman historians and others is a quest for a chimera. It might still be claimed that emphasis on the sentimental attachment of husband and wife increased during the Principate, but decisive evidence is hard to find. Pliny's letters demonstrate that marriages were still arranged with a view to family honour and advancement much more than to the compatibility of the couple or the wife's happiness (e.g. *Ep.* 6.26). But of course arranged marriages do not preclude marital affection.[25]

The third virtue for which Calpurnia received praise was her effort to follow and appreciate Pliny's endeavours. While she and many other wives may have done so as youthful admirers rather than as equal companions, upper-class Roman women did share in more of their husbands' activities than, for instance, their Athenian counterparts, who were segregated from male political and social activities.[26] Roman wives

[22] Carcopino (1940), 100; Veyne (1978).
[23] *FIRA* III, no. 69, 1. 22; translated with commentary by Wistrand (1976).
[24] Humbert (1972), 72ff.
[25] Treggiari (1982) (1984); Dixon (1985b).
[26] Pomeroy (1975), ch. 5.

were educated, attended dinner parties with their husbands and in the Principate began to accompany husbands during their tenure as governors of provinces. But the companionship was not on terms of equality, and not only because of the usual seniority of husband over wife. Calpurnia could share in Pliny's public life only as a spectator at a distance because women were not allowed to participate directly in political life or the courts. Though some women displayed literary talent, they were not as a rule educated to the same level as their husbands (Calpurnia was said to have taken up an interest in literature 'out of fondness' for Pliny).[27] No doubt women older than Calpurnia had more credibility as companions and advisers. It is clear, particularly from Cicero's letters, that some older women such as Brutus' mother were respected participants in political discussions (*Att*.15.10-12, 17). On the other hand, the influence of a woman over her husband in public affairs was regarded as inappropriate, just like that of a slave or freedman. The governor's wife may have accompanied her husband, but, if virtuous, she did not allow provincials to approach lest they try to influence the governor through her (Tacitus, *Ann*. 3.33-4).[28] In private life it was thought praiseworthy for the wife to provide moral support for her husband. Pliny (*Ep*. 6.24) tells a story of a wife who convinced her terminally ill husband to commit suicide and so end his pain by jumping off a cliff into Lake Como (an honourable act in the Roman view). She persuaded him by setting an example and jumping first – the last act of a companionate marriage perhaps, but an asymmetrical companionship (we never hear of a husband bolstering his wife's courage by joining her in death).

The companionship ideal was summed up by Plutarch in his *Conjugal Precepts* (*Mor*. 139D) in the advice that husband and wife share in decisions about their common life, but that the husband lead. The reality of the husband's domination was not always so gentle. The husband was lord of the *domus* with the right to exercise his authority over his slaves and his children, by physical punishment if he wished. The fact that the wife was not in her husband's legal power may not always have exempted her from such domination. In his *On Anger* (3.35) Seneca asked how a man could complain of the state being deprived of liberty when he in his own household became angry at his slave, freedman, client and wife for answering back to him. The inclusion of the wife in this series of inferior members of the *domus* is suggestive. Much later St. Augustine wrote more explicitly that his mother meekly suffered regular beatings at the hands of his father, and that most other wives in the small African town of Thagaste had similar bruises to show

[27] Marrou (1956), 274; Bonner (1977), 107.
[28] Marshall (1975); Saller (1982), 162.

(*Confessions* 9.9).[29] The source is unique in the corpus of imperial literature, but not necessarily the wife-beating that it describes.

The wealthy in the Roman world lived off their property rather than their labour; as a consequence, a vital aspect of marriage was the property arrangement, which reflected the ambiguous position of the woman in the family. Though a wife was a physical and social member of her husband's family, her property was quite separate. In non-*manus* marriages only the woman's dowry went into her husband's ownership. The provision of a dowry was regarded as a duty of the father, but was not mandatory for a legitimate marriage (as in Athens). While dowries were sometimes large, up to one million sesterces, their value and function must be put into perspective. In some early modern societies, the dowry constituted the daughter's share of the family estate, or at least the bulk of it. This was not the case in Rome, where daughters could expect an equal or at least substantial share of their father's estate on his death. Insofar as we can judge from the limited figures available, Roman dowries were relatively modest in comparison with the father's estate – of the order of one year's income (5 to 10 per cent of the estate). Consequently, though dowries were reckoned as part of the daughter's share of the family estate, they probably represented only a fraction of her full share. According to legal texts, they were intended to be of a size to contribute to the household living expenses. Modest dowries make sense in the Roman context of early female marriage and frequent divorce. A father would have been reluctant to give his daughter a full share of the patrimony before his own death or to hand over a large dowry to a husband who might well divorce the daughter and keep some fraction of it. The modest size of dowries also helps to explain certain noticeable silences in our texts: in contrast with the early modern period in Europe, few complaints were voiced by Romans about extravagant dowries ruining family fortunes; furthermore, there is little evidence for dowry hunting, in marked contrast with the frequent reference to legacy hunting.[30]

The right of the wife to divorce and take much of the dowry with her, together with her independent right of ownership, gave some wealthy women considerable financial leverage and freedom in their marriages. This should be set against the paternalism inherent in the age difference and the ideology of the husband's superiority. Martial explained that he was not interested in marrying a rich woman lest she be a husband to him (*Epig.* 8.12). Juvenal wrote of a husband's incapacity to control his adulterous wife because of his fear that she would leave him and take her money (*Sat.* 6.136). These verses no doubt contain an element of satirical exaggeration, but such fears are an intelligible result of Roman rules and

[29] See Shaw (forthcoming a), on the evidence of Augustine for Roman family life, especially corporal punishment within the family.

[30] Saller (1984b).

mores regarding divorce and separation of property in marriage, rules that contrast sharply with other systems. In early modern English law, 'by marriage, the husband and wife became one person in law – and that person was the husband [who] acquired absolute control of all his wife's personal property, which he could sell at will'.[31]

With the exception of the age gap, the discussion so far has concerned husbands and wives of the leisured classes, because the literary sources offer virtually no useful information about marriages between humble Romans. This silence has recently provided the basis for an argument that marriages were not entered into by ordinary Romans until aristocrats disseminated the institution in the Principate.[32] However, the epigraphic evidence shows conclusively that from the time that funerary inscriptions began to be erected in the late Republic, husbands and wives of low station commemorated each other and their marriages (e.g. *CIL* 1².1221). The pattern of dedications from the imperial era shows that rank influenced the selection of mates in the lower classes: freeborn Romans occasionally took spouses from the servile population in *de facto* or *de iure* marriages, but more often freeborn and servile lived with partners of their own rank.[33]

Parents and children

The characteristic feature of relations between the generations in Roman families was authoritarianism, or such is the impression conveyed by the law, in which the *paterfamilias* enjoyed sweeping powers over his direct descendants. As Gaius wrote in his second-century textbook of law, *patria potestas* 'is the special characteristic of Roman citizens; for virtually no other men have over their sons a power such as we have' (*Inst.* 1.55). Though the father's powers were modified during the Principate, most remained essentially intact.[34]

Perhaps the most striking was the power of life and death (*vitae necisque potestas*). The legitimacy of the use of this power to punish adult children was affirmed by Augustus, but was later denied by Hadrian and then the jurist Ulpian (*Digest* 48.8.2). Roman fathers continued until the late fourth century to exercise the power of life and death in choosing whether their newborn children were to be exposed or raised.[35] If a father decided to bring up a child, he had considerable legal control over it until his death. For instance, his consent was required for

---

[31] Stone (1977), 195.
[32] Veyne (1978).
[33] Rawson (1966); Weaver (1974).
[34] Daube (1969), 79ff.
[35] Engels (1980) (1984) minimizes infanticide, but see Harris (1980) (1982) and Saller (1987b).

the legitimate marriage of a son or daughter, and only in the second and third centuries was his power to break up his children's marriages restricted.[36]

The power that would seem to have been most awkward and oppressive from day to day was the father's sole right to own property in his *familia*.[37] Sons could be given an allowance or, more formally, a *peculium*, but according to the legal rules the *paterfamilias* had the rights of formal ownership over all this property, including any accruing to his children through labour, gifts or bequests. Again, the rules were modified in minor respects by the emperors, notably, Augustus' grant of a fund to soldiers into which the income from military service was paid and over which the soldier had control (*peculium castrense*).[38] Because the law did not set an age of majority, this incapacity to own property extended to all adults, whatever their age or rank, whose fathers were still alive and who had not been freed from their father's power by the special legal process of emancipation.

The *paterfamilias* also had a good deal of latitude in disposing of the family property upon his death. In cases of intestacy the civil law called for partible inheritance in equal shares among all legitimate children (male and female), but Romans with property typically made wills that could alter the equal shares.[39] Some restraints on the testator's freedom came to be enforced. If a Roman chose not to institute his children as heirs, he had to disinherit them explicitly in the will. By the end of the first century BC such a disherison could be challenged in court (by the *querela inofficiosi testamenti* procedure) on the grounds that there was not adequate cause for depriving the children of their patrimony. Yet the father could preempt this procedure by leaving a mere fraction of his estate, a quarter, to his primary intestate heirs.[40] This latitude in disposition of the patrimony no doubt gave the father more real power to exact obedience from his adult children than the harsher power of life and death.

obedience was exacted by deciding how much to give children in will.

The consequences of this strong paternal authority have recently been stressed by various social historians. The oppressiveness of *patria potestas* is said to have provoked a marked hostility of sons toward fathers, the direct result of which was the Roman propensity for parricide.[41] The fortunate Romans, so it is said, were those whose fathers died young. *Patria potestas* has also been invoked to prove that Roman

[36] Matringe (1971).

[37] Emphasized by Daube (1969). On the difficulties that the law raised for sons holding municipal office, see Y. Thomas (1982).

[38] Buckland (1963), 280-1; J.A.C. Thomas (1976), 416-17; Crook (1967a), 110-11.

[39] Crook (1973).

[40] Buckland (1963), 327-31; J.A.C. Thomas (1976), 495-6; Crook (1967a), 122-3.

[41] Veyne (1978); Y. Thomas (1981). Crook (1967b) offers an excellent antidote to these views.

women were really not so free: though they were not subject to their husbands, they continued to be in the power of their fathers.[42] For various reasons these portrayals of Roman family relations tend toward caricature.

The demography of the family can provide some help in understanding the context of the legal rules and social behaviour. Comparative evidence for pre-industrial societies suggests that the average life expectancy at birth for Romans was in the range of twenty to thirty years; it was probably in the middle of that range to judge from the very inadequate Roman evidence.[43] Infant mortality must have been very common, with a quarter or more of newborns not surviving their first year, and perhaps as many as half not living to age ten. Those who did survive the childhood diseases of their first decade could expect to live another thirty-five to forty years on average. Because of the high infant mortality rate, Roman women who lived to adulthood had to bear five or six children on average, if the population was not to go into decline. Yet many couples had more children than they could, or wished to, raise. The father most often exercised the legal power of life and death in exposing unwanted children. In the literary sources, those peoples of the empire, such as the Jews, who did not expose unwanted children were regarded as anomalies (Tacitus, *Hist.* 5.5; Strabo 17.824).[44] ('Exposure', rather than 'infanticide', is used advisedly here, since the literary sources reveal a clear expectation that the exposed infant would not die immediately, but would be picked up and enslaved.)[45]

It has not been appreciated that the late marriage age of men reduced the effects of *patria potestas*. Marriage of men in their late twenties rather than their late teens had the consequence that the generation gap was rather large, and that relatively few fathers were alive to witness their sons' marriages. A computer simulation incorporating the Roman demographic variables suggests that the average difference in age between father and child was about forty years. By the time children reached their late teens or early twenties – when women usually married – more than half had already lost their fathers. It is unrealistic, then, to argue that a husband's lack of authority over his wife did not normally leave her free because she remained in her father's power. Only a fifth or so of men at the time of their marriage in their late twenties or early thirties were still in their fathers' power and had to tolerate their interference in a decision about marriage (a quarter of aristocratic men, who married younger). Obviously, no more than a small fraction of mature Romans (less than 5 per cent at age forty) lacked the capacity to own property because they were still in their fathers' power.[46]

[42] Gratwick (1984).

[43] Hopkins (1966); Frier (1982) (1983).

[44] On the importance of exposed children for the slave supply, see Harris (1980).

[45] Bosworth (1984).

[46] Saller (1987a).

Clearly we must use other, more conventional methods to discover whether the Roman family was as authoritarian in practice as in law during the lifetime of the *paterfamilias*. Latin literature offers a glimpse, and not much more, of the quality of family relations at progressive stages of the lifecycle. Parents and children in Rome, it has been argued, did not enjoy highly developed affective bonds for several reasons. On account of the high infant mortality rate, parents could not afford a heavy emotional investment in a baby who was unlikely to survive childhood.[47] In addition, it was customary among the elite to entrust their children to slaves for wet-nursing and rearing, a custom lamented by Tacitus as contributing to Rome's decline (*Dial.* 28-9). It would seem reasonable to posit greater distance in parent-child relationships than we expect today, and some evidence supports this generalization: infants rarely received funerary memorials and a few literary passages display callousness toward the death of newborns (e.g. Cicero, *Att.* 10.18). On the other side, Latin authors repeatedly attest the strength of parental affection. Fathers grieved immoderately the death of their children, according to Seneca, despite the fact that they should have been numb to a tragedy so often repeated (*Cons. ad Marciam* 9.2). The children who lived were a source of joy and pleasure (Seneca, *Ep.* 9.7, 99.23; Fronto, *Ad amicos* 1.12).

One of the most obvious shortcomings of our sources written by males is the lack of information about the mother-child bond from the mother's perspective. Fronto was able to neglect his wife's feelings to such an extent as to claim to have mourned the loss of their first four children alone (*De nepote amisso* 2.1-2). It is hardly surprising, then, that these male sources give us very little sense, for example, of how the pattern of frequent divorce and remarriage affected the bond between mother and child.[48] Since Roman children customarily remained with their father after his divorce, they must very often have had to live with a stepmother (*noverca*) and half-siblings. The *noverca* was assumed to have a greater interest in her own children at the expense of her stepchildren, and so became stereotyped as a source of ill will – a stereotype so deeply ingrained that even the normally dry legal sources repeat it (*Digest* 5.2.4). We know that the frequency of divorce and remarriage produced complicated problems in division of the patrimony, and it is reasonable to assume equally awkward complexities in bonds of familial affection also resulted. One way for a widower or divorcé with children to avoid such problems was to take in place of another wife a lower class concubine, whose children would not be legitimate.[49]

After childhood and years of education for children of parents who could afford it, what kind of relationship did older children have with

[47] Bradley (1986), 220; cf. Hopkins (1983c), 224-6.
[48] Humbert (1972), ch. 2; Bradley (1985).
[49] Saller (1987b); Treggiari (1981a).

their parents, and especially their father, in whose legal power they remained for his lifetime? Was the hostility between the generations as intense as the stories of parricide have led some to believe? Daughters married and left their natal home soon after reaching adulthood, even before in the case of aristocratic girls, who were often married at the age of twelve.[50] As noted above, the law gave the father power to arrange his daughter's marriage, and the evidence about the way in which husbands in first marriages were selected in elite social circles suggests that fathers did in reality take the initiative.[51] It has been argued that aristocratic Roman fathers enjoyed a special affective relationship with their daughters throughout their lives, and that this produced a 'filiafocal' kinship system in which kinship links through daughters were especially prominent. The stories of father–daughter affection, however, do not constitute an effective demonstration of such a broad generalization, nor do relatives linked through daughters appear to have been favoured (see below, pp. 145f.).[52]

For young men there was an extended gap between physical maturity and marriage.[53] This period was not as awkward as it might have been, because for one reason or another many young men left their parents' houses. Army service could take up some or all of these years for rich and poor citizens alike. Among the wealthy at Rome, it was expected that a young man remaining in the city would set up a separate household. In the countryside adult sons of local notables were often sent off to manage an outlying piece of property. Various ways were devised to circumvent the legal incapacity of those still in their father's power to own property. While legal rules were developed to govern the *peculium*, the literary sources, such as Cicero, appear to suggest that the formality of the *peculium* was often dispensed with, and the son was simply given an allowance which he spent as his own. Presumably legal questions about his 'ownership' of the money were rarely raised: it was no doubt assumed that, if the son had the money, he had been given it by his father and hence had his approval. In all of Cicero's correspondence about providing funds for his son in Athens, the legal technicalities of ownership or *peculium* were never raised. Only if a son's spending exceeded his allowance and he borrowed money without his father's knowledge, would legal and social problems arise. An attempt to suppress such problems was made in the mid-first century by the *senatusconsultum Macedonianum*, which took away from creditors of sons in their father's power the right to reclaim their loans in court, even after the father's death.[54]

[50] Hopkins (1965a); Shaw (forthcoming b)
[51] Treggiari (1982) (1984).
[52] Hallett (1984), reviewed by Saller, *CPh* 81 (1986), 354ff.
[53] For what follows, see Saller (1986).
[54] Daube (1947).

The financial dependence of an adult son on his father could result in serious tensions, particularly if the son fell in with a disreputable creditor. However, these tensions are not the peculiar consequence of *patria potestas*, but are found in many agrarian societies. The fundamental problem arose from the fact that more than one adult generation sometimes had to depend for support on a fixed unit of land rather than on the variable labour of each member of the family. Different societies adopted various strategies for reaching a modus vivendi between father and son. One, which the Romans apparently did not use, was for the aging father to retire and turn over his land to his son in return for support until his death. Such strategies, however, did not wholly resolve the tensions: neither parricide nor stories of parricide are unique to Rome.[55] In fact, very few actual cases of sons murdering fathers or fathers executing sons are attested for imperial Rome. No doubt parricide did occur, as in other societies, but Seneca's often cited generalization (*Clem.* 1.23) about the frequency of parricide is highly suspect.

Because men married later than women, a much higher proportion of them would have been independent and hence free to make their own decisions about when and whom to marry. There is also some reason to believe that their age and sex gave even those in their father's power more influence in arranging a marriage than their sisters had. Young Quintus Cicero appears to have made his own survey of the field of potential wives, but we cannot be sure that all young aristocrats enjoyed the same latitude (*Att.* 15.29). In any case, once married, the new couple were expected to establish a new household.

Inheritance and lineage

The Roman father's power over, and interest in, his children did not cease with his death. His will largely determined the future financial well-being of his children, who were his hope for posterity. The legal rules of inheritance have been briefly described, but, as in other societies, the rules and legal instruments allowed for flexibility and could be manipulated to achieve a family's goals in what have been called 'strategies of heirship' (that is, how to plan a family and distribute the patrimony to the next generation). It has already been pointed out in regard to the Roman vocabulary of family and lineage that the emphasis in Roman thinking shifted from the strictly agnatic *familia* and *nomen* in the Republic to the *domus*, which included relatives by marriage and descendants through females as well as males. With this change came an increased interest in daughters as perpetuators of the family line. Under

[55] Gaunt (1983).

the empire a daughter's children came to be spoken of as a man's 'posterity', as they were not in the Republic. Fronto, who had no surviving son, wrote of his choice of Aufidius Victorinus to be his daughter's husband as a wise one 'both for my own sake in regard to my posterity and for my daughter's whole life' (*Ad amicos* 2.11). In the same vein, a letter from Pliny to his wife's paternal grandfather, Calpurnius Fabatus, indicates a keen desire on the part of Fabatus to extend his line through his granddaughter's children, whose 'descent from both of us should make their road to high office easy' (*Ep.* 8.10). Of course, the reference to 'the road to high office' implies a preference for a male descendant, but in the absence of a son or grandson Fabatus was willing to place his hopes on the offspring of his granddaughter. This willingness to use females to continue the family line is reflected in the development of extended names in the Principate when the children of the family increasingly preserved the memory of both father's and mother's *domus* by taking both of their names. One blue-blooded senator of the mid-second century sported no fewer than thirty-eight names.[56]

The recognition of women as links rather than as dead-ends in family lines is one aspect of a more general change in 'strategies of heirship'. As pointed out earlier, any group in the population that was to be self-perpetuating would have had to produce five or six children per family in order to overcome the devastation of high infant mortality. Parents who gave birth to five or six children had a good chance of having a male heir survive to continue the family line and name. In many of the early modern European aristocracies, families were large on average, thus enhancing the chances of biological success. The incidence of death was unpredictable and so in having large families parents ran the risk of being left with too many surviving children and a consequent fragmentation of the patrimony. This dilemma was resolved in several ways. A primogeniture system of inheritance would ensure that the eldest son inherited most of the patrimony regardless of the number of children, and so would be able to carry on the family line at the same level of wealth and prestige. Another possibility was to discourage marriage of all children beyond one son and one daughter, so that no permanent fragmentation of the estate was necessary to support new family lines.

Roman law and custom do not seem to have adopted either of these options. The system of inheritance remained firmly partible among male and female offspring. Though the will could have been used to settle the patrimony on the eldest son, this does not seem to have happened; such, at least, is the implication of the assumption in our sources that disherison of a son was abnormal and a result of bad behaviour. Furthermore, all children were supposed to get married. This expectation seems to have been fulfilled in the case of daughters, and to the extent

[56] Saller (1984a), 349.

that men did not marry it was not part of a strategy to avoid initiation of additional family lines by younger sons. During the middle Republic the lack of such strategies did not generally put great pressure on aristocratic families: they had many children and could hope to provide for all out of the massive influx of wealth into Rome from conquest. The flow largely dried up under the emperors, and this, together with social changes (e.g. much higher living standards for aristocrats in Rome), caused many aristocrats to limit their families to just a few children. No figures of any use are available for family size, but various authors of the Principate point to a widespread belief that having large families was unpopular on account of the expense and trouble. Pliny praised one of his friends, Asinius Rufus, for his virtuous character, one indication of which was his decision to have several children 'in this age when for most people the advantages of childlessness make even one child seem a burden' (*Ep.* 4.15.3). For noble women as well, child-bearing was perceived to be unpopular (Seneca, *Cons. ad Helviam* 16.3). A fragment of Musonius Rufus (15b, ed. O. Hense) suggests that even wealthy families resorted to infant exposure to restrict the number of children for financial reasons.[57]

Some indication that Pliny's and Seneca's perceptions about the reluctance to have children were not exaggerated is to be found in the discontent aroused by Augustus' marriage laws. These laws established legal disabilities, particularly in matters of inheritance, for men and women who were unmarried or had had fewer than three children.[58] Augustus' aim was to force the aristocracy to have children, but he failed and the laws were a continuing source of irritation until Constantine abolished them. Several points about Augustus' measures are worth stressing. First, if Roman parents did no more than meet the legal standard of three children, aristocratic families would have died out very quickly. Only 40 per cent of fathers would have been survived by a male heir, and 35 per cent would have had no child to institute as heir, figures that belie the view that Augustus hoped to weaken the aristocracy by requiring so many children that aristocratic estates would have been fragmented.[59]

The second point is that state intervention to force the propertied classes to have children and to continue their families is unexpected. In many early modern European societies nobles displayed a veritable obsession with securing male successors for their lines,[60] whereas in Rome the emperor had to employ carrot-and-stick methods to convince aristocrats to have three children, a number that would not have resulted in full replacement of their numbers. It was not that all Romans had abandoned concern for perpetuation of the family line, as Pliny's and Fronto's interest in their own posterity shows. Rather, it seems likely

[57] Hopkins (1983c), chs. 2-3; on contraception, see Hopkins (1965b), Eyben (1980-1).
[58] Rejected by Wallace-Hadrill (1981).
[59] Goody (1976), 133-4.
[60] Cooper (1976) summarizes a great deal of material about later European societies.

that many Romans came to take a more individualistic view of life, giving correspondingly less effort to ensuring the success of family and lineage.[61] Besides, Roman law and custom offered attractive alternatives to large families for continuing the *domus*. If a Roman could be satisfied with a daughter to perpetuate his *domus* he need have only half the number of children to achieve the same probability of having a successor as if he required a son. Better still, a man could continue the family name without any of the cost and trouble of a family by adopting a son, usually an adult, in his will.[62] This technique had other advantages as well. The testator could choose a son whose character was already developed, thus avoiding the possibility of being burdened with a reprobate natural son. Furthermore, being childless until his death, the testator would attract the attention and favours of the crowd of legacy-hunters so often mentioned in our texts. Indeed, part of the rationale behind Augustus' restrictions on the capacity of the childless and unmarried to inherit from unrelated testators was precisely to neutralize the advantage that they enjoyed in the exchange of gifts and legacies.[63] The custom of distributing bequests widely outside the family, rather than concentrating the inheritance on natural children, is a distinctive feature of Roman society, resulting in a fluidity of wealth between aristocratic families that contrasts strikingly with the drive in other aristocracies to prevent dispersion of the patrimony. Its role in cementing relationships between unrelated Romans is considered in the next chapter.

These features of Roman society and family life – the relatively weak stress on natural sons as successors, the acceptability of daughters in this role, the recourse to adoption, the financial and other pressures to limit family size severely, the advantages of childlessness in an inheritance system that dispersed patrimonies widely – all contribute to our understanding of why the senatorial aristocracy failed to reproduce itself (i.e., failed to fill the ranks of the next generation of the senate with its own sons). It has been suggested that in this respect the Romans simply fall under the general law that aristocracies do not reproduce themselves. Certainly the statistical probabilities are that even in a fully reproducing population a significant proportion of families will fail in the male line.[64] But the Roman aristocracy's failure was on a much grander scale than in many later European societies. The English nobility was one of the more successful in the early modern period: yet in the three generations from 1558 to 1641, 65 per cent of the families failed to produce a direct male descendant in each generation, while 33 per cent failed in the male line altogether. The old Danish aristocracy, one of the least successful, suffered a decline in the total number of males of 73 per cent over the 170

[61] Hopkins (1983c), 79-81.
[62] Crook (1967a), 111-12.
[63] Wallace-Hadrill (1981).
[64] Hammond (1957); Wachter et al. (1978).

years after 1550.[65] The disappearance rate of Roman consular families (roughly the more successful half of the senate and the ones we are likely to know about) was about 75 per cent in each generation. Only one in four Roman imperial consuls had a son who reached the consulship.[66] Of course, these figures are not precisely comparable to those from later European societies – the Roman son had to reach middle age and win high office – but even allowing for that, it is clear that the Roman aristocracy's failure was at a markedly higher level, partly because some sons withdrew from public life but largely because many aristocrats did not have adult sons. Whatever Augustus may have wished, the senatorial order was far from hereditary. The corollary of the massive 75 per cent failure rate each generation was that 75 per cent of the consulships were open to men of upwardly mobile families. Italians and provincials moved in to take up the vacancies in the senatorial aristocracy and married into already established families.

Extended kinship relations

The *Digest* (38.10.10) preserves a long passage of the jurist Paul detailing the classifications of Roman kin. The list extends to the sixth degree of kinship, which, as the author says, includes no fewer than 448 categories of relations, beginning with the first degree of parents and children, and proceeding as far as the great-great-great-great-grandfather (*tritavus*) in one direction and the great-great-great-great-grandson or daughter (*trinepos* or *trineptis*) in the other. As Paul noted, the jurisconsult needed to know the grades of kinship in order to identify the nearest kin for purposes of inheritance and guardianship. The Latin terminology for kin made a clear distinction between uncles, aunts and cousins related through the father (*patrui, amitae* and *fratres/sorores patrueles*) and those related through the mother (*avunculi, materterae* and *[con]sobrini*).

Whatever the social relationships among the early Latins on which the classificatory terminology was based, by the classical period little pattern in Roman kinship relations existed that one could call a 'system'. The law did preserve some old agnatic rules, but they had begun slowly to break down under the Republic and continued to do so under the Principate, until the mother's relationship with her children in intestate succession was given full recognition in the Antonine era.[67] By this time the Romans had long since ceased to make strong distinctions between agnates, cognates and affines in daily social life. Indeed, the literary sources give the impression that Romans felt a duty to help

[65] Stone (1965), 168f.; Hansen (1965), 106.
[66] Hopkins (1983c), ch. 3.
[67] Crook (1986a), 67-8.

'kin', but the feeling of obligation did not discriminate between types of kin outside the immediate family. An indication of this can be found in the absence of distinctions in the vocabulary used by the prose authors. None of the words for cousin can be found in the letters of Pliny or the works of moral philosophy by Seneca, suggesting not only that the division between paternal and maternal cousins was unimportant, but that cousins did not loom very large in the thinking of Romans about their social relationships. The words for uncles and aunts do appear occasionally, though without any obvious difference in social roles between paternal and maternal uncles and aunts. General words for kin (*necessarius, propinquus,* and *mei, tui* or *sui*) seem to have been used more often than specific classificatory designations. Words meaning 'mine' or 'yours' were particularly common in reference to relatives, and they did not distinguish kin from unrelated dependants such as freedmen. Kin outside the immediate family came into consideration as one group among others deserving protection and help, with no special classification of kin enjoying a privileged position.

The literary sources point to several types of services that kin provided for one another in Roman families. The high mortality rate meant that many children lost their fathers before adulthood: the computer simulation suggests that perhaps a third of Roman children had lost their fathers by age ten, and one in ten was an orphan. In cases of such misfortune, relatives of all types were natural candidates to take in and raise the children (Pliny, *Ep.* 2.18, 4.19, 6.20; *FIRA* III, no. 69, 11.42ff.). In looking for help and support in public or private affairs a Roman naturally considered kin by blood or by marriage as a potential source. A senior brother, a former mother-in-law, almost any relative could be called on to provide anything from a loan, to support for a candidature, to a connection to secure citizenship from the emperor (Pliny, *Ep.* 3.19.8, 3.8, 10.51). The point to be made about these favours and services is that they do not serve to distinguish kinship from friendship or patronage. Rather, kinship was intertwined in a broader network of social relationships and reciprocal obligation.

The provision of a dowry for a kinswoman was another common form of support (Pliny, *Ep.* 2.4, *FIRA* III, no. 69, 11.42ff.) and raises the more general question of the place of kin in marriage and property considerations. It has been argued that the desires to keep the dowry and women's property in the family and to reinforce clan unity inclined Romans to choose spouses from among kin, particularly parallel cousins. Marriage of first cousins was legal in Rome until the fourth century, but close scrutiny shows marriage among close kin to have been exceptional. Stemma after stemma of aristocratic families yields no case of marriage between cousins, nor do the letters of Cicero and Pliny concerning marriage arrangements give any thought at all to the kinship of the proposed husband or wife. In this respect, then, there is no reason to believe that Christianity, with its wider incest prohibition, forced a change in familial behaviour for most Romans.[68]

Conclusion

In a classic article, Hajnal drew a basic distinction between a pattern of late marriage for men and women who typically lived in nuclear family households in western Europe and the pattern of early marriage and large, extended family households in eastern Europe. In an expansion of the typology, a 'Mediterranean' type has been added, characterized by much later marriage for men than for women and a significant proportion of extended family households.[69] The Roman family described in this chapter seems to fit the Mediterranean classification in certain important respects, particularly the pattern of late male/early female marriage with the consequent age gap between husband and wife. But the Romans diverged from the Mediterranean type insofar as multiple family households were neither the norm nor common in practice.

The family offers the Roman historian a promising subject for an analysis of the complex relationship between the law and social behaviour. On the one hand, the emperors and the jurists did move with the current of changing attitudes and practices in their legal innovations, though rather belatedly in cases like the recognition of the mother's legal relationship with her children and the limitation of the father's power of life and death. On the other hand, a fundamental conservatism in regard to basic legal principles led to a substantial disjunction between those principles and widespread *mores*. Insofar as the literary sources provide insights, the legal powers of the *paterfamilias*, oppressive as they were in theory, did not dominate the Roman family experience. *A fortiori*, if *patria potestas* is of limited value in understanding the Roman family, we may be sceptical of broad arguments that explain basic differences in later Europe between northern and Mediterranean patterns of family life by the reintroduction of Roman law into Mediterranean lands.

Wives had much legal freedom but were still under hubs
Children were completely under father
Inheritance - fewer children + women + adoptees.

---

[68] For the claim that cousin marriage was common, see Goody (1983), 51-5; Y. Thomas (1980); *contra*, Saller and Shaw (1984b).

[69] Hajnal (1965) (1983); Laslett (1983); Smith (1981).

CHAPTER EIGHT

Social Relations

The place of a Roman in society was a function of his position in the social hierarchy, membership of a family, and involvement in a web of personal relationships extending out from the household. Romans were obligated to and could expect support from their families, kinsmen and dependants both inside and outside the household, and friends, patrons, protégés and clients. In the eyes of Seneca, whose longest moral essay was devoted to the subject, the exchange of favours and services (*beneficia*) which underlay these relationships 'most especially binds together human society' (*Ben.* 1.4.2).[1] Seneca's emphasis on reciprocal exchange is justifiable on several grounds: it eased tensions and conflicts provoked by divisions and inequalities; and it provided many of the services for which today we turn to impersonal governmental or private institutions.[2]

Honour, status and the reciprocity ethic

Despite the general comment about human society quoted above, Seneca's *On Benefits* is not a work of sociology or anthropology, but an ethical treatise about how men ought to conduct themselves in the giving and receiving of favours and services. His central premise is that a man in receipt of a favour owes his benefactor gratitude and a return in kind. Of the man who neglects this ethical precept, Seneca wrote: 'Homicides, tyrants, traitors there always will be; but worse than all these is the crime of ingratitude' (*Ben.* 1.10.4). A century earlier Cicero expressed the same view: 'To fail to repay [a favour] is not permitted to a·good man' (*Off.* 1.48). The ideal benefactor was supposed to act without thought of what was due to him, but this was unrealistic. It was understood by both the author of the *Handbook on Canvassing* attributed to Q. Cicero and by Tacitus in his *Dialogue on the Orators* that the orator and politician would succeed by distributing benefits that would subsequently be reciprocated. Consequently, Seneca could use the metaphor of treasure for benefits that could be recalled in time of the benefactor's need (*Ben.* 6.43.3), and the language of debt and repayment regularly appeared in discussions of exchange between friends or patrons and clients.[3]

[1] Kaufman (1974), 286-7, on the cohesive effects of patronage.
[2] Hands (1968), 32ff.; Michel (1962), 562; Veyne (1976), 17.
[3] Saller (1982), 21 and, more generally, ch. 1 for the language of exchange.

Just as a loan created a relationship between creditor and debtor, so a favour or service gave rise to a social relationship between Romans. Because benefaction and requital were matters of honour, the dynamics of the exchange partially determined the relative social standing of the men involved. Very little pretence was made about egalitarianism in friendships. A man might have 'superior friends', 'equal friends', 'lesser friends' and humble 'clients', and the categorization of others into one or another of these depended on their resources (Pliny, *Ep.* 7.3.2, 2.6.2; Seneca, *Ep.* 94.14). Those who could exchange comparable benefits were friends of equal social standing, whilst most stood higher or lower in the hierarchy by virtue of their capacity to provide superior or inferior services in return. Some Romans tried to conceal the favours done for them precisely to avoid the implication of social inferiority arising from the fact that they had to turn to someone else for help. The proper conduct of a recipient was to acknowledge and advertise his benefactor's generosity and power.

Three rough categories of exchange relationships can be distinguished for analytical purposes according to the relative social statuses of the men involved (though the dividing lines between them were not clear and were sometimes intentionally obscured by the Romans themselves): patrons and clients, superior and inferior friends (or patrons and protégés), and equal friends.

The emperor as patron

Augustus sought to establish his legitimacy not only by restoring the social order, but also by demonstrating his own supremacy in it through the traditional modes of patronage and beneficence. Much of the *Res Gestae*, his own account of his reign, was an elaboration of the staggering scale of his benefits and services to the Roman people (15-18). In Pliny's *Panegyric* (e.g., 2, 21), the ideology of the good emperor was one not so much of an efficient administrator as of a paternal protector and benefactor.[4] Since subjects could not repay imperial benefactions in kind, the reciprocity ethic dictated that they make a return in the form of deference, respect and loyalty. Consequently, as Seneca pointed out, the emperor who played the role of great patron well had no need of guards because he was 'protected by his benefits' (*Clem.* 1.13.5).

The emperor distributed his benefits individually to those who had access to him and, more broadly, to favoured groups, notably the Roman plebs and the army. Proximity to the emperor opened up to a privileged circle, including friends of high rank, relatives, and servile members of his household, a wide range of benefits from offices and honours to

[4] Béranger (1953), 259.

financial assistance to citizenship and the right of tapping the water supply. The norms guiding the distribution of these goods and services were openly particularistic, in contrast to the universalistic rules associated with modern bureaucracies. They were treated as personal favours granted to the loyal, not as governmental services and positions to be distributed on the basis of impersonal competition and universally available to all qualified citizens or subjects. In return, devoted service and gratitude were expected, one manifestation of which was the naming of the emperor in the will. T. Marius Urbinas caused a scandal by failing to acknowledge Augustus' generosity to himself in this way (Valerius Maximus 7.8.6). From more conscientious friends and clients Augustus received 1.4 billion sesterces in bequests over the last twenty years of his reign (Suetonius, *Aug.* 101).[5]

The emperor also took on the role of benefactor of the plebs, in the cause of order and the security of his regime. Augustus' interest in the tribunate, the prerogatives of which he gradually assumed between 36 and 23 BC, is to be explained in these terms. The appeal of the tribune lay in its historic role as the champion of the common people. More important, Augustus saw to the material needs of the masses by tending to their supply of food, water and housing, by providing public shows and by occasional distributions of considerable sums of money to all male citizens of the city. The sums cited in *Res Gestae* were the equivalent of at least several months' rent for the poor (15). Whatever their feelings about these handouts, later emperors felt compelled to continue in this role. Though the plebs lost all semblance of constitutional power with the transfer of elections to the senate in AD 14, they still possessed means of making their discontent known and the emperor's position awkward, whether through protests at public spectacles or riots in the streets.[6]

Emperors did not and could not monopolize patronage. They did not attempt to be universal patrons to all their subjects, since universality would have undermined the incentive for personal gratitude on the part of the subjects.[7] Far from contemplating the suppression of the patronal networks of the aristocratic houses in Rome, emperors positively encouraged them by providing some of the resources that helped aristocratic patrons like Pliny to reward their clients. The letters of Pliny show Trajan granting offices and citizenship at Pliny's request, thus bolstering Pliny's status as an effective mediator. The successful emperors were the ones who kept the imperial aristocrats content by allowing them to maintain their exalted social status, and that implied a willingness to permit the great houses to display their patronal influence in the traditional way.

[5] Millar (1977), pp. 153ff. and chs. 6, 8; Saller (1982), chs. 1-3.

[6] Yavetz (1969), chs. 2, 5-6; Kloft (1970).

[7] Pliny, *Pan.* 23.1, with Saller (1982), 68, 73-4, and P.A. Brunt, *TLS* 19 Nov. 1982, 1276.

Patrons and clients

Tacitus in writing of the 'part of the populace ... attached to the great houses' (*Hist*. 1.4.) attests the patronal ties linking aristocrats and members of the lower classes in the city of Rome. The *salutatio* and other Republican customs characteristic of patronage continued throughout the Principate, though with a different complexion. After AD 14 the relationship could no longer revolve around the electoral process. In the *Handbook on Canvassing* (11) it was stressed that a Republican candidate for high office had to make every effort to win followers of all ranks, even to the extent of lowering himself by mixing with and flattering members of the lower classes who would ordinarily be beneath his dignity. In the imperial era the impotence of the popular assemblies deprived the ordinary people of their political leverage and, with it, the incentive for aristocrats to treat their humble clients with a modicum of respect.[8] The patron's arrogance toward his clients was a common motif in imperial literature (e.g. Martial, *Epig*. 2.68).

Nevertheless, some *quid pro quo* was still possible and provided the basis for patronal exchange. Clients could contribute to their patron's social status by forming crowds at his door for the morning *salutatio* (Tacitus, *Ann*. 3.55) or by accompanying him on his rounds of public business during the day and applauding his speeches in court. In return, they could expect handouts of food or *sportulae* (small sums of money, customarily about six sesterces in Martial's day) and sometimes an invitation to dinner. Martial lists attendance on a patron as one way that an immigrant to the city of Rome might hope to support himself, though he warns that the *sportulae* were not enough to live on. They must have been just one of the possible supplements to the grain dole (*Epig*. 3.7 and 8.42). These epigrams were written after the inauguration of Vespasian, whose more austere habits were supposed to have set an example for a retreat from the lavish clientèles of the Julio-Claudian era (Tacitus, *Ann*. 3.55). Martial's verses and other evidence, however, leave no doubt that the *salutatio* and other patronal customs continued to characterize life in Rome throughout the Principate.[9]

Patron-client bonds extended out from Rome to the provinces. Like the emperor, governors and other officials representing his power had a patronal role. In a speech before a governor of Africa Proconsularis, Apuleius claimed that provincials esteemed governors for the benefits they conferred (*Flor*. 9). This is corroborated by a number of north African inscriptions dedicated by provincials to governors as their 'patrons'. In their official capacities governors could help provincials secure citizenship, offices and honours from Rome, and they could also

---

[8] De Ste. Croix (1954), 33, 40.
[9] Friedlaender (1908-13), I, 195ff.; Saller (1982), 127-9.

make administrative and legal decisions in their favour. The public dedications to governor 'patrons' from lawyers (*advocati*) may strike the modern reader as an ominous sign of corruption, but in fact highlight the differences between ancient and modern ideologies of administration (e.g., *CIL* VIII.2734,2743,2393).[10] Governors also received from grateful provincials gifts (or, differently interpreted, bribes) and support in case of a prosecution for maladministration after the governor's term of office. For his part in discouraging a prosecution against a senatorial ex-governor of Gaul, T. Sennius Sollemnis received from the former governor a tribunate on his staff in Britain (salary paid in gold), several luxury garments, a sealskin and jewelry (*CIL*XIII.3162).[11] The advertisement of all these details on a public monument demonstrates that the exercise of patronage in government was not considered dishonourable or corrupt.

As the provincialization of the Roman aristocracy progressed in the late first and second centuries, a steadily increasing number of provincials had fellow townsmen well placed in Rome to serve as patronal mediators between themselves and the Roman rulers. This gave them alternative means of access to the benefits distributed from Rome, and also a means of influencing the administrators sent out to rule them. No longer were they governed by foreign conquerors, but by friends of friends. The increasing integration into the patronal networks centred on Rome was naturally most advantageous to the well-connected – that is, the local elites. The plight of the tenants on the imperial estates of the *saltus Burunitanus* illustrates how the patronal links between local magnates and imperial officials could result in collusion whereby the former drew on the force of the latter to reinforce their own ability to exploit the *humiliores* (see above, p. 112).

Patrons and protégés

The relationship between patron and protégé, or superior and inferior friends, falls between that of friendship on equal terms and that of patron and humble client. Because the label *cliens* was regarded as demeaning, considerate patrons generally avoided using it in references to their junior or less powerful friends.[12] Since the extant Latin literature was written largely by the 'superior friends', the word *cliens* rarely appears in descriptions of protégés, with the consequence that some historians have argued that the Romans did not consider these relationships to be patronal nor should we analyse them as such. But if we define patronage as 'a reciprocal exchange relationship between men of unequal status and

10 De Ste. Croix (1954), 43-4; Saller (1982), 151-2 and Table III.
11 Pflaum (1948).
12 Cicero, *Off.* 2.69; White (1978), 80-1; Saller (1982), 8-15.

resources', then bonds between patrons and protégés clearly qualify.
Further, the contrary argument minimizing the dependence of 'lesser
friends' on their 'superiors' goes astray by taking the polite language of
the superiors at face value. Young and ambitious men behaved in ways
typical of *clientes* in their search for powerful supporters: Plutarch refers
to aristocrats in search of high office as those who 'grow old haunting the
doors of other men's houses', a reference to attendance at morning
salutationes (*Mor.* 814D). Finally, the argument from the absence of the
particular words *patronus* and *cliens* in descriptions of these
relationships fails to take account of all the evidence. While courteous
patrons generally did not wish to highlight the inferior social position of
their protégés by calling them *clientes*, the latter did use *patronus* in
dedications to their benefactors. For example, C. Vibius Maximus,
starting out in his equestrian career, honoured his *patronus*, the senior
equestrian governor of Numidia, L. Titinius Clodianus, for his support in
securing office (*Ann. Epigr.* 1917-18, 85).

The question of how to categorize these relationships is more than a
quibble over words, insofar as it draws attention to the issue of whether
they were characterized by the dependence and deference associated
with patronage. Pliny's relationship with his supporter, the senior
senator Corellius Rufus, suggests that they were. Corellius Rufus paid
Pliny the compliment of treating him as an equal, but his behaviour was
taken as complimentary only because they were not equal (*Ep.* 4.17.4).
Pliny showed a deferential attitude in seeking and following the advice of
his supporter on nearly every issue (*Ep.* 9.13.6). In their unequal
exchange Corellius provided support that Pliny, as a new man, depended
on for advancement in his career, while Pliny displayed respect,
extended his patron's influence after the completion of the latter's career
by acting on his advice, and finally provided help for Corellius' family
after his death (*Ep.* 4.17.4-7). The quasi-paternal quality of these
friendships stands out in Pliny's description of his own protégés, who
used him as a model, accompanied him on his daily business and even
assumed the toga with the broad stripe (*latus clavus*) in his house (*Ep.*
8.23.2, 6.6.5f.).

Several features of imperial society gave this type of patronage a
special importance in the Principate. Patronal support was essential in
the recruitment of the imperial elite, because no bureaucratic
mechanisms were developed to supply the next generation of aristocratic
officials. The emperor's role in making these appointments is often
emphasized, but in the absence of training schools or application
procedures the emperor had to appoint those brought to his attention by
senior friends like Corellius Rufus. The mediators who supported the
careers of young senators and equestrians were generally patrons rather
than fathers, because most young aspirants were from new families and
only a small fraction of those in the early stages of their careers (perhaps

a fifth of thirty-year-olds) had a living father on account of the relatively late age at marriage for men.[13] Thus, the imperial elite was renewed, and the new families from across the empire were introduced to traditional Roman ways, in large part through the patron-protégé bonds.

The exchange between patron and protégé extended beyond the political sphere. Pliny's letters show him offering lesser friends support in a legal matter related to an inheritance (*Ep.* 6.8), a gift of 300,000 sesterces (*Ep.* 1.19) and other financial favours. The smaller resources of these protégés normally precluded a comparable return – that is what made them 'inferior friends' – but they could honour their patron with gratitude and, more concretely, with bequests after their death.

The literary talents of some protégés gave a few of these relationships a cultural dimension. While some authors and poets of the Principate were men of substantial means and high rank, others hoped to support themselves by writing for patrons. In return for the fame that would accrue to the patron of a successful author, the latter might hope that his patron would draw attention to his work and improve his material position with gifts ranging from an estate and an apartment in the city to an official salaried appointment, money, clothing and food. Many writers were disappointed by lack of generosity and others had no need of it, but that should not obscure the fact that important literary figures from Virgil to Martial did receive significant material support from patrons, such as Maecenas, Seneca and C. Calpurnius Piso, who viewed themselves as supporters of literature.[14]

The patron helped his protégé

Friends

Roman philosophers placed great value on friendship, stressing that ideal friends should share common interests and values without thought of self-interest.[15] Though the philosophers eschewed material advantage as a motive for friendship, for other Romans (and indeed for the philosophers in their more pragmatic moments) the exchange of services was a foundation for friendship (Fronto, *Ad M. Caesarem* 1.3.4f.). The exchange between friends of comparable social standing and resources had a different character from those described above. Though neither party was in a permanent position of superiority, one or the other might be better placed at a particular time to confer a favour.

The glittering prizes of late Republican senatorial politics were no longer available, yet support in the competition for magistracies and other posts before the emperor and in senatorial elections remained essential. Governors had staff offices to bestow not only on their own

[13] Saller (1987a) and (1982), ch. 4.
[14] Pliny, *Ep.*8.12. White (1978) (1982); Morford (1985); Saller (1983).
[15] Brunt (1965).

'lesser friends', but also on those of their peers. Pliny introduced a request that his friend Priscus confer such a post on a protégé of his with the comment that Priscus had had time to reward his own friends and should now be prepared to spread his favours more widely (*Ep.* 2.13.2).[16]

The financial favours exchanged between friends of comparable resources were generally more sporadic than the continuing dependence of a humble client on a patron. Despite their wealth, even senators occasionally found themselves with temporary liquidity problems, which they solved by turning to friends and kin for gifts or loans. The praetorian games expected of senators, for example, required heavy outlays of cash to which friends often contributed (Seneca, *Ben.* 2.21.5). If a wealthy Roman suffered a catastrophe, such as a fire in his home, it was customary for his friends to contribute to reestablishing the household (Juvenal, *Sat.* 3.220). The wealthiest Romans also used friends to look after their widely dispersed property (see above, pp. 66ff.). As a final gesture, the services of friends were customarily acknowledged by means of bequests in wills. To leave friends out of a will, or worse, to criticize them in a will, was an insult that drew public attention (e.g. Fronto, *Ad Pium* 3.3). Legacies could be very valuable, allowing some Romans to make fortunes from them and giving rise to the literary topos of the base legacy-hunter who courted favour with the old and childless (Pliny, *Ep.* 2.20; Seneca, *Ben.* 4.20.3).[17]

The custom of distributing large bequests to valued friends helps us to understand why forensic oratory continued to be an avenue to success, as in the Republic. The impact of the new political regime can be judged by a comparison of Cicero with the imperial orator M. Aper, as portrayed in Tacitus' *Dialogue on the Orators* more than a century later. Forensic oratory could no longer be the path to electoral success for Aper as it had been for Cicero. Nevertheless, because effective oratory was still needed to win civil and criminal cases, the successful orator could win valuable friends, especially the influential and the wealthy childless, to promote his career or to enrich himself. All of this has to be understood in the context of reciprocity in friendships, since, in contrast to the lower-class advocate who made his living through fees, the gentleman orator relied on his friends' generosity in returning his favours (Quintilian, *Inst.* 12.7.12).

The benefits exchanged in friendship resemble those given between patrons and protégés, but the tone of friendship on an equal footing is different. Pliny's relationships with men like Priscus were characterized by courteous cooperation. Behind the facade of cooperation lay competition: if a friend failed to make a return of the same order, he

[16] Recommendations (*commendationes*), the standard vehicle of patronal mediation, are discussed by Cotton (1981).

[17] On the size of Cicero's and Pliny's inheritances, Shatzman (1975), 409ff., and Duncan-Jones (1982), 25ff.

risked slipping into the position of a 'lesser friend' and losing honour in the process. In contrast, Pliny's relationship with Corellius was not competitive, because genuine equality was not possible. Corellius was the backer, and the roles were not reversible. Pliny eventually surpassed his supporter, but his success as a new man was not a foregone conclusion, and he needed whatever help he could get from senior senators like Corellius and Verginius Rufus.

The personal exchange relationships described above effectively mitigated cross-order conflict and tension, the importance of which has often been exaggerated. Specifically, the old view that emperors preferred as administrators equestrians, who were directly dependent on them for offices and honours, rather than senators, who were potential competitors for power, is no longer tenable. Many senators were as dependent on imperial favour as equestrians, many equestrians were more directly tied to the senatorial mediators who won them offices and honours than to the emperor, and senators and equestrians were generally integrated through kinship, friendship and patronage into a single social network. Consequently, equestrians as a group were not noticeably more loyal than senators.

The plebs: patronage, self-help and coercion

Patrons did not enter into relationships with their social inferiors indiscriminately. In his division of the ordinary people of the city of Rome into the good and the bad (*Hist.* 1.4.), Tacitus characterizes the former by their attachment to the great houses – an implicit commitment to the social order as it was.[18] The latter were not caught up in patronal relationships with the rich, because they were thought to have nothing to contribute to a reciprocal exchange relationship or because they wished to avoid the humiliation of dependence.

Upper-class writers show little interest in vertical links between the high and the low, but have even less to say about horizontal bonds between the latter. A plethora of informal relationships between individual neighbours and work associates have gone largely unrecorded. However, one institutional manifestation of these relationships, the *collegium*, is well known from numerous inscriptions and some largely hostile references in the literary sources.[19]

Collegia, made up of a few score or few hundred urban residents, were essentially mutual aid societies formed to meet basic needs of their members. Organized around cults to patron deities or by occupation, these associations provided for decent burial of the dead as well as

[18] A parallel in Livy 9.46.13.
[19] J.P. Waltzing (1895-1900); de Robertis (1955); Ausbuettel (1982); Hopkins (1983c), 211-17.

periodic festive dinners for the living. Unable to rely on family, many Romans took the precaution of arranging burial before their death by joining a *collegium* and paying small monthly dues. In a long inscription detailing the rules of a *collegium* in the small Italian town of Lanuvium, the membership fee was specified as 100 sesterces, with dues of slightly more than one sesterce per month, which guaranteed a funeral attended by club members.[20] These fees were meant for modestly prosperous men, as were the club dinners with a menu of good wine, two asses worth of bread and four sardines per member. Lower down in the social hierarchy was another stratum, the impoverished who could not afford club membership and whose bodies, consequently, were dumped unceremoniously into mass graves.

Though these *collegia* were associations of humble men, they still exhibit some of the hierarchical features so characteristic of Roman society. Like the larger community, *collegia* were often patronized by the wealthy.[21] In the case of the association in Lanuvium, Caesennius Rufus provided an endowment of 15,000 sesterces to finance club dinners honouring the birthdays of himself and his family. Further, the club rules show a typically Roman appreciation for rank and the authority of office: the chief magistrate of the club, the *quinquennalis* (the title taken from municipal office), received double portions at the banquets and was protected from 'insolent language' by a special fine of twenty sesterces.

Despite the conservative attitudes implied by such rules, the authorities were always suspicious of these associations and fearful lest they become sources of unrest. In the late Republic, demagogic tribunes like P. Clodius had made use of the *collegia* in their campaigns to undermine the authority of the Roman magistrates by violence. Under the Principate, those *collegia* that had achieved respectability because of their long histories and the special public services they were held to perform (apparently in the area of fire fighting, building construction and religious ceremonial) were allowed a continuous and even a privileged existence.[22] Religious and burial clubs were also authorized. But the emperors remained suspicious of plebeian organizations as seedbeds of undercover political activity. Hence, an imperial rule prohibited meetings of these associations more often than once a month. Pliny, Trajan's special envoy in Bithynia/Pontus, a province with a bad reputation for disorder, was instructed to issue a decree prohibiting associations. Christian gatherings were assumed to fall under the general prohibition (Pliny, *Ep.* 10.96.7), and also groups with an apparently utilitarian function. Trajan rejected a request from the people of Nicomedia for a fire brigade. Pliny, who had viewed the proposal sympathetically, was reminded by the emperor that 'this province and

[20] *CIL* XIV.2112=*ILS* 7212, translated in Lewis and Reinhold (1955), 273-5.
[21] Clemente (1972)
[22] *AE* 1966, 277.

especially these cities have been troubled by cliques of this type. Whatever name we may give for whatever reason to those who come together for a common purpose, political clubs emerge quickly from them' (Pliny, *Ep.* 10.34).

Imperial regulation of urban gatherings and distribution of benefits were not enough to prevent violence in the cities. Republican magistrates had had no police forces to suppress urban unrest, and military units were by tradition forbidden from crossing the 'sacred boundary' (*pomerium*) around the city. In the midst of recurring urban violence the senate in 52 BC dispensed with tradition and summoned Pompey to reestablish order in the city with troops.[23] Augustus then organized the first standing forces in Rome: the praetorian guard, the urban cohorts and the night watch (*vigiles*). The initial impetus for these organizations was partially political in the beginning – to support Augustus against challenges – but they did come to perform various policing functions in the city. Despite their presence, pervasive street crime aroused constant fear among urban residents (Pliny, *HN* 19.59). The military units were more effective in controlling the crowds at public spectacles. When a theatre crowd in AD 32 abused Tiberius for allowing grain prices to rise, the emperor resorted to the traditional Republican response of asking the senate and the magistrates to use their authority to suppress the verbal insolence (Tacitus, *Ann.* 6.15). To prevent vocal protest from developing into a riot, the presence of a praetorian cohort became a regular feature of public spectacles. In AD 55, Nero experimented by removing the guard at the games, 'in order that there might be a greater show of freedom, that the soldiery too might be less demoralized when no longer in contact with the licence of the theatre, and that it might be proved whether the populace, in the absence of a guard, would maintain their self-control' (Tacitus, *Ann.* 13.24-5). The soldiers were brought back the following year, but it is noteworthy that a consideration in Nero's initial decision was freedom of expression.

Away from Rome, the authorities had both less to offer urban populations in the manner of subsistence and entertainment, and less institutional apparatus for repressing disorder or other activities classified as undesirable. Army detachments were sometimes available for policing purposes, especially in provincial or regional centres. Thus soldiers are much in evidence in accounts of actions taken by authorities against Christians. To a large extent, however, communities were left to police themselves. Many Greek cities of the East had magistrates, irenarchs, charged with the maintenance of order, but they had only small forces at their disposal and no power to punish. In addition, sources as diverse as the New Testament (Acts 18.12-17) and Apuleius' *Golden Ass* (*Met.* 10.28) testify to initiatives taken by ordinary local men to

---

[23] Nippel (1984).

capture criminals and troublemakers and bring them before Roman officials for imprisonment and punishment. The local or imperial authorities (away from military zones) established full control only in and around the cities. In the countryside, especially in rough terrains, banditry was a constant problem.[24]

---

[24] Jones (1940), 211-13; Millar (1981), 71; MacMullen (1966), app. B; Shaw (1984b).

PART IV

CHAPTER NINE

Religion

The official Roman religion was a cluster of beliefs expressed in an elaborate system of institutions and rituals. The Romans accepted that the safety and prosperity.of their communities depended upon the gods, whose favour was won and held by the correct performance of the full range of cult practices inherited from the past. Supervision of the state religion was in the hands of the political authorities. Priesthoods were held by the same men who held political office. In Rome, as in other societies, religious institutions and practices reflected the power relations within the community and provided the justification for the existing order.[1]

Given that religion was embedded in the political structure of the state, the transition from oligarchy to monarchy inevitably brought changes in the framework of the official religion. Religious offices, as all others, fell under the control of the emperor. The life office of high priest (*pontifex maximus*), won by Julius Caesar with heavy bribery against the senior conservative aristocrat Lutatius Catulus in 63 BC, was taken over by Augustus in 12 BC without contest; only his political sensitivity delayed his assumption of the post until the death of the incumbent. Succeeding emperors were high priests *ex officio*. The priestly colleges were deprived of their influence over political decision-making and reoriented toward service of the emperor. The main task of the Arval Brothers, for example, was to intercede with the gods for the welfare of the emperor and his family. Religious practices with Republican political associations were phased out. Thus public divination went into disuse, whether the regular consultation of the gods by senior magistrates that preceded important decisions or actions, or the interpretation of unusual natural phenomena by professional diviners. In the past, the senate had presided over such operations. Under the new regime, the taking of the auspices, notably by generals, was treated as an imperial prerogative; while divine wrath, as manifested, for example, in 23-22 BC in the onset of epidemic disease accompanied by alarming prodigies (Cassius Dio 54.1.1), was met not with the customary expiatory procedures, but with

---

[1] Books on Roman religion especially to be recommended include Beaujeu (1955), Liebeschuetz (1979) and Price (1984). See also Latte (1960), Bayet (1969), Le Gall (1975), MacMullen (1981), Wardman (1982).

We are grateful to Graeme Clarke, Richard Gordon and Simon Price for fruitful discussion of matters raised in this chapter.

practical measures taken on imperial initiative, the revival of ancient cults, brotherhoods and ritual practices, moral reform and a concentration of power in the emperor's hands.

These developments were of minor significance in that they did not alter the religious culture of Rome. Augustus was a religious conservative. Traditional religious forms provided a vehicle by which he was able to express his policies and conceptions of revival and restoration. The rebuilding of temples, the reorganization of sacerdotal colleges, ever stricter limitation of their membership to the high elite, and the rejection of new cults were signals that nothing had changed. The main innovation in the area of cult associated with the Principate, the cult of the emperor, was easily grafted onto the traditional state religion. The imperial cult was a product of internal political developments, and its introduction compromised the political, not religious, sensibilities of the more traditionalist Romans. For this reason it was instituted in Rome only after Augustus' death, although Augustus had been an object of worship in his lifetime in Italy and all over the empire.

In this chapter we pursue two main themes, the influence of Rome on the local religions of the enlarged Roman empire, and the stability of the official state religion itself. How extensively was Roman religion transplanted in the enlarged empire, by whose initiative and with what effect on indigenous cult systems? Secondly, how was it that the official religion remained more or less impermeable and unresponsive to new religious movements until the end of the second century? This despite claims by historians that the 'constant receptivity' of the Romans to new religious forms is one of the 'best attested general characteristics' of their religious life.[2]

The impact of Rome

Rome's main export to the empire was the cult of the emperors. This was the only Roman intrusion in the area of cult that was tolerated in the Greek world, whose cultural superiority was asserted by Greeks and conceded by leading Romans through much of our period. The acceptance of the imperial cult in the eastern Mediterranean did not involve the displacement or subordination of the cults of the traditional gods. The Greek-speaking provinces already knew ruler cults celebrating Hellenistic kings, cults of individual Roman officials, typically proconsuls, and other cults which recognized Roman power, of which the cult of Rome is simply the best known. The domination of the East by Rome, and of Rome by Augustus, put an end to the creation of new cults

---

[2] See North (1976), who raises and resolves the problem for the period of the Republic.

of kings and governors, while the cult of Rome was easily transformed into a cult of Rome and Augustus or a cult of Augustus alone. The latter was offered Augustus by the Asians and Bithynians as soon as he had emerged as victor in the civil war, it was refused, and instituted none the less; the former was pronounced acceptable for non-Roman citizens only (Cassius Dio 51.20.7-8; Suetonius, *Aug.* 52). This response was in character. Augustus was at once making allowance for the sensitivities of the Roman upper classes, and discreetly asserting the inseparability of emperor and state. Certain of his subjects saw no merit in moderation in this context. The exceptional honours paid to Augustus by Greeks, their enthusiastic appreciation of the benefits of his rule, the overt and detailed comparisons made between the emperor and the gods, and the organization of the cult at both provincial and local level together make it possible to identify the reign of Augustus as a crucial turning-point in the history of ruler cult. The cult continued to diffuse and prosper over the next two centuries. There was a change in tone and in superficial characteristics. Augustus' successors, at least until the Severan age, received flatter and shorter honorific decrees and fewer cults, generic cults tending to replace cults in the name of an individual. But these are indications of routinization, not lack of vigour.[3]

The imperial cult appealed to Augustus, as it did to later emperors, as a way of focusing the loyalty of provincials on the imperial *persona*. In the East, the initial impetus came from the provincials themselves, as communities, anxious to eradicate the memory of their support for Antony in the civil war, transformed existing cults and institutions to accommodate it. But the work done by Roman governors in encouraging and even orchestrating these moves, or by the authorities in Rome, including the emperor, in approving proposals forwarded to them and occasionally taking the initiative, should not be neglected. In the West, the part played by the Roman authorities and their representatives in the provinces in propagating the cult was much more central. Proconsular prompting can be shown or suspected to lie behind the public expression of devotion to Augustus at provincial or regional capitals like Carthage and Lepcis Magna in north Africa.[4] Provincial as opposed to local city cults of the emperor in the West likewise originated in imperial initiatives. It is noticeable that the cult was established at the provincial level in newly conquered, un-Romanized provinces before its introduction into peaceful, relatively Romanized provinces. This signifies that the provincial cult of the emperor was first employed as an instrument for the promotion of the military and political might of Rome. It was used by the first emperor in no other way.

The foundation of the provincial cults near Lyon and in Cologne define

[3] Price (1984), chs. 2-3.
[4] Smadja (1978) and (n.d.); in general, Fishwick (1978).

the character and limits of Augustan policy in this area. The imperial cult for the provinces of the Three Gauls at Condate, at the confluence of the Rhône and the Saône, was instituted on Augustus' birthday in the year of his assumption of the office of high priest, 12 BC. Drusus, the emperor's stepson, was at hand just before his German war to convoke and direct the inaugural meeting of the provincial council (Livy, *Epit.* 139), of which the local leader and first high priest was Gaius Iulius Vercondaridubnus, a notable from the Aeduan tribe based on Autun. The cooperation of the tribal leadership was not always assured. In AD 9 the Aeduan's counterpart at the city of the Ubii (Cologne), Segimundus of the Cherusci, absconded to join the German rebels (Tacitus, *Ann.* 1.39.1, 57.2). The Aeduan and Treveran chiefs who led the revolt of AD 21 might have included former high priests of Rome and Augustus at Condate (Tacitus, *Ann.* 3.41). In Britain, too, the institution of the imperial cult by Claudius at Colchester (Camulodunum) at the inauguration of the new province in AD 43 predated the pacification of the people and the winning of the loyalty of the local leadership. The temple to the Divine Claudius subsequently erected on the site was represented by Tacitus as a symbol of domination in perpetuity. This description misrepresents neither the sentiments of the rebellious Britons in AD 60 nor the intentions of the Romans. Tacitus lets slip the detail that the expensiveness of the priesthood was a grievance (*Ann.* 14.31). The message had not yet sunk in among the native leadership that the prestige of the priesthood more than compensated for its cost.[5]

In contrast, Augustus left the older and more Romanized Iberian provinces and Gallia Narbonensis without a provincial cult. Tarraco, the capital of Hither Spain, received a civic cult of Augustus in about 26 BC. It may have been difficult for the city to avoid requesting one, and for Augustus to avoid granting its request, given that ambassadors from Mitylene bringing a decree conferring divine honours on Augustus found him there (*IG* IV 39). This happy coincidence may also explain the relatively early award of a cult of the Divine Augustus to the province of Tarraconensis, following representation by the provincials at the court of Tiberius in AD 15 (Tacitus, *Ann.* 1.78). Augustus had not given it to them a generation earlier. Despite the comment of Tacitus that Tiberius in conceding the cult had created a precedent, no province apart from Lusitania is known to have followed suit (*AE.* 1966,177). It was left to Vespasian to establish the imperial cult in Baetica, Narbonensis and Africa Proconsularis, as part of a drive by an uncharismatic, arriviste emperor to bind the empire in loyalty to him and to the Flavian family. Tarraconensis was a deviant case.[6]

The imperial cult is important for its novelty, (eventual) ubiquity and

---

[5] See *ILS* 5163 (AD 177, Gaul), for later recognition of the cost of the office.
[6] Fishwick (1978), 1219ff. For the Iberian peninsula, see Etienne (1958)

its functions as a conveyor of imperial ideology, a focus of loyalty for the many, and a mechanism for the social advancement of the few. The widespread diffusion of the traditional gods of Rome was a complementary and closely associated phenomenon. The development was not confined to Roman colonies and municipalities abroad, although in the early stages the transplantation of gods, priesthoods and major festivals into these communities served to mark them off from others of lower status. The prominence of the capitoline triad of Jupiter, Juno and Minerva is marked, particularly from the time of Trajan. The building of capitols in north Africa is a second-century phenomenon, spilling over into the third.

Under the influence of Trajan and Hadrian and later emperors, the triad became an essential element of the imperial ideology and propaganda.[7] The capitol in the forum at Dougga in Africa Proconsularis, where a native city coexisted with a new urban agglomeration, was dedicated for the safety of the emperors Marcus Aurelius and Lucius Verus. The pediment, depicting the apotheosis of their predecessor, Antoninus Pius, underlined their present status and future prospects. Jupiter's connection with the emperor and the imperial cult was particularly close. A contract inscribed on a wooden tablet found at London was sealed by an oath to Jupiter Optimus Maximus and the Genius of the Emperor Domitian. Trajan began a fashion when he shared the face of coins with Jupiter. A certain Fortunatus set up a monument at Maktar in Numidia in the Severan period consecrated to Jupiter for the safety of the emperors. In the East, the cult of Zeus, the Greek equivalent of Jupiter, prospered. The temple of Olympian Zeus at Athens was completed under the direction of the emperor Hadrian, who took the title Olympios as the earthly representative of the god.[8]

What was the effect of the massive exportation of Roman gods on native religions? The question, framed in this way, has very limited relevance for the East, outside Roman colonies and the Roman army, which were certainly outposts of Roman religion and culture. Augustus and his successors set about breaking the independent political and economic power of the large sanctuaries, but in Asia Minor, at least, the cults themselves were unaffected. This is unsurprising, in view of the substantial degree of overlap between Roman and Greek religion, and Rome's 'failure' to make any impression on Hellenic culture in general. In this case, moreover, the emperors showed their commitment to the spread of Hellenism by turning over the temples and their priesthoods to the authority of the cities, the seats of Hellenic culture. There was no question of subjecting them to direct Roman control, much less altering or deforming the cults by introducing the more obviously Roman aspects

[7] Fears (1981); Février (1976); Smadja (1985); Beaujeu (1955), 69ff.
[8] Henig (1984), 84; Fears (1977), 225ff.; *CIL* VIII 6353; Beaujeu (1955), 76ff., 200ff.

of Roman religion. In Egypt, considerable damage was done to local cults, as the priesthood was gradually shorn of its wealth, independence and privileges and the less powerful temples went into decline. In this, the circumstances of Augustus' rise to power, the distaste of Romans for animal-worship, and the strong tradition of bureaucratic government as opposed to local, civic autonomy in Egypt each played a part.[9]

What occurred in Egypt was rather less than the repression of cults judged to be 'non-Roman'. In general, Rome's contact with alien religions was marked by peaceful penetration rather than coercion. The consequence of Roman cultural dominance outside the East was none the less the disintegration, or at best the simplification, of local religions. Coexistence of Roman and native cults can be illustrated, as in the high plains of Sitifis in Mauretania Caesariensis, where a market was placed under the protection of Jupiter, the deified king Juba and the local guardian spirit the Genius Vanisnesi (*ILS* 4490). But syncretism or fusion was the more common phenomenon. In north Africa, Saturn was increasingly associated with Jupiter, Caelestis with Juno. The Roman-Celtic Mercury was Lug in another guise, and Taranis was readily identified with Jupiter. Minerva found counterparts in a number of local deities, including Sulis, the water goddess of Bath (Aquae Sulis). Mars coalesced with and then absorbed the Iberian Cosus. Local gods that never received Roman names can be assumed to have faded out, at least in the urban environment, which was the stage where the Roman-native religious and cultural confrontation was played out. The gods that disappeared in Roman Gaul include those connected with sovereignty and war, prominent in the period of independence.[10]

The Romans, however, did encounter cults and institutions that they were unwilling to absorb. Strabo employs a rough three-fold distinction among cults and practices between the *politika*, that is, those characteristic of a *polis*, the savage and those in an intermediate grade (165). The first are praiseworthy, and the third could be tolerated. The second, however, are disapproved of, and, says Strabo, have been suppressed where possible. Sacrifices, divination and other practices involving human victims are in question. Why were they suppressed? Strabo gives no reason beyond the bland statement that they were un-Roman. After describing the Gallic custom of nailing heads of enemies to the entrances of homes, he continues: 'But the Romans put a stop to these customs, as well as all those connected with the sacrifices and divinations that are opposed to our usages. They used to strike a human being whom they had devoted to death in the back with a sabre and then divine from his death struggle. But they would not sacrifice without the Druids' (198).

[9] Debord (1982); Whitehorne (1980); Beaujeu (1955), 209ff., 297ff.
[10] See Février (1976); Henig (1984); Clavel-Lévêque (1972), cf. Letta (1984); Lambrino (1965); Etienne (1973); Etienne et al. (1976).

Writing a century after Strabo, Tacitus in his remarkably evenhanded treatment of German religion in the *Germania* – giving credit where it was due for piety, respect for tradition, devotion to divination, absence of anthropomorphism – employs the *religio-superstitio* distinction to mark off Roman from un-Roman elements. But the distinction, which could in any case be turned against official Roman religion itself, as by Varro and Seneca (Augustine, *de Civ.D.* 6.10), is not applied rigorously and lacks explanatory force.

Sheer moral repugnance, which surfaces more conspicuously in Tacitus than in Strabo or Caesar, contributed to the decision to suppress. The Romans moved against human sacrifice everywhere, in north Africa, where it was associated with Saturn (Baal-Hammon), as well as in Gaul. But the essential explanation is political. 'But they would not sacrifice without the Druids,' says Strabo. Religious, social and political authority were intermeshed in Celtic and German society. Suppression of Druids in Gaul and Britain, and hostility toward the prophetesses of Germany, are manifestations of the traditional Roman policy of stamping on those elements of an indigenous religion that impeded the advance of their empire.[11]

Judaism was another ethnic religion whose autonomy was at risk, though in quite different circumstances.[12] Again it is the political aspect of the Jewish problem which should hold our attention. The origin of Rome's failure to coexist peaceably with the Jews does not lie in the incompatibility of this exclusive, monotheistic religion with the official religion, or in the distaste felt for Jewish religious practices by members of the cultural elite including Cicero, Tacitus and Strabo (who, however, has praise for the Jewish religion and state in the time of Moses). Similarly, the earlier policy of toleration, enunciated by Julius Caesar, confirmed by Augustus and carried on by Claudius, was not a response to the antiquity of the Jewish religion and the steadfastness with which it was clung to by its adherents, though these were given due acknowledgement. It was from political considerations that toleration was adopted and later abandoned in favour of confrontation.

Toleration of the Jews had its origin in an approach to the Romans by envoys of Judas Maccabee in 161 BC after Antiochus IV's unprecedented attack on the Jewish religion. The Romans were interested in embarrassing and weakening Syria, and agreed to a declaration of friendship. In the following century, the Jews lent valuable military assistance first to Caesar and subsequently to Octavian in the civil wars, moved by outrage at Pompey's capture of Jerusalem and violation of the

[11] Druids: Strabo 197-8; Caesar, *BG* 6.14; Suetonius, *Claud.* 25.5; Tacitus, *Hist.*4.18.3, 54.2; Chadwick (1966). German priestesses: Strabo 298; Tacitus, *Germ.*8.3; *Hist.* 4.61.2. Saturn: Leglay (1966).

[12] Schürer (1973-79); Juster (1914); Smallwood (1976); Rabello (1980); Rajak (1984). See Cicero, *Flacc.* 53ff.; Tacitus, *Hist.* 5.1ff.; cf. Pliny, *HN* 12.113,13.46; Strabo 760-2.

Holy of Holies, and by the diplomatic necessity of rallying to the victor of Actium. The outcome was a series of official edicts and letters to Greek cities in the East instructing them to permit resident Jews to observe their traditional religion. These documents were the fruit of brilliant diplomacy on the Jewish side, not Roman initiative. In time, moreover, memories of Jewish favours to Rome's rulers grew dim and were replaced by a current perception, spiced with prejudice, of the nuisance-value of Jews both in their homeland and abroad. From the Roman point of view, the Jews proved themselves congenitally incapable of either cooperating with the Roman provincial authorities within their home territory, or coexisting peaceably with Greeks in the cities of the eastern Mediterranean.

Continuity and change in the official religion

Did the Roman authorities in the period of the Principate show any interest in appropriating foreign cults that were in principle compatible with their own? How accessible was the state religion to foreign influences?

The Romans are often credited not only with a tolerance of foreign cults in their local setting, but also a readiness to adopt them as their own. Yet under the empire no new gods were given official status as gods of the Roman state before the emperor Caracalla secured the admission of the Egyptian Isis and Serapis in the early third century.

Roman receptiveness to alien religions is a feature of the early and middle Republic and of no other period.[13] The early Romans expanded their Pantheon in two main ways: they 'captured' the tutelary deity of an enemy state (typically by the ritual of *evocatio*), or they 'summoned' a prestigious foreign divinity (Asclepius, Magna Mater) to cope with a national emergency (epidemic, invasion). The series of innovations came to a climax but also to an end with the importation of the Great Mother of the gods, Cybele or Magna Mater, at the time of the invasion of Italy by Hannibal. This was a Phrygian goddess whose worship was marked by ecstatic dancing, culminating, at least when practised at the cult centre of Pessinus, in self-castration. The senate quickly purged the cult of its more extreme features and made it unavailable to Roman citizens.

Thereafter, no more exotic cults came in by invitation, and those that arrived in Rome and Italy uninvited were liable to be attacked as subversive. The cults in question – beginning in the 180s BC with the worship of Bacchus, and proceeding through the Egyptian gods, Judaism and Christianity to Mithraism, well entrenched by the mid-second century AD – were subversive in two ways. First, they threatened to break

---

[13] For the Republican background, see North (1976) and (1979).

the exclusive control of the political authorities over religious activities. The senate, and later, the emperors, were confronted with a series of autonomous, exclusively religious organizations devoted to divine service. The Bacchanalians, for example, had their own cell structure, oath of membership, treasury, and lay and priestly hierarchies. Secondly, the new cults threatened to undermine rather than supplement the ancestral religion. Whereas the gods of the Roman state made, no demands on the individual, and promised him no rewards except in his capacity as a member of a political collectivity, the so-called mystery religions required conversion and ritual purification, and offered revelation, redemption, and to the few, the prospect of deeper religious experience. The cult of Mithras freed the incorporeal soul from the material body and enabled it to rise gradually through the seven planetary spheres to Saturn and thence to the realm of the fixed stars.

The 'failure' of Roman governments of the Principate to expand the official state religion to accommodate alien cults is therefore quite predictable. Yet the arrival of an emperor at the head of the government created the possibility of change. To put the matter at its simplest, some day an emperor with pronounced monarchical tendencies might take office, one who was a devotee of a personal religion, and who would set about bringing the official religion into line with his own. Two questions are of interest: what factors delayed that development, and how did governments cope with the intrusion of new cults in the interim, that is to say for the major part of our period?

To answer the first question we need to scrutinize the policies of the creator of the Principate. In Augustus, a sensitivity to the political traditions of Rome was combined with a backward-looking religious policy and a social conservatism. The essential facts are well known, and a brief summary can suffice. First, the Augustan constitution was a monarchy, but it was built on the political structures of the old Republic. The constitutionality of the position of the emperor, and the continued (if in practice diminished) roles of the established organs of government, were central planks. The second and third points are closely linked. The depth of Augustus' religious conservatism is beyond debate. But in addition, the senate as rebuilt by him was likely to share his views; it was as close to the old senate in social composition and values as it was possible to get after a decade and a half of destructive civil wars.

The heritage of Augustus was hard to shake off. In the first place, the status of the emperor and the imperial ideology do not show a decisive change before the end of the second century. We might contrast the relation between on the one hand the Flavian dynasty, on the other the Severan, and the Egyptian gods. The devotion of the Flavians to Isis and Serapis was exceptional.[14] Vespasian represented himself as the elect of

[14] Malaise (1972), pt.V; briefly, Liebeschuetz (1979), 179ff.

Serapis on the basis of certain miraculous experiences he had undergone in Alexandria in the critical early days of his bid for power. Domitian owed his life to Isis, having escaped Vitellius' men by dressing as a priest of the goddess. Yet the Flavians, a new family lacking charisma and authority, drew a firm line between their personal religious choices and the official religion. The Severans were also *arrivistes*, but their conception of themselves and of the imperial *persona* was sufficiently elevated to enable them to reorganize the state religion in accordance with their own preferences. The uninhibited (or megalomaniacal) behaviour of the last Antonine emperor, Commodus, in his last years had shown the way. Commodus had represented himself as Hercules, participated fully and openly in the festivals of the Egyptian gods, incorporated a prayer to Serapis in the official prayers of the new year, and saluted Serapis *Conservator Augusti* on his coins. All that was left for Caracalla to do was to introduce the Egyptian gods into sanctuaries within the sacred boundary of Rome (the *pomerium*) and reconstruct the official Pantheon around them. Where the gods of Egypt had entered, Syrian gods could follow.[15]

Secondly, the conservative governing class that Augustus bequeathed to the Roman state acted as a restraint on religious innovation. In the two centuries that followed his death, the social base of the upper classes broadened, but not the social outlook and religious values of their members. Isis and later Mithras as new, lower-class religions had virtually no appeal for the senate of the Principate.[16] The antipathy of senators of the late Antonine and Severan age for the religious developments of their period can be read in the pages of Cassius Dio. The advice offered by 'Maecenas' to 'Augustus' in Dio's history is at one level an endorsement of Augustan religious conservatism by a Severan senator reacting against the rapid pace of political and religious change in his world:

> Therefore, if you desire to become in very truth immortal, act as I advise; and furthermore both yourself worship the Divine Power everywhere and in every way in accordance with the traditions of our fathers and compel all others to honour it. Those who attempt to distort our religion with strange rites you should abhor and punish, not merely for the sake of the gods, but because such men, by bringing in new divinities in place of the old, persuade many to adopt foreign practices, from which spring up conspiracies, factions and cabals, which are far from profitable to a monarchy. Do not, therefore, permit anybody to be an atheist or a sorcerer. (52.36)

Whatever was in Cassius Dio's mind when he wrote this passage, the plan of action attributed to Maecenas does resemble Augustus' actual religious policy. Augustus did champion the traditional religion. He did

---

[15] Halsberghe (1972) on Sol Invictus Elagabal.

[16] Malaise (1972), 75ff., Gordon (1972), 103ff. on the social catchment of Isis and Mithras, respectively. For a brief introduction to the cult of Mithras, see Nock (1937), and for a full

move against Isis and her kindred deities, for reasons unstated but not mysterious (Cassius Dio 53.2.4; 54.6.6). Conservative forces in the late Republican senate had engineered the banning of Egyptian religions on several occasions, and their cult followers were implicated in the political violence of the 50s and perhaps again in the late 20s, the first decade of Augustus' reign. Finally, Augustus was to some extent a prisoner of his own propaganda war against Egyptian gods and their champions or personifications Antony and Cleopatra.[17]

But the statement in Dio is deficient as a summary of the policies of later emperors. In particular, repression was selective, sporadic and short-lived. Emperors typically moved against a suspect cult or practice when an actual or threatened breach of law and order had been brought to their attention. After the reign of Tiberius, imperial hostility to the Egyptian gods simply faded away, while a number of emperors were fascinated by or devoted to them. Mithras, the last of the mystery cults to establish itself in Rome, Italy and beyond, was never in danger of persecution, because it fostered acceptance of the status quo. It won a following especially among soldiers and slaves, both imperial and private, callings in which submission to authority was given special emphasis. Leaving aside Judaism, which in any case received protection from Augustus and Claudius, no cult was as actively persecuted as were the practices of astrology and magic.

Unlike other alien ideological influences, astrology and magic invaded all sections of Roman society.[18] Emperors were disturbed by the political implications of the popularity of astrology among the Roman upper classes. If emperors could use astrology freely, as they did, for aid in decision-making and for information about their span of life, then covertly disloyal members of the political classes could do the same as a preliminary step to revolution. Magic was, and is, a complex phenomenon. At one level it was a set of practices designed to secure success in the law-courts, in love or at the races, or injury to or destruction of another person. In a more 'scientific' version, as practised by members of the cultural elite like the African Apuleius, it appears as a form of practical philosophy. We do not know who was banned for sorcery by the authorities (nor what practices they followed). What lay behind such coercive action was the fear of the potential use of magical arts by members of the upper classes to jeopardize the safety of the emperor.

The official reaction to astrology, magic and for that matter Stoic and Cynic philosophy, which also secured a following at the highest level of

---

survey, see Beck (1984), espec. 2063ff., where, *inter alia*, it is argued, with reference to Gordon (1975), that Mithras did not come from 'the East'.

[17] References in Malaise (1972), 378-89, cf. 244-51.

[18] Cramer (1954); Liebeschuetz (1979), 119-39; Xella (1976) (studies by Garosi and Sabbatucci); Annequin (n.d.)

Roman society, were untypical. They do not help us define the attitude of the state authorities to the alien theodicies in their midst. We have seen that the permeability of the Roman state as measured by the enrolment of aliens as citizens, as soldiers and as members of the governing class itself, was not matched by a broadening of the base of the state religion. The official response to innovation was either negative, or more often, passive. Unauthorized religious cults and organizations that could not be controlled or eradicated were simply allowed to exist. This attitude falls far short of the policy of toleration with which the Roman state is usually credited.[19] Meanwhile, the steadfastly maintained impermeability of the ancestral religion deprived it of the infusion of strength it needed to face a new foreign cult that was monotheistic, universal, exclusive and intolerant.

The rise of Christianity

Christianity was the main beneficiary of the failure of the defenders of the state religion to control innovation. Christians invited persecution by their denial of the gods of Rome, which earned them the label of atheists.[20] They even refused to take an oath by the emperor's guardian spirit, thus giving rise to the suspicion that they did not accept his earthly supremacy. However, no emperor before Decius in the mid-third century tried to root out the Christians. Instead, they were inclined to follow the policy established under Trajan not to hunt down the Christians (*conquirendi non sunt*, Pliny, *Ep.* 10.96). When the authorities did become involved in confrontation with Christians, this was in individual, local contexts, where law and order, the supreme Roman desiderata, were placed in jeopardy, thanks to the agitations of opponents among the pagans and less often among the Jews. Justin Martyr claimed that the Christians were innocuous (*Apol.* 1.68). Melito, bishop of Sardis, produced the bold, sophistic argument for the benefit of Marcus Aurelius that Christianity was worthy of protection because its fortunes and those of the Principate were linked in history from a shared beginning and mutually guaranteed:

> Our philosophy first grew up among the barbarians, but its full flower came among your nation in the great reign of your ancestor Augustus, and became an omen of good to your empire, for from that time the power of the Romans became great and splendid. You are now his happy successor, and shall be so along with your son, if you protect the philosophy that grew up with the empire and began with Augustus. Your ancestors nourished it

---

[19] Garnsey (1984), 1-12.

[20] On atheism, Drachmann (1922); on the persecution of Christians, de Ste. Croix (1974); Barnes (1968); Frend (1965).

along with other cults, and the greatest proof that our doctrine flourished
for good along with the empire in its noble beginning, is the fact that it met
no evil in the reign of Augustus, but on the contrary everything splendid
and glorious according to the wishes of all men.' (Eusebius, *Hist.Eccl.*
4.26.7ff.)

Nevertheless, Christians did become from time to time the centre of civil
disturbance. Insofar as a religious factor lay at the root of the problem, it
was the traditional view that the welfare of the state and its subjects
depended upon divine favour, and that the *pax deorum* (peace with or
from the gods) was secured by the performance of established rituals and
jeopardized by their non-performance, with dire consequences. The gods
showed their anger by sending plague, famine and other natural
disasters, plus civil and foreign war – responsibility for which was
sometimes attributed to the Christians.

There was, however, no general persecution prior to the reign of Decius.
What had changed? According to the conventional view, the Decian
persecution took place against a background of political and military
disaster. The political order had all but collapsed, and enemies were
invading on all sides. The survival of the empire as an entity was at
stake, and the emperor in reaction sought to regain the favour of the gods
by organizing a massive demonstration of the loyalty of the empire. But
we may question whether it was so obvious to Decius that the empire was
falling apart. The great calamities, including the death in battle of
Decius himself, lay in the future. Decius, it might be argued, had
restored the northern frontier and now set out to strengthen his position
by bidding for the support of the empire at large. His imperial edict was a
thoroughly old-fashioned gesture, to cap the millennial games of his
predecessor Philip: the people of Rome were summoned to a *supplicatio*
in the old style, an act of corporate veneration of the tutelary gods of the
state.[21] But in addition, Decius had the mentality of an emperor from the
Balkans. These were hard men with a narrowly realistic view of the
priorities of the imperial office, and a firm determination to impose order
and discipline on the world. Diocletian is the model, and, unlike Decius
and Valerian, he persecuted from a position of strength.

Our major interest, given the chronological limits of our study, is in the
pre-persecution period, in which the church was permitted an extended
period of relatively unimpeded growth. Its rate of growth should not be
exaggerated; it was not sufficiently fast or dramatic to raise concern in
the minds of emperors and other statesmen before the second half of the
third century. Marcus Aurelius in his *Meditations* mentions the
Christians only once, and not in such a way as to imply that he viewed
them as a threat. Marcus sanctioned minor persecutions of Christians, as

[21] An effective critique of the traditional view in G.W. Clarke, *The Letters of St. Cyprian of Carthage* (1984), I 21-25.

at Lyon in AD 177 (Eusebius, *Hist. Eccl.* 5.1.4ff.), but on request, and without departing from the Trajanic directive. It is striking how little we hear about early Christianity from non-Christian writers. In the Severan era alone, sometimes seen as a period of significant growth, Christianity is not mentioned in Cassius Dio, Herodian or Philostratus, that is, the major historical and biographical sources for the period.[22] Christians impinged more on the world by the time of Decius, but were still a small minority, and predominantly of low or modest status. It is not even clear that the original edict of Decius was aimed at Christians as such, although the authorities would certainly have been aware that there were 'atheists' abroad who would absent themselves from the great religious jamboree planned by the emperor.

But Christianity was already a success, and we should try to understand why. Explanations have been offered in terms of its ability to meet the social and psychological needs of the individual,[23] and again in terms of the power of the Christian god as displayed in miracles.[24] These explanations have merit but should not be seen as mutually exclusive. The role of the Christian community in supporting the individual and nurturing spiritual growth may be readily admitted. But the part played by miracle is also undeniable. In a superstitious age Christians as well as pagans (and Jews) found evidence of the interaction of the world of the spirit and the terrestrial world in signs, symbols and dreams, and held wonder-workers in awe, or condemned them as sorcerers and magicians.[25] Other interpretations point to weaknesses in polytheistic paganism that facilitated the growth of Christianity. In one formulation, paganism, 'a very spongy, shapeless, easily penetrated structure', was always vulnerable to attack from 'a sharply focussed and intransigent creed'.[26] This is unexceptionable, but lacks a specific historical reference.

The solution to the problem of Christianity's success is not to evoke an alleged weakening in the fabric of polytheism (for example, a supposed increased tendency toward syncretism), which reduced its appeal and gave additional impetus to Christianity.[27] On the contrary, paganism at the level of personal religious experience was manifesting considerable vitality, especially near the end of our period. It would be consistent with the argument of this chapter to suggest that the source of the problem lay in the ambivalent attitude of the Roman authorities to religious change,

[22] See Brunt (1979) on Marcus, Wilken (1984) and in more detail Labriolle (1948) on pagan discussion of Christianity. For the Severan era as the period of 'take off' for Christianity see Frend (1984), 272ff.

[23] Nock (1933), e.g. 210; Dodds (1965), passim; Brown (1978), 1ff. (critique of Dodds).

[24] MacMullen (1984), 17-42. Support in e.g. Origen, 8.47 cf. 1.46.

[25] For superstition among Christians see e.g. Cyprian *Ep.*16 (a timely divine monition), 22 (cult of martyrs), 39 (a vision), with Clarke, *Cyprian*, ad loc. Other references, also for Jews and pagans, in Brunt (1979), 497-8.

[26] MacMullen (1984), 16.

[27] Frend (1965), e.g. 456.

which was permitted in the private, but not the public, sphere. An ossified official religion fitted the image of changelessness and stability that Roman emperors were concerned to project. Meanwhile, however, they failed both to control the forces of innovation, pagan and non-pagan, that were active at an unofficial level, and to harness those operating within paganism against the challenge of Christianity.

Cult of Emperor - popularize leader, Rome, and new people are in awe

other Roman cults don't have too much affect in E

Romans did not like new religion but did little

christianity

CHAPTER TEN
Culture

Following the victory of Augustus, institutions, values and cultural life in
Rome gradually adjusted to the monarchy. Augustus' exercise of political
patronage had its counterpart in the cultural sphere. As loyalty to the
emperor became the key to office and high status, so those writers and
artists who were the beneficiaries of the emperor's patronage were
expected to treat Augustan themes and to do so in a sympathetic
manner.

The provinces were less directly exposed than the capital city to the
processes of cultural transformation stimulated by the installation of an
emperor; nor was there any grand design emanating from the emperors
and their advisers to spread the culture of Rome through the empire at
large. Nevertheless, in the expanding western empire, emperors stepped
up the traditional Roman policy of imposing metropolitan political and
cultural institutions as an essential complement to military conquest.
The consequence of Roman imperialism, however, was not so much
Romanization as the forging of distinctive Romano-Iberian, African,
Gallic or British cultures through the fusion of imperial and local
elements.

Moreover, Roman customs and ideas circulated mainly in the cities;
where urbanization remained underdeveloped, and in the countryside in
general, the impact of the imperial culture was much reduced. Similarly,
in the eastern provinces, where an indigenous civic culture was already
entrenched and flourishing, no attempt was made to disturb it. In
general, Romanization was deep-rooted and lasting only where a local
elite were zealous in espousing Roman culture, and this spirit was
entirely lacking in the eastern empire.

Finally, the imperial or metropolitan culture was itself a blend of
indigenous and foreign elements. Receptiveness to the cultures of others,
especially that of the Greeks, whose cultural superiority was not
contested by the Roman governing classes, was enhanced as a result of
the political integration of the Mediterranean by Augustus, and given
specific encouragement by philhellene emperors.

Rome

The obsession of the early emperors with their personal safety and the
security of their regimes set new limits on freedom in the realm of ideas.

We saw that magic and astrology became fashionable ways of foretelling the future, but could be treated with suspicion by emperors because of their potential links with conspiracy. Harassment of philosophers was not unknown under the Republic. But the problems that some emperors had with philosophers, particularly Stoics, require a special explanation.

Stoicism dominated the world of ideas for much of our period.[1] It was the ethical system, not the theoretical speculations, of Stoicism that appealed to Romans, including many of aristocratic lineage, and eventually an emperor, Marcus Aurelius. Stoic ethics had lost their earlier rigidities, having passed through a period of doctrinal compromise and simplification, and were now available to ordinary mortals. Seneca, Epictetus, and others saw it as their task to help anyone earnestly seeking moral improvement. The goal was progress, not perfection. The condition of the sage was now acknowledged as an ideal. Late Stoicism accepted sound moral teaching from any source; Seneca's *Letters* are liberally sprinkled with the sayings of Epicurus, while Epictetus went as far as to applaud the Cynics, especially their doctrine of freedom. It was freedom of the spirit that they celebrated, not free birth, which was viewed as an external, of little account. Epictetus, himself an ex-slave, wrote: 'Zeus has set me free: do you think he intended his own son to be enslaved? But you are master of my carcass; take it' (Arrian, *Epict. Diss.* 1.19.9). A philosophy for which the salvation of the soul was everything generated solidly conservative social attitudes among its adherents. In political terms, too, Stoicism supported the status quo, and had in fact taken the lead in transposing Hellenistic kingship theory into a Roman setting. In general, Stoicism played an important role in the articulation and consolidation of traditional beliefs and practices.

Stoicism should have been acceptable to the monarchy. But there were ambiguities in the Stoic position. The doctrines of 'the appropriate' (*to kathêkon, officium*) and 'constancy' (*constantia*), which in combination involve holding steadfastly to one's predetermined station in life and the conduct it requires, could lead to martyrdom. The suicide of Cato in the cause of Republicanism was an embarrassment to Caesar. The attack on Stoicism under Domitian, which produced a martyr in Helvidius Priscus and conferred a Stoic halo on Nero's victim Thrasea Paetus, is to be seen as an aspect of the political confrontation between emperor and senate. A Stoic might phrase his opposition to the political and ethical conduct of a particular emperor (or even to the Principate itself) in Stoic terms. But the mere possession of Stoic beliefs in a public figure might be enough to inflame a suspicious emperor who was on the look-out for hints of disloyalty, especially among members of senatorial families who had already fallen foul of emperors.

[1] Hicks (1911); Long (1971); Sandbach (1975); Brunt (1975b); M. Griffin (1976); Shaw (1985).

The imperial system imposed new constraints upon literature.[2] Historians, with few exceptions men of high rank for whom politics was a central concern, were most obviously vulnerable to criticism or attack. Augustus burned the works of the provocative T. Labienus; Tiberius burned those of Cremutius Cordus, historian of the proscriptions stage-managed by Augustus himself (as Octavian). According to Tacitus (*Ann.* 1.1; cf. *Hist.* 1.1), after Augustus contemporary history was acceptable only if adulatory.

The relations between emperors and the writers of imaginative literature were complex. Writers needed patrons. An emperor interested in supporting literature was a patron to outbid all rivals. Like any patron, he required praise. An emperor offered unusual scope for praise, but he could make unusual demands. Augustus required nothing less from his clients (and from those authors patronized by his confidant of the 30s and 20s, Maecenas) than the organization of opinion in support of his regime. His attitude to those not involved in his patronage network is unclear. Did he exile Ovid for the *carmen* or the *error*, for a poem (*Ars Amatoria*) conspicuous for its un-Augustan view of love and marriage, or for some indiscretion, perhaps complicity in the scandal of the younger Julia? Or for both? At the least Augustus expected of public figures, whether writers or politicians, that they not actively undermine his regime and its values.

The response of the Augustan poets to pressure from above is difficult to measure. Did Virgil and Horace undermine their own panegyrics (if panegyrics they were)? Is Propertius revealed in his poems as an admirer or a dissident? What was the effect on contemporary writers of Ovid's fate, and more generally, of the experience of creative writers under the Augustan Principate? The great days of personal elegy came to an end with Ovid. Is this a vindication of the verdict of Velleius Paterculus, a firm supporter of the Principate and a contemporary, that literary genres by a natural law enjoy only a brief efflorescence (1.16-17)? Or was the death of elegy not entirely natural?

The history of Latin literature as a whole under the Principate poses the same dilemma. The rich vein of imaginative literature that produced the Augustan writers, Petronius, Lucan, Martial, Juvenal, Tacitus and numerous other substantial figures, was worked out by the end of the 120s. It is arguable that Latin literature had no distinguished representative (with the possible exception of Apuleius) between the first quarter of the second century and the last quarter of the fourth. It is tempting to argue that the attitudes of emperors and the changed political climate in general had a dampening effect on artistic creativity

[2] Syme (1939), ch. 30; Williams (1968), ch. 2; Johnson (1976), esp. 135-54; J. Griffin (1976); Sullivan (1976); Otis (1970), ch. 9; Syme (1978); Williams (1978); Kenney (1982), chs. 15-42; Gold (1982); Woodman and West (1984). We gratefully acknowledge the advice of Ian DuQuesnay and Richard Hunter. Culpability for the views expressed is ours.

in Rome. Yet the age of Augustus witnessed a remarkable flowering of Latin literature, and there were minor peaks in the reigns of Nero and Domitian, no champions of freedom. The beneficial and inhibiting effects of monarchy have to be weighed against each other.

While the classic genres of Latin literature – epic, elegy, drama, satire and history – faded out, oratory, or rhetoric, was flourishing. The monarchy contributed to this development and to the transformation that oratory underwent, which in the view of critics from the elder Seneca to Quintilian amounted to a qualitative decline.

The promotion of rhetoric by emperors was an aspect of their support for education in general, which in turn signalled their commitment to the Graeco-Roman literary culture: rhetoric was the keystone of the educational system.[3] Education, traditionally a private matter for those families who could afford it, became increasingly a concern of the government. Augustus set up public libraries in Rome, Vespasian financed chairs in Greek and Latin rhetoric again in Rome, Marcus Aurelius chairs in philosophy in Athens, and Vespasian began a policy of exempting teachers from local, civic services. Oratory flourished, but was conventionally held to have changed for the worse. The trend away from rhetorical theory toward declamation in the form of *suasoriae* (speeches of advice to some historical or mythological figure) and *controversiae* (speeches in imaginary court cases) accelerated under the emperors. Public declamations were designed to entertain, not persuade; themes were remote from real life, their treatment was over-ornate and sententious. Students imitated this style in their exercises and went on to use it in public life. But public life had changed in character, and for a number of writers this was a fundamental cause of decline in oratory. Important political issues were no longer debated in public. The fierce competitiveness among politicians that had produced the great oratorical efforts of the last century of the Republic in senate house, assembly and law-court was eliminated under the Principate. The 'free oratory' of men like T. Labienus and Cassius Severus, which had contributed materially to their downfall at the hands of Augustus, came to an end. More degenerate forms of public oratory took their place, as a direct result of the operation of imperial patronage: the denunciation of a defendant in a political trial by an accuser seeking personal advancement and material reward, or the flattering speech addressed to the emperor by a newly elected consul (Pliny's *Panegyricus* is a surviving exemplar).

So much for the contemporary critique of rhetoric. It is useful for its documentation of change and the way change is accounted for. In particular, the political explanation seems to be in general valid (not

---

[3] The system is described by Quintilian in *Instit. Orat.* (early 90s). See Marrou (1956); Bonner (1977). On rhetoric/oratory, see Bonner (1949); Syme (1958), ch. 9; Kennedy (1972); Fairweather (1981), esp. 132-50. On second-century developments, Champlin (1980); Bowersock (1969).

uniquely so) and relevant to our theme, though we need not accept all the details. For example, political rhetoric under the Principate was not uniquely self-serving or destructive in intent.

Moreover, 'modern' oratory had its supporters, such as M. Aper in Tacitus' *Dialogus*, as well as its detractors. The most authoritative of the critics, Quintilian, is measured in his criticism, conceding the usefulness of *controversiae* and *suasoriae*, and distancing himself from the Ciceronian view that rhetoric should be based on academic philosophy. The gaps that opened up between Cicero and the elder Seneca or Quintilian, or between Quintilian and the fashionable orators of his day, are to be analysed in terms not of decline, but of differences of taste.

Oratory did not decline; it flourished. Indeed, profiting from the absence of distinguished exponents of the conventional genres of Latin literature, epideictic oratory had achieved the status of the most popular literary form by the mid-second century. Fronto, the leading littérateur at Rome in the Antonine age, and the tutor of princes, was famous as an orator. It is symptomatic that, unlike Tacitus, the foremost orator of an earlier age, Fronto's literary distinction extended no further than this.

However, the most brilliant representatives of second-century oratory, the 'sophists' (also known as rhetors or philosophers) of the so-called Second Sophistic, came from the Greek East.[4] These itinerant rhetoricians fascinated crowds with their verbal pyrotechnics and won riches for themselves and friendships with the great. Their eloquence was also harnessed to political objectives, including the securing of favours and rewards for individuals and communities from Roman emperors and their representatives.

The popularity of the sophists reflects the general dominance of Greek culture in the Mediterranean in the second and early third centuries. The use of Greek as the medium for the *Meditations* of the Stoic emperor Marcus Aurelius may perhaps be dismissed as an aberration, in the sense that the depth of his immersion in Greek culture cannot be regarded as typical of the western elite of this or any other period of Roman history; for this reason it is unwise to talk in terms of the existence of a unified Graeco-Roman literary culture characteristic of a bilingual elite.[5] On the other hand, one can accept that the superiority of Greek culture, long acknowledged, directly or indirectly, by the elite of Rome, became more pronounced than ever in the Antonine and Severan periods. The slump in Latin literature coincided with a period of vitality in Greek literature, of which the sophistic movement was only one aspect.[6] This Greek literary renaissance produced, among others, genuine littérateurs such as Lucian, Alciphron and Philostratus, historians of the calibre of Arrian and Appian, the antiquarians Pausanias and Athenaeus, the novelist Longus,

[4] Boulanger (1923); Bowersock (1969).
[5] Cf. Kenney (1982), 5ff.
[6] Reardon (1971); Palm (1959); brief discussion in Easterling and Knox (1985), 642ff.

and the medical writer and philosopher Galen. While many of these writers are remarkable for their self-conscious lack of interest in Rome, stemming from a desire to preserve the integrity of their cultural heritage, others were openly eulogizing Rome, or at least devoting their energies to charting the rise and progress of the Roman empire. For the best part of a century, from Appian to Cassius Dio and Herodian, Roman history was written by Greeks or Greek speakers, in Greek. Greek schizophrenia on the subject of the Romans was not novel, but reached new heights in the second century. The benefits of Roman rule were never so obvious, the vulnerability of Hellenic culture – the danger that bad culture would drive out good – was never more clearly perceived. That both attitudes, and the Greek literary culture in general, were able to flourish, was a consequence of the sympathetic attitudes and policies of Roman emperors, and the political integration of the Mediterranean that they achieved.

In the visual arts, the chief feature of the period was the development of an official imperial art with its own recognizable message and repertory of art forms. By drawing together certain traditions and stylistic conventions already much employed in the late Republic, art in the Augustan period provided a strong basis for this new and specific use of official art as propaganda. Works of art (whether sculpture or 'minor arts' such as silverware and cameos) and architecture served to reinforce the emperor's own claims and purposes. The desired image of the emperor and his family was carefully built up through portraiture. He was shown as idealized and noble, and was depicted making sacrifice, extending clemency and carrying out other particularly significant acts. The contrasting themes of victory and peace are conspicuous in the triumphal arches and commemorative and decorative reliefs on buildings and the Ara Pacis, as well as on other 'minor' or 'non-official' works of art. The Ara Pacis sums up all the themes of Augustan propaganda, in its suggestion of continuity with the great traditions of the past, and in its allegorical reference to the contemporary role of the imperial family and to the general political and social situation.[7]

The type of eclectic, classical style used for these official purposes is strongly reflected in private art in Rome and elsewhere in Italy. It can be seen, for example, in the decoration of certain houses belonging to the late Pompeian 'second style' and early 'third style', such as the House of Livia on the Palatine, the House of the Villa Farnesina at Rome, and the villa at Boscotrecase outside Pompeii. The formal classicism of the 'third

[7] Strong (1961), pl.35; Ryberg (1955), ch. 4 and *passim*. On developments in art and architecture, Strong (1961); Brilliant (1963); MacDonald (1965); Pollitt (1966); Boethius and Ward-Perkins (1970); Strong (1976). We owe thanks to Janet Huskinson for assistance in this area.

style' in general may be linked with the prevailing tastes of Augustus and his circle.[8]

Augustus' successors were concerned to stress dynastic continuity through the medium of art. The most probably posthumous Primaporta statue of Augustus uses a basically classical pose (recalling the Doryphorus of Polycleitus), enhanced by complex imagery on the cuirass, perhaps alluding to the emperor's diplomatic success at the expense of the Parthians, which was dressed up as a victory. The Boscoreale silver cups have historical scenes showing aspects of Augustus' rule in war and peace, and Tiberius in triumphal procession. Again, the Ravenna relief of Claudian date shows members of the imperial family, including Augustus, in divine or heroic guise.[9]

After Augustus, there was a resurgence of less hellenized forms, which had been somewhat displaced by the idealized classical preferences of Augustus. A constant progression of style in this tradition is the main feature of both representational arts and architecture up to the early second century, despite occasional renewed emphasis on the classical tradition. In sculpture this is reflected in the appearance of portraits that are more realistic and vigorously modelled, in the increasing interest shown in chiaroscuro and contrasting textures, and in the preference for bolder forms of relief. In wall-painting this movement finds a parallel in the introduction of the 'fourth style' that revives the idea of spatial recession, and in some individual paintings which show the use of an impressionistic technique with less fully modelled forms.

Augustus carried out a major programme of rebuilding and construction, of which the Forum Augustum was the most striking achievement, and was praised for his civic sense by Vitruvius. In contrast, Nero's Golden House was a product of his own ambitious tastes rather than any public spirit. This fantastic architectural concept involved a complete landscape setting with a lake, and a complex building richly decorated with wall-paintings (which find parallels in some of the Campanian designs of the 'fourth style') and housing a colossal statue of Nero as well as collected works of art. Domitian's huge Domus Augustana on the Palatine (dedicated in AD 92), which replaced parts of the Golden House, stands in the same tradition of imperial self-glorification. In contrast, the Colosseum (opened by Titus in AD 80), on the site lately occupied by Nero's lake, and the baths of Trajan on the Esquiline (opened in 109), which replaced another section of the Golden House, were straightforward bids for popularity. Other buildings striking

[8] For portraiture, see the herm of L. Caecilius Felix from the house of L. Caecilius Iucundus in Pompeii (Naples Museum 110663); Ward-Perkins and Claridge (1976), fig. on p.39; and in silverware, cups with Greek mythological scenes (etc.), Strong (1966), 136ff. For the paintings, Strong (1976), 50ff.

[9] Augustus: Vitruvius 1, pref. 2; Suetonius, *Aug.* 28.3ff., 31.5; Pollitt (1966), 104ff. Nero: Suetonius, *Nero* 31; Tacitus, *Ann.* 15.38ff.; Boethius (1960); Nash (1968), vol. 1, 339ff.

for their vigour of form and imagination that were contributed to the city by imperial architects from Vespasian to Trajan include Vespasian's Temple of Peace next to the Forum of Augustus (a large complex comprising porticoes, temple and library), Trajan's Market on the Quirinal and below it Trajan's Forum – a large colonnaded court, with a triumphal arch at the south end and the Basilica Ulpia at the north, behind which stood Trajan's Column, and before long, Hadrian's temple of the deified Trajan. These building programmes were designed to display the power, wealth and civic spirit of the emperors.[10]

In official art from the second half of the first century AD there was increased use of standard motifs and scenes such as the imperial *profectio* and *adlocutio*, that is, the departure of the emperor on a military expedition and his address to the soldiers. This trend, and a parallel development, the appearance of allegorical figures to back up the emperor, are well illustrated in the Arch of Trajan at Benevento, the Trajanic Frieze and Trajan's Column, both of which represented Trajan's Dacian war in continuous frieze.[11] Later emperors, especially Marcus Aurelius and Septimius Severus, celebrated their military triumphs with sculptured reliefs depicting now conventional martial scenes on arch or column; but these monuments reveal significant new developments in imperial iconography that can be traced back to the reign of Hadrian, or earlier.

The Hadrianic 'classical revival' was a product of the personal tastes and patronage of this most cultivated of emperors.[12] Hadrian's classicism was not the bleak and academic traditionalism of his Antonine successors. Received and novel artistic conceptions were creatively combined in the architectural design and decoration of the brilliant and extravagant 'villa' at Tivoli and of the Pantheon, rebuilt as a huge brick-faced concrete dome with an elaborately decorated interior. Hadrian ('the Greek') introduced a new style in imperial portraiture, the emperor as bearded Greek hero. More significant for the future development of Roman art was his active encouragement of the importation of techniques of sculpture and artistic representation that would gradually subvert the classical tradition. A comparison between the Trajanic and Severan arches (and even the Trajanic and Aurelian columns) reveals a retreat from realism and a widening of the gap between emperor and subjects: the emperor is presented on the later monuments not in profile but frontally, and towering above groups of undifferentiated soldiers. The distinctive Asiatic or Oriental style of these reliefs, on display on the Severan arches in Rome and (even more

[10] For buildings of this period, Boethius and Ward-Perkins (1970), 217ff.; MacDonald (1965), 47ff.

[11] Brilliant (1963), 89ff., 105ff., 113ff., 118ff.

[12] Post-Trajanic developments: Strong (1976), chs. 8-10; Boethius and Ward-Perkins (1970), 264ff.

so) Lepcis Magna, expresses to perfection the new dynasty's view of its elevated religious and political position in the world.

Rome and the empire

In focussing on the capital city, we have put off discussion of the spreading outwards of the cultural institutions and practices that had developed in Rome through the fusion of Romano-Italian and provincial, especially Greek, elements. Romanization was the joint product of central government initiative and local response. In many parts of the West, what occurred was the transplantation into an artificially created urban setting of a metropolitan language, educational system, religion, architecture and art through the agency of emperors and their representatives. Even in these areas of the empire, however, the speed and depth of Romanization were crucially dependent upon the willingness of local elites to take the initiative in transforming the institutions and values of their communities. Otherwise, the impact of Rome on underlying native cultural traditions varied according to such factors as distance and accessibility from Rome, degree of urbanization, extent of immigration from Italy, proximity of a resident army and the tenacity of local conventions.

The growth of cities is the key development. Romanization was most resoundingly successful in those areas where urban growth was most pronounced: the Iberian peninsula (especially in the south and east), the south of France and north Africa. The urbanization of these areas generated a race of politicians and officials of native or immigrant origin who were capable of being absorbed into a traditional social hierarchy in Rome. Urbanization also produced poets in Spain, orators in Gaul and, beginning with Suetonius, an astonishing crop of African littérateurs, who, whatever their quality, prided themselves on their Latinity.

The Roman administration imposed Latin as the official language in the cities it founded in the West, ignoring all local languages, whether Iberian, Celtic, Punic or Libyan. Urban elites were introduced to Roman-style education, as we know from key passages in Tacitus and other Rome-based writers, from the inscriptional evidence for educators (such as the *grammaticus* Demetrius of Tarsus who taught at York) and for the composition of bad poetry (notably in north Africa), and from the careers and literary creations of the most distinguished products of the educational system.[13]

As with politics, so with learning, the most ambitious provincials (and Italians) transferred their base to Rome, and the best of them dominated the Roman intellectual scene. Romans in the Flavian period witnessed

[13] See e.g. *CIL* II 4319 (a Greek 'educator' at Tarraco), *RIB* 662-3 (Demetrius cf. Ogilvie and Richmond, Comm. on Tacitus, *Agricola*, 32ff.), and about 300 metrical inscriptions surviving from north Africa, Champlin (1980), 17, 148 n. 86.

the spectacle of a Spaniard, Quintilian, the leading rhetor and first incumbent of the state chair of Latin rhetoric, championing traditional Roman literary and educational standards against the innovations of Silver Age baroque, represented by among others his fellow Spaniards Seneca and Lucan, who are described by Martial, another Spaniard, as the glories of Cordova together with their father the elder Seneca. (*Epig.* 1.16). In the second century, Africa displaced Spain as the main exporter of intellectual luminaries to Rome: Suetonius the biographer, Fronto the orator, Sulpicius Apollinaris the grammarian are the best-known representatives. What is remarkable is not that all these men, and many others, responded to the magnetic pull of Rome, but that, Martial apart, their writings carry so little mark of their provincial origins. For this reason, doubt lingers over the African origins of Suetonius, the addressee of an honorific inscription from Hippo Regius in eastern Algeria, and over the hypothetical south Gallic origins of Tacitus, for whom no such convenient evidence exists.[14]

Born two generations after Suetonius and one after Fronto, Apuleius was different, a provincial who composed worthwhile Latin literature elsewhere than in Rome. As such, he was the first of a series of Africans extending through Tertullian, Nemesianus and Lactantius to Augustine, who found Carthage an acceptable centre of intellectual excellence. Apuleius symbolizes the creativity and self-confidence of African society in the late Antonine and Severan periods. The more representative product of Africa in this period was, however, not Apuleius but Fronto. Apuleius saw himself as a (Platonic) philosopher. He is more accurately described as a sophist. It does not matter which term is used: they overlap. It is more significant that these interests were something of a rarity in north Africa, and that they led him to Athens. The natural destination of Fronto the advocate was Rome, and Africa, as Juvenal commented, was 'the wetnurse of advocates'.[15]

The prosaic norm is often as revealing as the brilliant exception. For every Fronto, Martial or Favorinus, the sophist from Arles, there were thousands of uninspired littérateurs, the 'Ciceros' and 'Virgils' of their communities, or ambitious mediocrities whose talents made no impact in Rome, or small-town products exploiting within their provinces the opportunities for social and political advancement that education afforded.

At an even lower level, the educational attainment of the average product of a municipal school, whether in Apuleius' home town of Madauros or in Isona in Spain (*CIL* II 4465), was not high. While every city had its *grammatici* equipped to give a basic literary education, teachers of rhetoric were far from ubiquitous, and only the upper echelon of the elite could afford to pursue the standard rhetorical education – let

[14] Spain: Griffin (1972). Africa: Champlin (1980), ch. 1; Suetonius: Wallace-Hadrill (1983), with *CRAI* 1952, 76-85 (Hippo Regius).
[15] Apuleius: Tatum (1979); Winkler (1985).

alone a legal training – in the larger towns. The deficiencies of the schools of Pliny's Como meant that the more talented – and well-to-do – youth were drawn away to the regional centre Milan (*Ep.* 4.13). Again, although Greek was taught as well as Latin, literary and inscriptional evidence suggests that erudition and fluency in both languages (not the same thing) was a rarity, worth boasting about on an inscription or in a public speech.[16] Finally, there was an enormous gap between an Apuleius and the average townsman, who had no access to the educational system, and who could only have attained a smattering of Latin.

Metropolitan architecture and art, along with the language and educational system of the Romans, were exported through governmental initiative to the underdeveloped western provinces. New foundations, cities promoted to Roman status, and tribal capitals were equipped, not usually all at once, with an orthogonal street grid, and a selection of public buildings for administrative, political and religious ends, and for entertainment.[17] However, urban construction and renovation were a quite general phenomenon. Nowhere was urban embellishment undertaken so enthusiastically as in the Greek world, where long-established cities sought to outstrip one another in ambitious building projects, financed for the most part by the local elite through official payments and donations, supplemented by the generosity of ostentatious philanthropists like Herodes Atticus of Athens or Opramoas of Rhodiapolis in Lycia in the middle of the second century.[18] Direct imperial initiative can sometimes be traced. Hadrian's travels prompted a rash of new building wherever he went; in particular, he transformed the urban landscape of Italica in Spain, his place of origin, and of Athens, his spiritual home. Septimius Severus refurbished his city of origin, Lepcis Magna. In general, however, the example and general inspiration provided by emperors was sufficient to stimulate the local elites into activity that was in any case in tune with their political aspirations, systems of values and life-styles.

In areas of rapid urban growth such as southern France and southern and eastern Spain, the metropolitan and Italian influence was very pronounced, as imported artists and craftsmen created replicas in miniature of Roman public buildings, artefacts in clay and metal from Italian workshops circulated, and crafts hitherto unknown such as mosaic and wall-painting took root.

Provincial styles and art forms were sometimes scarcely affected by foreign importations or adapted only late. In other instances, there was free borrowing, and essentially derivative crafts grew up and flourished, as for example the pottery industry of Gaul which produced the red-glazed Samian ware, a development of Hellenistic ceramic art. In

[16] E.g. *ILAlg* I 1363-4 ('learned in both languages'); Apuleius, *Flor.* 9.29.
[17] Grew and Hobley (1985).
[18] Graindor (1930); Veyne (1976), 279ff.; *Fouilles de Xanthos* VII ch. 7 (Balland).

still other cases, the blending of foreign and native elements produced a distinctive local style. Thus in British sculpture, a basic classical structure is combined with a stylized, 'conceptual' Celtic treatment. In mosaic, which was established in the north-western and African provinces by the middle of the second century, African craftsmen show an inventiveness unrivalled anywhere else in the empire. While Italy never broke away from the black and white mosaic with traditional, purely ornamental, design, mosaicists in Africa were employing from the Severan period free composition combined with polychromy, and favouring realistic scenes that reflected the pursuits and interests of their patrons (hunting, circus and amphitheatre, rural life).[19]

The limits of Romanization: cities

It was in the context of the city, for the most part in the western empire, that Roman and native came into contact and combined to form Romano-African, Romano-British, or some other particular and original culture. Cities expanded and multiplied also in the East, but in the tradition of Hellenic, not Roman, culture. When villagers such as the Tymandeni of Galatia petitioned an emperor for promotion to city status, they wanted a *polis*, not a *colonia* or *municipium*. Similarly, when emperors created cities in eastern areas where before there were none, or promoted communities of lower status, as Septimius Severus did in Egypt, they gave them Greek, not Roman institutions. It was Greek, not Latin, that replaced Nabataean as the official language in Trajan's newly created province of Arabia.[20]

The earlier colonies, those founded by Caesar for Roman civilians and by Augustus for discharged Italian veterans, as opposed to the later 'titular' colonies where promotion did not involve Romanization, are the exception. The Augustan colony at Beirut, Colonia Julia Augusta Felix Berytus, was founded, as the coins indicate, in accordance with a traditional Etruscan rite supposedly employed by Romulus at the foundation of Rome itself. The city was laid out according to a grid plan like other veteran colonies (Timgad in Numidia was typical). It was equipped with forum and capitol located at the intersection of the two main arteries, and was adorned with a fine array of public buildings, including the typically Roman amenities of hippodrome, theatre and amphitheatre, with the aid of friendly kings, notably Herod the Great and his grandson Herod Agrippa I. The city was likewise endowed with

[19] Oswald and Davies Pryce (1920); Toynbee (1964); Dunbabin (1978).
[20] Bowman (1971); Millar (1971), 2-3. Trajan founded on the Lower Danube both Roman colonies (Ratiaria and Oescus) and Greek *poleis* (Nicopolis ad Istrum and Marcianopolis): Gerov (1980), 21ff.

Roman-style political institutions, and its citizens were enrolled in a Roman tribe, the Fabia.[21]

Much remains obscure about the cultural development of the early eastern colonies, Italian islands in a Greek sea. In the six Pisidian colonies planted by Augustus inland in southern Asia Minor, Latin remained the official language (for dedications to the emperor and his representatives, for example) but otherwise steadily lost ground to Greek. The pattern of development in the Augustan veteran colony of Heliopolis at Baalbek was broadly similar, to judge from the largely epigraphical evidence.[22] Inscriptional material from nearby Beirut is scanty. However, for the resilience of the Roman educational system in that city, we can cite the career of one of its citizens, M. Valerius Probus, eminent Latin grammarian and editor of Virgil, Horace and Terence in the mid-first century, and more strikingly, the presence from the late second century, if not earlier, of what was to become a famous law school. Roman law was a luxury subject in the East, but appears to have been a specialty of the Phoenician cities, which produced the great Severan jurisprudents Ulpian and Papinian. The wider significance of a law school, as both Gregory Thaumaturgus (c. AD 239) and Libanius (c. 370) bear witness, is that it stimulated instruction in Latin in places near and far. Gregory recalls that he had learned Latin in distant Cappadocia with a view to studying law 'at Berytus, that most Roman of cities, centre of instruction in the law'.[23]

Roman culture did make progress in the East. We can cite among relevant factors the numerous establishments of Italian traders and financiers in eastern cities from the second half of the second century BC, the presence of around twenty-five pockets of Italian colonists from the age of Caesar and Augustus, the existence of Roman educational institutions in those colonies and to some extent elsewhere, the use of Latin as the official language of the army and the civil and judicial administration, the institution of the cult of Rome from the early second century BC and subsequently the spread of the imperial cult, the popularity of some Roman entertainments, in particular, gladiatorial games and wild-beast shows (normally linked with the imperial cult), and the diffusion of Roman-style podium-mounted temples, baths and theatres, as well as amphitheatres. Occasionally, there was open imitation of buildings in Rome. The Herodian theatres in Jerusalem, Caesarea and elsewhere were inspired by the theatre of Pompey in Rome, seen by their donor within two decades of its construction. Local initiative, the pressing desire to exploit a city's special connection with Rome, lay behind the unique early Tiberian Sebasteion complex in

[21] Mouterde (1964).

[22] Levick (1967); *IGLS* 6: 34ff. (Rey-Coquais).

[23] Mouterde (1964), 173-4 (Probus), 175-6 (law school), with Migne, *PG* 10, 1065-6 (Gregory), Libanius, *Or.* 62.21-3, and Collinet (1925).

Aphrodisias. This was a processional way entered through a propylaeum, and leading between three-storied walls to a temple. It drew on the forum of Augustus at Rome, and, for its extensive relief decoration, on recent events in Rome, specifically, the funerals of Augustus and Drusus, son of Tiberius.[24]

It remains the case that the cultural tradition of the Greeks was much too powerful to be undermined on home ground, even had successive Roman governments been inclined to mount a frontal attack. As it was, imperial governments were inclined to protect and promote Hellenic civic culture at the expense of local eastern cultures. It was precisely this policy that to the educated Greek constituted the major benefit of Roman rule. It also explains the acceptance by the intellectual and political leadership of a permanent condition of political subservience, and its attentiveness to particular Rome-originating directives and initiatives – or, for that matter, changes of fashion. A production of sarcophagi, beginning in Rome and Ostia in the early second century in response to a growing preference for inhumation as opposed to cremation among the Roman upper classes, quickly spread to the East; but, predictably, the great demand for these sculptured coffins in the East was met by local craftsmen (operating in Athens and several centres in Asia Minor), and with decorative relief work that was purely Greek in idiom.[25]

There is much more to be said about the mixture of cultures in the eastern empire in the urban environment, but this properly belongs to a prior investigation into the limits of Hellenization. The uniqueness and durability of Jewish and Egyptian cultures, the continuously evolving and influential Oriental cultures, are familiar themes to students of the East and Near East. The diverse Anatolian cultures largely escape notice until later Christian sources partially lift the veil, but in the Phoenician cities continuity with the pre-Greek past in the areas of language, political institutions, cults, literary and documentary tradition, and historical consciousness can be identified with different degrees of certainty. Moreover, toward the end of our period there were emperors and courtiers who, because of their backgrounds, were particularly well informed about the vitality of Phoenician and other Near-Eastern cultures. The jurist Ulpian, who boasted Tyre as his place of origin, entertained the idea that Punic and Aramaic ('Assyrian') might be chosen as alternative languages to Latin or Greek for certain legal transactions (*Digest* 45.1.1.6). Punic-speaking Tripolitania produced the family of Septimius Severus, and an Aramaic-speaking area of Syria that of his second wife, Julia Domna.[26]

[24] See Hatzfeld (1919); Price (1984); Robert (1941); Frézouls (1959) and (1961); Reynolds (1981). We are extremely grateful to Joyce Reynolds for sharing her interpretation of the Sebasteion.

[25] Strong (1976), 102-6, etc.; Toynbee (1971), 270-7.

[26] Momigliano (1975); Schlumberger (1970); Avi-Yonah (1961); Colledge (1976); Millar (1968), (1971), (1983b).

The survival of Phoenician culture has important implications for the extent not only of Hellenization in the East but also of Romanization in the West. The potency of Greek culture is established by its continuous and lasting influence on the culture of Rome, and also its survival in various outposts in the West from Sicily to Spain, most dramatically in Naples, 'a Greek shop window 150 miles from Rome'. The survival in north Africa of the other 'colonial' culture, Phoenician, is proven by hundreds of Neo-Punic inscriptions (many of them official, as in first-century Lepcis Magna and first- and second-century Maktar) and by literary evidence from Statius in the second half of the first century to Augustine in the early fifth. Apuleius' disparaging comment about his renegade stepson Pudens of Oea in Tripolitania, that he never spoke anything but Punic, may not be fair to Pudens, but is acceptable for its implication that Punic in the mid-second century was a living language among the propertied classes as well as the unlettered townsfolk. Elsewhere, evidence of the staying-power of Phoenician culture in an urban setting is harder to find, but the neo-Punic inscription from Bitia in Sardinia should occasion no surprise. Finally, even without the evidence of the inscriptions in Libyan, or Ulpian's remark that the Celtic language might be admissible in Roman civil law (*Digest* 32.11 pref.), or the quantity of onomastic evidence from the north and north-western provinces, it would be reasonable to expect indigenous languages to have survived the impact of Romanization as languages of ordinary discourse, and not only among the lower classes, in the urban setting.[27]

The limits of Romanization: countryside

City and country formed to some extent a continuum. Cities typically served as the geographical and economic axis of a rural territory, as the domicile of a portion of the agricultural work-force, and as a social and religious centre for all and sundry. Again, the city and the 'villa-belt' around it may be thought of as a unity from the point of view of the landowning urban aristocracy. Yet in Antioch and Hippo Regius, Syriac- and Punic-speaking rustics stood out from other members of the congregations of, respectively, John Chrysostom and Augustine.[28] In what follows, we treat city and country as distinct categories for purposes of analysis.

Some cultural penetration of the countryside was inevitable. Peasants

[27] Citations from Hardie (1983), 3, and ch. 1, *passim* (Naples), and Millar (1983b), 57 (Sardinia), Apuleius, *Apol.* 98.8-9. In general, Millar (1968).

[28] John Chrysostom, *Hom. ad pop. Ant.* 19.1 with Millar (1971), esp. 5-8; Brown (1968), 88 n.22. It is a theme of Leveau (1984), that the city and the nearer territory, organised by the villas, form an 'ensemble', to be clearly separated from the outer territory. For urban-rural as a cultural distinction, see MacMullen (1974).

were brought into contact with Roman influences through taxation, conscription, money, cults, rural markets, customs stations, and itinerant soldiers and civilian officials. But their commitment to the vernacular languages and their native customs in general remained firm. In the Danubian provinces of Pannonia and Upper Moesia, the 'archaeologically and epigraphically traceable' sector of the tribal communities (the more prosperous members) betray their origins in their wagon graves and *tumuli* (which are much more widespread in the Roman period than previously), tombstone sculpture (depicting local costume and astral symbolism) and funerary inscriptions, on which Celtic, Illyrian (Pannonian) and Thracian names abound. The very act of setting up an inscribed stone, and the use of Latin, even if it is bad or rudimentary Latin, are manifestations of Roman cultural influence. But this is not to say very much, especially when it is borne in mind that the inscriptions are heavily concentrated in the comparatively few urban centres of the provinces concerned, in the frontier areas and along the main roads. As for the wide dispersion of local burial customs in the Roman period, this is a reflection not of Roman cultural influence, but of the political achievement of the imperial power in imposing settled conditions in a frontier area. When suddenly at the end of the second century, Romanization did make something of a breakthrough in the Danubian provinces in response to the enhanced political importance of the region, it was colourless, shallow-rooted and ephemeral.[29]

Latin received the same kind of token recognition from inhabitants of the pre-desert zone in Tripolitania, who transliterated their Punic into Latin for epigraphic purposes, as from the Pannonian and Moesian tribesmen. Closer to the coast, at El-Amronni in the south-west Gefara, a prosperous farmer laid claim to Roman citizen status in his funerary inscription of uncertain date, when he recorded his name as Q. Apuleius Maxssimus (everyday name, Rideus), but the names of his father (Iuzale), grandfather (Iurath) and wife (Thanubra) were Libyan, and beside his inscription his heirs provided a neo-Punic version. Romanization in his case was at best skin-deep, and that of his sons (who bear stock Latin names) no different, unless they had emigrated to the city (Gigthis and Sabratha were the least remote). Some Latin had crept into the vocabulary of the countryfolk around St. Augustine's see of Hippo Regius. The word *salus* in their usage was heavy with religious symbolism, since it combined the Latin 'salvation' with the Punic 'three' (compare the Hebrew, *shalosh*). But these peasants were still Punic-speakers, six centuries after the Roman conquest.[30]

---

[29] Mócsy (1970) and (1974), e.g. 147ff., 247 ff.; Gerov (1980), 21ff. For Spain, see Le Roux and Tranoy (1973); Etienne et al. in Pippidi (1976) – contributions in the same volume by Beaujeu, Pippidi and Protase are of value. On non-Roman names, see L'onomastique latine (1977), pt. 4.

[30] Brogan (1965); Brogan and Reynolds (1985); Millar (1968), 132; Brown (1968), 88.

The degree to which rural areas were Romanized was severely circumscribed by the character of Roman imperial policy, and the nature and limited extent of the contact that was deemed necessary between Rome's representatives abroad and the subject peoples. The elitist and town-centred character of Roman civilization have been recurrent themes of this book. There was no *mission civilisatrice* undertaken in the interests of the mass of the subject population. Agricola's conduct as governor of Britain is symptomatic (Tacitus, *Agr.* 19-21). His aims did not include the imposition of the Roman educational system on Britons of all classes. This would not have been a practical proposition in Britain or anywhere else. In any case, Agricola would not have believed in it. His civilizing efforts were aimed exclusively at British chieftains and their sons: it was they who were led to live a comfortable urban life, receive a Roman education and adopt Roman customs. He had no programme for ordinary Britons, in town or country, beyond administering justice equitably, moderating requests for taxes, supplies and military manpower, and maintaining a close supervision through the army. In brief, if rural populations gave no trouble and fulfilled their essential obligations, then the imperial administration was content to leave them in peace.

The army, where it existed in substantial numbers, was arguably the main official instrument of rural Romanization, to the extent that it 'recycled' peasants after exposing them to the dominant culture. There was, however, a growing tendency for the army to recruit from soldiers' families 'in the camp', and to form a closed order, cut off from both the local population and the rest of provincial society.[31]

The local elites were potential disseminators of Roman culture beyond the city boundaries. They, if anyone, were in contact with the mass of Rome's subjects, that is, the inhabitants of the countryside, in their capacities as landlords and employers of labour, patrons, creditors and representatives of urban authority. An index of the Romanization of British or Gallic chieftains was the replacement of timber huts, circular or rectangular, by stone-founded corridor villas, increasingly improved with baths, underfloor heating and mosaics. These Roman-style country-houses signalled their owner's allegiance to the new order and pointed to their enhanced status within it.[32]

By the same token, the villa symbolised the accentuation under Roman influence of the social divisions that were present in pre-conquest provincial society. The possession of Roman culture was seen and valued by the local elite as an additional criterion of social superiority. They had no more interest than central government officials in transforming the style of life of the mass of the population. It is symptomatic of this

[31] A theme of Shaw (1983), at 144-8.
[32] Miles (1982); Wightman, (1970), 139ff., 150ff.

attitude that villas and native farmsteads coexisted in south and south-east Britain, a relatively Romanized rural area. The indigenous settlements were subordinate to or formed part of the villa estates. Their survival implies that the material culture of their occupants had not changed *pari passu* with the transformation of their social and economic relationships with the villa proprietors.[33]

In addition, villas were not everywhere: whether in Britain, Gallia Belgica, Mauretania Caesariensis or Tripolitania, they occupied the inner ring of a city's rural territory. Beyond, rural life continued relatively undisturbed, and retained its traditional character.

Finally, cities and Romanizing urban elites were not everywhere. The Celtic area, an extensive belt of land from the Iberian peninsula through France to Germany and Britain, remained under-urbanized. The cities of the north African provinces were concentrated in the coastal zone and near-interior, and in inland Mauretania the main unit of organization was the tribe. In inner Anatolia, Syria or Egypt, the population lived principally in scattered villages that retained their distinctive, local character.[34] In Syria Palestina, Jerusalem disappeared under the straight line and right angle of Hadrian's Aelia Capitolina, but Galilee, like other rural areas all over the empire, was allowed to follow a path of separate development.[35]

Emperors cared about educ. + helped orators
Greek lit big as is architecture

Big culture movement to western cities
Some to Eastern cities, but more Greek
Very little to countryside

[33] Branigan (1982), at 94.
[34] Harper (1928); Boak (1935); Hobson (1985).
[35] Goodman (1983).

Conclusion

The spreading outwards of Rome was a process almost as old as Rome itself. But the transition from oligarchy to monarchy at the beginning of our period (27 BC to AD 235) ushered in a new phase of expansion, extending Roman rule well beyond the Mediterranean basin.

Rome's rulers pursued contrasting aims in the Mediterranean world and in the world removed from the Mediterranean. In the former, a level of political and cultural unity was achieved not previously known in antiquity. Rome reconciled the Greek East to its rule by protecting Hellenic civic culture and encouraging its diffusion; meanwhile immigration, colonization and cultural penetration which had begun in the Republican period narrowed the gap between Italy and those regions of north Africa, France and the Iberian peninsula that were already part of the empire. In the latter, Rome's mission was conquest and pacification rather than the spread of Graeco-Roman civilization. Measured in terms of the incidence of urbanization and the extent of assimilation of local urban elites into the Rome-based governing class, imperial institutions and culture (Romanization) made relatively little impact on indigenous structures and ways of life in these newly conquered areas. The hegemony of the political and cultural elite of the Mediterranean was not broken until the mid-third century, when endemic frontier insecurity placed the direction of the Roman empire in the hands of military men from the Balkans. This vast empire was administered by a few officials. The emperors instituted a modest expansion in the number of administrative posts and diversified the social background of officials, but this marked rather less than a departure from the tradition of government without bureaucracy. Officials owed their appointment and promotion to personal factors, not rules, and were directly responsible to the emperor. The aims of government remained limited to the enforcement of law and order and the raising of revenues for the support of capital city, court, administration and army. To achieve the first of these aims, Augustus organized for the first time a professional army. In respect of administrative practices, however, there was substantial continuity with the past. Revenues were raised more efficiently and from a wider area, but no attempt was made to impose a uniform tax system.

Instead of reforming the central and provincial administration, emperors followed the traditional policy of building up an infrastructure of centres of local government which could render practical services to the imperial power. In the Greek East it was a matter of winning or confirming the loyalty and cooperation of an existing urban elite, though the under-urbanized hinterland received some new foundations. In many parts of the West, however, an urban elite had to be fashioned out of the remnants of defeated tribal aristocracies.

The extraction of the resources of the provinces remained the responsibility of the cities under the supervision of the provincial governors. Imperial governments showed their interest in the proper performance of this task not by multiplying officials, but by exercising closer supervision over those already there. Governors suffered a reduction in both formal powers and discretionary authority. The income and expenditures of cities were subjected to certain restrictions (no new taxes, no new public building without permission), while the compulsory and voluntary contributions and services of the local elite – the main mechanism by which both local and central government demands were met – were subjected to tighter regulation. However, it would be wrong to exaggerate the extent of central government concern and pressure. Interference by emperors or their delegates was sporadic and ad hoc, usually elicited by interested individuals or groups in the localities themselves. There was no rash of general enactments, nor any systematic reorganization of local government. However inefficient and corrupt, it served the limited purpose of the state.

Roman and provincial society, economy and culture did undergo transformation despite the constraints imposed by the limited expectations of the government, the sheer size of the empire, the range and diversity of cultures within it and the relatively primitive level of development of economic life. The task is to make a realistic assessment of the pace and extent of change and to explain how it was effected.

II

The economy was underdeveloped, as measured by the poverty of the mass of the people, the predominance of agricultural labour, the backward state of technology, the importance of land as a source of wealth and power, and the dominance of the value system of the landed aristocracy. The establishment of peace and stable government made possible economic prosperity and growth on a modest scale. The impact on the economies of the 'developing' provinces of the West of immigration, urbanization, military occupation and the fiscal demands of the government is undeniable. But we do not accept the bolder estimates of the extent and effects of monetization and the growth of trade and commerce; we believe that expanded agricultural production was achieved in the western provinces through intensification (higher labour input per unit area) and crop-specialization rather than technological innovation; and we hold that despite provincial 'competition', Italian agriculture (including viticulture) enjoyed moderate prosperity and contributed significantly to the provisioning of Rome throughout our period.

In this agrarian economy, rich landowners are more visible than poor, so that there is a temptation to deny altogether the existence of a significant number of owner-occupiers operating at or near subsistence level. This view and the associated assumption that low productivity and primitive methods made subsistence farming unviable should be rejected. The commonly accepted doctrine of a rapid and decisive shift from slave labour and management to tenancies in consequence of the 'internal contradictions' of slavery or declining interest among landowners in their estates is also dubious. First, the reduction in the numbers of agricultural slaves was a much longer and slower process than is envisaged in the conventional argument. Secondly, the evidence suggests the wealthy were actively concerned with, rather than uninterested in, landed investment and income. Similarly, with regard to patterns of landholding, only a few wealthy landowners held land in the form of huge tracts of arable-turned-pastureland, the *latifundia* of the moralising literature of the early Principate. Their property was typically dispersed and fragmented, a product of inheritance, marriage patterns and economic forces.

An 'underdeveloped' agrarian economy was able to meet the demands of the Roman government without jeopardizing the survival chances of Rome's subjects. The burdens imposed were greater in aggregate than ever before, but were also distributed throughout the empire. A three-fold division operated, without substantial overlap, between areas supplying tax- and rent-grain to Rome, food and equipment to the army and money for civilian and military salaries and other cash expenditures. Rome's subjects were no less able than previously to cope with the food shortages endemic in the region. Subsistence farmers were vulnerable but also resilient. In the urban context 'euergetism', the willingness of the local elite to contribute money, goods and services, continued to perform its function of staving off catastrophe in the absence of any organized system of 'famine relief'. However, local elites included in their ranks speculators as well as benefactors. There are signs that profiteering in essential foodstuffs became more common than in the past, and that local government was less able to control it and more ready to seek outside intervention. These were ominous developments, but local patriotism was seriously undermined not by the normal operation of Roman government under the Principate, but by the collapse of central authority combined with chronic insecurity in the localities in the mid-third century.

III

Augustus restored stability to Roman society. Social divisions and tensions persisted, but the social order was held together by the family, by other vertical and horizontal relationships, and by the ideological, legal and coercive power of the state.

The historian can usefully employ the conceptual apparatuses of both Marx and Weber in analyzing social divisions in classical Rome. In class analysis, the search for the precise membership of classes, conceived as specific social entities, is a less fruitful approach than the identification of the processes by which social inequalities arose and were perpetuated. The property system ensured that access to productive property (the means of production) was limited and passed down within the family. The legal system established property rights and in general underpinned the dominance of the propertied classes. The social system was marked by the direct personal dependence of workers (slave or free) on employers, a basis for exploitation. In our period, the major developments are the appearance of ex-soldiers in the ranks of the propertied under the sponsorship of the imperial government, and the strengthening of the position of local elites entailed in the (uneven) extension of the Roman legal system beyond Rome and Italy. The colonate, involving the radical downgrading of the free peasantry, was an innovation of the late empire.

Roman society was obsessed with status and rank; a Roman's place in the social hierarchy was advertised in the clothes he wore, the seat he occupied at public entertainments, the number and social position of his clients and followers, and his private expenditures on slaves, housing and banquets. Hierarchies of status and rank were not precisely congruent; the one reflected values and outlook, the other legal or customary rules. There were significant status variations within the same ranks at all levels, even among slaves, a far from homogeneous group in terms of occupation and economic resources. These differentials led to ideological conflict when they threatened to upset the pyramid of rank, as when equestrians and especially freedmen attained wealth and power that were thought to be incongruent with their station.

The Republican system of ranks (or orders) was taken over, extended and given sharper definition by Augustus. The senate was rebuilt and its social superiority emphasized through a property qualification, special clothing, and restrictive regulations governing marriage and behaviour. The equestrians were established as a second aristocratic order with similar criteria for membership (birth, wealth), and restrictions on conduct (but not marriage). The military and administrative responsibilities given to equestrians produced in time a hierarchy of rank within the order and at the top honour deriving from rank rivalling that of leading senators. The decurions, or members of local governments, formed a third aristocracy. Below the three aristocratic orders came the humble free and the slaves. The humble free were differentiated from one another from the viewpoint of the law in terms of birth (whether slave or free) and rights (whether citizens or aliens). An important development in our period for which the emperors were responsible was the progressive overshadowing of this ancient juridical distinction by a status distinction between *honestiores* and *humiliores*, which won formal recognition in imperial rescripts from the early second century or earlier. Slaves were chattel; their humanity was given some limited recognition in the law, again through the decisions of emperors.

Turnover in senatorial and equestrian families was extremely high by any historical standards; these orders and to a lesser extent the urban elites were in constant need of replenishment from below. Ex-soldiers and ex-slaves formed two upwardly mobile groups. The promotion of veterans was an outcome of the professionalization of the army. Pay and donatives were sufficient to enable veterans to retire with modest, and in the case of officers, substantial, wealth and assume positions of responsibility in local government. In contrast, the emancipation of slaves was a private affair; Augustus regulated but did not block the practice. Thus ex-slaves, selected as suitable recipients of property by wealthy men who lacked natural heirs or adopted sons, contributed a steady trickle of sons to the local aristocracy. In this way manumission played a part in the wealth-transferring process. In the East, where for technical reasons men of servile origin are less easy to pick out in the relevant Greek-language documents, it is a safe inference that the local elite replaced itself with select clients, freed or freeborn. In a society where wealth was in land and transmitted through the family, a propertied class that could not reproduce itself was replenished through controlled cooptation.

Augustus was aware of the importance of the family in society; he tried to reduce social mobility at the top of the social hierarchy by encouraging senators to marry, bear children and keep their property within the family. He was attempting the impossible, essentially because senators had devised what were to them satisfactory alternatives to constant childbearing, in particular, recourse to natural daughters as successors and the adoption of adult sons. In general, emperors were unwilling to bring Roman law as it related to the family into line with social behaviour. The contrast between legal principles and social realities is nowhere clearer than in the matter of parental authority, though the scale of the contrast has escaped modern commentators. The standard image of the Roman family as a patriarchal household ruled by an authoritarian, elderly *paterfamilias* and including his wife, sons and unmarried daughters, plus his sons' children is untenable. In particular, low life expectancy at birth (about twenty-five), the late age of marriage of men (the late twenties), and therefore the generational age gap (about forty) substantially reduced the effects of paternal authority over sons. Few fathers, around 20 per cent (25 per cent in the case of aristocratic men), were alive at the time of their son's marriage. Women married younger, at 13 or 14 if aristocrats, in their late teens or early twenties otherwise. Many lacked fathers to witness their marriages (in the case of non-aristocratic women, this was true of more than half). As to husband-wife relationships, the effects of the ideology of inferiority and the age differential between wives and husbands have to be weighed against the wife's independent control of her own property after her father's death, her right to divorce and to take much of the (typically modest) dowry.

Given the high rates of parental mortality, extended kinship links and personal reciprocal exchange relationships outside the family assume considerable importance. The latter fall into three main categories: patron/client, patron/protégé (or superior/inferior friends) and equal friends. The emperor was patron to individuals with access to him and to the army and the plebs of Rome in general. Far from trying to eradicate traditional patronage relationships, emperors encouraged their continuation, in part because they were the main mechanism for the recruitment of new members of the imperial elite. A development of the Principate was the wider extension of patronage relationships encompassing the provinces, where imperial officials and successful provincials acted as patronal mediators for the younger generation of potential Roman aristocrats. Vertical patronal links also embraced the 'respectable' sections of the plebs and their social clubs or *collegia* (which provided mutual assistance for their memberships), but bypassed the unemployed and underemployed poor. Nevertheless, the extensiveness of the patronage network was a powerful force for social cohesion.

IV

The religious history of the Principate revolves around three main themes: the stability of the official religion, the confrontation of official and indigenous gods and cults in the localities, and the rise of Christianity. Rome as the increasingly cosmopolitan capital of a vast empire was ever more accessible to religious influences from abroad. Augustus was a religious conservative, as were some of his successors and the senatorial aristocracy as a whole. However, even emperors who were devotees of foreign, especially Egyptian, deities (for example, the Flavians) drew a firm line between their personal religious preferences and the public religion of Rome. Until the early third century no new gods were admitted into the Roman Pantheon with the exception of the Deified Emperors, whose admission was a natural outcome of the transition to monarchy. The admission of Isis and Serapis by Caracalla is an important innovation to imperial tradition, reflecting the Severan dynasty's more elevated view of its religious and political status. For much of our period, however, the commitment of emperors to a changeless state religion which projected an image of stability was unqualified.

The ruler cult was the only Roman cult to become more or less universal. It served three main functions: the diffusion of imperial ideology, the focusing of the loyalty of subjects on the emperor and the social and political advancement of those provincials who presided over its operation. In addition, the western provinces were invaded by the traditional Roman gods, especially the Capitoline Triad (Jupiter, Juno and Minerva), with which emperors and the ruler cult were closely associated. Indigenous religions disintegrated, were simplified and reinterpreted under the impact of Roman religion, particularly in the urban environment, the main area of imperial/local confrontation. However, religious transformation was on the whole the product of long-term peaceful penetration rather than coercion. Unless their moral sensibilities were outraged, as in the extreme case of human sacrifice, the Romans intervened with force only against cults and priesthoods held to be politically subversive. Political considerations led some of Rome's rulers (Caesar, Augustus, Claudius) to favour the Jews, and others (Vespasian, Titus, Hadrian) to repress them. Christianity, identified as a subversive force but not regarded as dangerous, was the main beneficiary of the Roman government's passive acceptance of innovation, the licence it gave to the individual to follow his own religious preferences. Emperors did not 'tolerate' Christianity, they looked the other way. Christianity was officially tolerated only in the aftermath of official persecution, and there was none in the period of the Principate.

Rome the imperial capital felt the full impact of the ensuing changes at all levels when monarchy emerged out of the wreckage of the Republic. In the realm of culture, emperors looked to writers, artists, educators and philosophers, and to their own clients in particular, to promote or at least not undermine the imperial regime and its values. The results are visible in the poetry of Virgil and Horace and the oratory of Pliny, the fates of Ovid, Demetrius the Cynic and Helvidius Priscus the Stoic, the burning of the books of T. Labienus, the career of Quintilian the professor of rhetoric and the overt use of official art as propaganda. But the history of literature, education or architecture cannot be reduced to a study of the personal preferences and relationships of emperors.

Roman emperors lacked any grand design to spread the culture of Rome through the empire. Romanization, better described as the fusion of imperial and local institutions and cultures, was the joint product of central government actions and local initiatives. In the West, a crucial factor was the incidence and depth of urbanization. In African, Spanish and Gallic cities, a Roman-style educational system produced men of culture, many of the most able and ambitious of whom moved to Rome to pursue literary, forensic and political careers. The career of Apuleius, who wrote Latin literature from a provincial base, is one indicator of the special vitality of Romano-African civilization in the latter part of our period – to be set alongside, for example, the brilliant innovations of African mosaicists.

What were the limits of Romanization? The position of Hellenic culture in the East provides a useful parallel. This was predominantly a civic culture. It made little impact on the indigenous cultures of the countryside. Moreover, its advance was resisted by the unique and durable Jewish, Egyptian and Oriental cultures, and by the resilient native traditions of Phoenicia. Finally, the Greek world proved susceptible in a limited way to Roman cultural influence. In the western provinces Rome was the dominant but far from ubiquitous cultural influence. Roman cultural hegemony was exercised principally in the cities and their immediate hinterlands. The possession of Roman culture was another symbol of the status of a community and its leading members, many of whom continued to use the vernacular as the language of common discourse. Roman rule accentuated rather than broke down the divisions between city and country, rich and poor, local elites and the urban and rural masses.

V

The limited cultural penetration of Rome, the cultural diversity of the empire, even in the West, confirm an important feature of Roman rule. By tradition the Romans conceived of the role of government as a limited one. In this regard, there was an essential continuity between Republic and Principate. Emperors were fundamentally conservative: their administrative innovations were limited and betray more interest in controlling their officials than in directing the lives of their subjects. The Augustan conquests were consolidated by the institution of permanent garrisons and the extension of urbanization. These were also the main mechanisms of change in the areas concerned, but the pace and extent of change depended crucially on local initiative. After Rome made its initial impact, Romanization was largely self-directed, a response of local elites to the prospect of enhanced status, wealth and power under the protection of the imperial authority. Finally, soldiers, functionaries and Romanizing elites were not everywhere. Many inhabitants of the empire had little experience or conception of Rome.

Bibliography

Alföldy, G. (1968) *Die Hilfstruppen der römischen Provinz Germania Inferior.*
    Epigr. Stud. 6. Düsseldorf
Alföldy, G. (1980) 'Die Stellung der Ritter in der Führungsschicht des Imperiums
    Romanum', *Chiron* 11: 169-215
Alföldy, G. (1985) *The Social History of Rome.* London
Ampolo, C. (1980) 'Le condizioni materiali della produzione. Agricoltura e
    paesaggio agrario', *Dial. d. arch.* 1: 15-46
Anderson, M. (1980) *Approaches to the History of the Western Family,
    1500-1914.* London
Andreau, J. (1983) 'A propos de la vie financière à Pouzzoles: Cluvius et
    Vestorius', in *Le dernier siècle de la République romaine et l'époque
    augustéenne,* Strasbourg, 47-62
Andreau, J. (1985) 'Les financiers romains entre la ville et la campagne', in
    Leveau (1985), 177-96
Annequin, J. (n.d.) 'Magie et organisation du monde chez Apulée', in *Religions,
    pouvoir, rapports sociaux.* Centre de recherches d'histoire ancienne, 32, no.
    237: 173-208
Armées et Fiscalité (1977) *Armées et fiscalité dans le monde antique, Paris 14-16
    Octobre 1976.* Paris
D'Arms, J.H. (1981) *Commerce and Social Standing in Ancient Rome.*
    Cambridge, Mass.
D'Arms, J.H. and Kopff, E.C. eds. (1980) *Roman Seaborne Commerce, MAAR*
    36. Rome
Ausbuettel, F. (1982) *Untersuchungen zu Vereinen im Westen des römisches
    Reiches.* Frankfurt
Avi-Yonah, M. (1961) *Oriental Art in Roman Palestine.* Rome
Aymard, M. (1973) 'Mesures et interprétations de la croissance: Rendements et
    productivité agricole dans l'Italie moderne', *Annales ESC* 28: 475-98
Baillie-Reynolds, P.K. (1926) *The Vigiles of Imperial Rome.* Oxford
Barbagallo, C. (1904) 'La produzione media relativa dei cereali e della vite nella
    Grecia nella Sicilia e nell'Italia antica', *Riv.Stor.Ant.* 8: 477-504
Barker, G.W., Lloyd, J., Webley, D. (1978) 'A classical landscape in Molise',
    PBSR 46: 35-51
Barnes, T.D. (1968) 'Legislation against the Christians', *JRS* 58: 32-50
Barnes, T.D. (1974) 'Who were the nobility in the Roman empire?', *Phoenix* 28:
    444-9
Bayet, J. (1969) *Histoire politique et psychologique de la religion romaine,* ed. 2.
    Paris
Beaujeu, J. (1955) *La religion romaine à l'apogée de l'empire I: La politique
    religieuse des Antonins (96-192).* Paris

Beck, R. (1984) 'Mithraism since Franz Cumont', *ANRW* II 17.4: 2002-2115

Benabou, M. (1976) *La résistance africaine à la romanisation*. Paris.

Béranger, J. (1953) *Recherches sur l'aspect idéologique du Principat*. Basel

Bérard, F. (1984) 'La carrière de Plotius Grypus et le ravitaillement de l'armée impériale en campagne', *MEFR* 96: 259-324.

Bernhardt, R. (1971) *Imperium und Eleutheria*. Hamburg

Bird, H.W. (1984) *Sextus Aurelius Victor. A Historiographical Study*. Liverpool

Birley, E. (1953) 'Senators in the emperor's service', *PBA* 39: 197-214

Blagg, T.F.C. and King, A.C. eds. (1984) *Military and Civilian in Roman Britain, BAR* 136

Boak, A.E.R. (1935) *Soknopaiou Nesos: the University of Michigan Excavations at Dime in 1931-32*. Ann Arbor

Boethius, A. (1960) *The Golden House of Nero*. Ann Arbor

Boethius, A., Ward-Perkins, J.B. (1970) *Etruscan and Roman Architecture*. London

Bonner, S.F. (1949) *Roman Declamation in the Late Republic and Early Empire*, Liverpool

Bonner, S.F. (1977) *Education in Ancient Rome*, London

Boswell, J.E. (1984) '*Expositio* and *oblatio*: the abandonment of children and the ancient and medieval family', *AHR* 89: 10-33

Boulanger, A. (1923) *Aelius Aristide et la sophistique dans la province d'Asie au IIe siècle de notre ère*. Paris

Boulvert, G. (1970) *Esclaves et affranchis impériaux sous le Haut-Empire romain: rôle politique et administratif*. Naples

Boulvert, G. (1974) *Domestique et fonctionnaire sous le Haut-Empire romain: la condition de l'affranchi et de l'esclave du prince*. Naples

Bowersock, G.W. (1965) *Augustus and the Greek World*. Oxford

Bowersock, G.W. (1969) *Greek Sophists in the Roman Empire*. Oxford

Bowman, A.K. (1971) *The Town Councils of Roman Egypt*. Toronto

Bowman, A.K. (1983) *The Roman Writing Tablets from Vindolanda*. London

Bradley, K.R. (1984) *Slaves and Masters in the Roman Empire*. Brussels

Bradley, K.R. (1985) 'Child care at Rome: the role of men', *Historical Reflexions – Reflexions historiques* 12: 485-523

Bradley, K.R. (1986) 'Wet-nursing at Rome: a study in social relations', in Rawson (1986)

Branigan, K. (1982) 'Celtic Farm to Roman Villa', in Miles (1982), 81-95

Braudel, F. (1975) *The Mediterranean and the Mediterranean World in the Age of Philip II*. London

Brilliant, R. (1963) *Gesture and Rank in Roman Art*. New Haven

Brockmeyer, N. (1968) *Arbeitsorganisation und ökonomisches Denken in der Gutswirtschaft des römischen Reiches*. Bochum

Brogan, O. (1965) 'Henscir El-Ausaf by Tigi (Tripolitania) and some related tombs in the Tunisian Gefara', *Libya Antiqua* 2: 47-56

Brogan, O., Reynolds, J.M. (1985) 'An inscription from the Wadi Antar', in Buck, D.J., Mattingley, D.J., eds., *Town and Country in Roman Tripolitania: papers in honour of Olwen Hackett, BAR* 274: 13-21

Brown, P. (1968) 'Christianity and Local Culture in Late Roman Africa', *JRS* 58: 85-95

Brown, P. (1978) *The Making of Late Antiquity*. Cambridge, Mass.

Brunt, P.A. (1961) 'The lex Valeria Cornelia', *JRS* 61: 71-83

Brunt, P.A. (1965) ' "Amicitia" in the late Roman Republic', *PCPhS* 11: 1-20 (repr. in Seager, R., ed., *The Crisis of the Roman Republic*, Cambridge, 1969, 199-218)

Brunt, P.A. (1966a) 'The "Fiscus" and its Development', *JRS* 56: 75-91.

Brunt, P.A. (1966b) 'Procuratorial Jurisdiction', *Latomus* 25: 161-89

Brunt, P.A. (1969) 'The equites in the late Republic', in Seager, R., ed., *The Crisis of the Roman Republic*, Cambridge, 83-115

Brunt, P.A. (1971) *Italian Manpower, 225 BC – AD 14*. Oxford

Brunt, P.A. (1975a) 'The Administration of Roman Egypt', *JRS* 65: 124-47.

Brunt, P.A. (1975b) 'Stoicism and the Principate', *PBSR* 43: 7-35

Brunt, P.A. (1975c) 'Two great Roman landowners', *Latomus* 34: 619-35

Brunt, P.A. (1976) 'The Romanization of the Local Ruling Classes in the Roman Empire', in Pippidi (1976), 161-74

Brunt, P.A. (1978) 'Laus Imperii', in Garnsey and Whittaker (1978), 159-92

Brunt, P.A. (1979) 'Marcus Aurelius and the Christians', in Deroux, D., ed., *Studies in Latin Literature and Roman History I*: 483-520

Brunt, P.A. (1980) 'Free labour and public works at Rome', *JRS* 70: 81-100

Brunt, P.A. (1981) 'The Revenues of Rome'. Review Discussion of Neesen (1980), *JRS* 71: 161-72

Brunt, P.A. (1983) 'Princeps and Equites', *JRS* 73: 42-75

Buckland, W.W. (1908) *The Roman Law of Slavery*. Cambridge

Buckland, W.W. (1963) *A Text-book of Roman Law from Augustus to Justinian*, 3rd ed. rev. P. Stein. Cambridge

Buckler, W.H. (1923) 'Labour disputes in the province of Asia', in Buckler, W.H., Calder, W.M., eds., *Anatolian Studies presented to W.M. Ramsay*, Manchester, 27-50

Burnand, Y. (1982) 'Senatores Romani ex provinciis Galliarum orti', in *Atti del Colloquio Internazionale AIEGL su Epigrafia e ordine senatorio*. Roma, 14-20 maggio 1981. 2 vols. Rome

Burton, G.P. (1975) 'Proconsuls, Assizes, and the Administration of Justice under the Empire', *JRS* 65: 92-106

Burton, G.P. (1976) 'The issuing of mandata to proconsuls and a new inscription from Cos', *ZPE* 21:63-8

Burton, G.P. (1979) 'The curator rei publicae', *Chiron* 9: 465-88

Cagnat, R. (1913) *L'Armée romaine d'Afrique*. Paris

Campbell, J.B. (1975) 'Who were the "Viri Militares"?', *JRS* 65: 11-31

Campbell, J.B. (1984) *The Emperor and the Roman Army, 31 BC – AD 235*. Oxford

Carandini, A. (1981) 'Sviluppo e crisi delle manifatture rurali e urbane', in Giardina and Schiavone (1981), II 249-60

Carandini, A. (1983) 'Columella's Vineyard and the Rationality of the Roman Economy', *Opus* 2, 1: 177-204

Carandini, A., Ricci, A. (1984) *Sette Finestre: una villa schiavistica nell' Etruria Romana*, 3 vols. Modena

Carandini, A., Tatton-Brown, T. (1980) 'Excavations at the Roman villa of "Sette Finestre" in Etruria, 1975-9: First Interim Report', in Painter, K., ed., *Roman Villas in Italy*, London

Carcopino, J. (1940) *Daily Life in Ancient Rome*. New Haven

Carrié, J.-M. (1977) 'Le rôle économique de l'armée dans l'Egypte romaine', in Armées et Fiscalité (1977), 373-93

Cartledge, P.A., Harvey, F.D., eds. (1985) *Crux: Essays presented to G.E.M. de Ste. Croix on his 75th birthday*. Sidmouth, Devon

Cary, M. (1949) *The Geographic Background of Greek and Roman History*. Oxford

Casson, L. (1954) 'The grain trade of the Hellenistic World', *TAPA* 85: 168ff.

Casson, L. (1971) *Ships and Seamanship in the Ancient World*. New Jersey

Casson, L. (1980) 'The Role of the State in Rome's Grain Trade' in D'Arms and Kopff (1980), 21-33

Chadwick, N.K. (1966) *The Druids*. Cardiff

Champlin, E. (1980) *Fronto and Antonine Rome*. Cambridge, Mass.

Champlin, E. (1981) 'Owners and Neighbours at Ligures Baebiani', *Chiron* 11: 239-64

Champlin, E. (1983) 'Figlinae Marcianae', *Athenaeum* 61: 257-64

Chastagnol, A. (1971) 'Les modes d'accès au sénat romain au début de l'Empire', *Bull. Soc. Antiq. France*, 283-310

Chastagnol, A. (1973) 'La naissance de l'ordo senatorius', *MEFR* 85: 583-607

Chastagnol, A. (1975) 'Latus clavus et adlection. L'accès des hommes nouveaux au sénat romain sous le Haut-Empire', *RHD* 53: 375-94

Clark, C., Haswell, M. (1970) *The Economics of Subsistence Agriculture* ed. 4. London

Clarke, M.L. (1971) *Higher Education in the Ancient World*. London.

Clavel-Lévêque, M. (1972) 'Le syncrétisme gallo-romaine, structures et finalités', in F. Sartori, ed., *Praelectiones Patavinae*, Univ. Padova, Pubbl. Ist. di Storia antica, 9: 51-134

Clemente, G. (1972) 'Il patronato nei collegia dell'Impero Romano', *SCO* 21: 142-229

Cohen, B. (1975) 'La notion d'"ordo" dans la Rome antique', *Bull. Assoc. Budé* 4th Ser. 1: 259-82

Colledge, M.A.R. (1976) *The Art of Palmyra*. London

Collinet, P. (1925) *Histoire de l'école de droit de Beyrouth*. Paris

Cooper, J.P. (1976) 'Patterns of inheritance and settlement by great landowners from the fifteenth to the eighteenth centuries', in *Family and Inheritance: Rural Society in Western Europe, 1200-1800*, ed. J. Goody et al. Cambridge

Corbett, P.E. (1930) *The Roman Law of Marriage*. Oxford

Corbier, M. (1978) 'Dévaluations et fiscalité (161-235)', in *Les Dévaluations à Rome: époque républicaine et impériale* (Rome, 13-15 Nov. 1975), 227-48

Cotton, H. (1981) *Documentary Letters of Recommendation in Latin from the Roman Empire*. Königstein

Cramer, F.H. (1954) *Astrology in Roman Law and Politics*. Philadelphia.

Crawford, D.J. (1976) 'Imperial Estates', in Finley (1976), 35-70

Crawford, M.H. (1970) 'Money and Exchange in the Roman World', *JRS* 60: 40-48

Crawford, M.H. (1978) 'Greek Intellectuals and the Roman Aristocracy in the first century BC', in Garnsey and Whittaker (1978), 193-208, 330-8

Crawford, M.H., ed. (1983) *Sources for Ancient History*. Cambridge

Crawford, M.H. (1985) *Coinage and Money under the Roman Republic: Italy and the Mediterranean Economy*. London

Crawford, M.H., ed. (1986) *L'Impero Romano e le strutture economiche e sociali delle province.* Como

Crook, J.A. (1955) *Consilium Principis.* Cambridge

Crook, J.A. (1967a) *Law and Life of Rome.* London

Crook, J.A. (1967b) *'Patria potestas', CQ* 17: 113-22

Crook, J.A. (1973) 'Intestacy in Roman society', *PCPhS* 19: 38-44

Crook, J.A. (1986a) 'Women in Roman Succession', in Rawson (1986)

Crook, J.A. (1986b) 'Female inadequacy and the *Senatusconsultum Velleianum*', in Rawson (1986), 83-92

Csillag, P. (1976) *The Augustan Laws on Family Relations.* Budapest

Darling, M.J. (1977) 'Pottery from early military sites in West Britain', in Dore and Greene (1977), 57-100

Daube, D. (1947) 'Did Macedo murder his father?', *ZSS* 65: 261-311

Daube, D. (1969) *Roman Law: Linguistic, Social and Philosophical Aspects.* Edinburgh

Davies, J.L. (1984) 'Soldiers, peasants and markets in Wales and the marches', in Blagg and King (1984), 93-127

Davies, R.W. (1971) 'The Roman Military Diet', *Britannia* 2: 122-42

Debord, P. (1982) *Aspects sociaux et économiques de la vie religieuse dans L'Anatolie Gréco-Romaine.* Leiden.

Demougin, S. (1982) 'Uterque ordo: les rapports entre l'ordre sénatorial et l'ordre équestre sous les Julio-Claudiens' in *Epigrafia e ordine senatorio, Tituli* 4: 73-104

Den Boer, W. (1972) *Some Minor Roman Historians.* Leuven

Devijver, H. (1976-80) *Prosopographia Militiarum Equestrium quae fuerunt ab Augusto ad Gallienum.* 3 vols. Leuven

Dilke, O.A.W. (1985) *Greek and Roman Maps.* London

Dixon, S. (1985a) 'Polybius on Roman women and property', *AJP* 106: 147-70

Dixon, S. (1985b) 'The marriage alliance in the Roman elite', *Journal of Family History* 10: 353-78

Dobson, B. (1974a) 'The centurionate and social mobility during the Principate', in Nicolet, C., ed., *Recherches sur les structures sociales dans l'antiquité classique*, 99-115

Dobson, B. (1974b) 'The significance of the centurion and "primipilaris" in the Roman army and administration', *ANRW* II 1: 392-434

Dodds, E.R. (1965) *Pagan and Christian in an Age of Anxiety.* Cambridge

Dore, J., Greene, K., eds. (1977) *Roman Pottery Studies in Britain and Beyond. BAR* 30

Drachmann, A.B. (1922) *Atheism in Classical Antiquity.* London

Drinkwater, J.F. (1979) 'A note on local careers in the Three Gauls under the early Empire', *Britannia* 10: 89-100

Drinkwater, J.F. (1983) *Roman Gaul. The Three Provinces, 58 BC – AD 260.* London

Duff, A.M. (1928) *Freedmen in the Early Roman Empire.* Oxford

Dunbabin, K.M.D. (1978) *The Mosaics of Roman North Africa: Studies in Iconography and Patronage.* Oxford

Duncan-Jones, R.P. (1963) 'Wealth and munificence in Roman Africa', *PBSR* 31: 159-77

Duncan-Jones, R.P. (1967) 'Equestrian rank in the cities of the African provinces under the Principate: an epigraphic survey', *PBSR* 35: 147-88

Duncan-Jones, R.P. (1972) 'Patronage and city privileges – the case of Giufi', *Epigraphische Studien* 9: 12-16

Duncan-Jones, R.P. (1976a) 'Some Configurations of Landholding in the Roman Empire', in Finley (1976), 7-34

Duncan-Jones, R.P. (1976b) 'The price of wheat in Roman Egypt under the Principate', *Chiron* 6: 241ff.

Duncan-Jones, R.P. (1982) *Economy of the Roman Empire*. Rev. ed. Cambridge

Durry, M. (1938) *Les Cohortes prétoriennes*. Paris

Duthoy, R. (1974) 'La fonction sociale de l'Augustalité', *Epigraphica* 36: 135-54

Duthoy, R. (1978) 'Les Augustales', *ANRW* II 16.2: 1254-1309

Duthoy, R. (1979) 'Curatores rei publicae en Occident durant le Principat', *Ancient Society* 10: 171-239

Easterling, P.E., Knox, B.M.W., eds. (1985) *The Cambridge History of Classical Literature, I: Greek Literature*. Cambridge

Eck, W. (1974) 'Beforderungskriterien innerhalb der senatorischen Laufbahn, dargestellt an der Zeit von 69 bis 138 n.Chr.' *ANRW* II 1 158-228

Eck, W. (1979) *Die staatliche Organisation Italiens in der hohen Kaiserzeit*. Munich

Engels, D. (1980) 'The problem of female infanticide in the Greco-Roman world', *CP* 75: 112-20

Engels, D. (1984) 'The use of historical demography in ancient history', *CQ* 34: 386-93

D'Escurac, P. (1974) 'Pour une étude sociale de l'Apologée d'Apulée', *Ant.Afr.* 8: 89-101

D'Escurac, P. (1976) *La préfecture de l'annone, service administratif impérial d'Auguste à Constantin*. Paris

Etienne, R. (1958) *Le culte impérial dans la péninsule ibérique d'Auguste à Dioclétien*. Paris

Etienne, R. (1973) 'Les syncrétismes religieux dans la péninsule ibérique à l'époque impériale', in *Les Syncrétismes dans les religions grecque et romaine (Colloque de Strasbourg, 9-11 juin, 1971)*, Paris, 153-63

Etienne, R., Fabre, G., Le Roux, P., Tranoy, A. (1976) 'Les dimensions sociales de la romanisation dans la péninsule ibérique des origines à la fin de l'Empire', in Pippidi (1976), 95-107

Evans, J.K. (1980) 'Plebs rustica II', *Am.Jl.Anc.Hist.* 5: 134-75

Evans, J.K. (1981) 'Wheat production and its social consequences in the Roman world', *CQ* 31: 428-42

Eyben, E. (1980-81) 'Family planning in Graeco-Roman antiquity', *Ancient Society* 11-12: 5-82

Fairweather, J. (1981) *Seneca the Elder*. Cambridge

Fears, J.R. (1977) *Princeps a diis electus. MAAR* 26. Rome

Fears, J.R. (1981) 'The cult of Jupiter and Roman imperial ideology', *ANRW* II 17.1: 3-141

Février, P.-A. (1976) 'Religion et domination dans l'Afrique romaine', *DHA* 21: 305-36

Fink, R.O. (1971) *Roman Military Documents on Papyri*. American Philological Association

Finley, M.I. (1965) 'Technical Innovation and Economic Progress in the Ancient

World', *Ec.Hist.Rev.* 18: 29-45. Reprinted with corrections in Finley (1981)

Finley, M.I., ed. (1968) *Slavery in Classical Antiquity*. Cambridge

Finley, M.I., ed. (1974) *Studies in Ancient Society*. London

Finley, M.I., ed. (1976) *Studies in Roman Property*. Cambridge

Finley, M.I. (1980) *Ancient Slavery and Modern Ideology*, London

Finley, M.I. (1981) *Economy and Society in Ancient Greece*, Shaw, B.D., Saller, R.P., eds. London

Finley, M.I. (1985a) *The Ancient Economy*. Rev. ed. London

Finley, M.I. (1985b) *Ancient History: Evidence and Models*. London

Fishwick, D. (1978) 'The development of provincial ruler worship in the western Roman empire', *ANRW* II 16. 1, 1201-53

Flandrin, J.-L. (1979) *Families in Former Times*. Cambridge

Flory, M. (1978) 'Family in *familia*: kinship and community in slavery', *Am. Jl. Anc. Hist.* 3: 78-95

Foxhall, L., Forbes, H.A. (1982) 'Sitometreia: the Role of Grain as a Staple Food in Classical Antiquity', *Chiron* 12: 41-90

Frederiksen, M.W. (1976) 'Changes in the patterns of settlement', *Hellenismus in Mittelitalien, Koll. in Göttingen, Juni 1974, Abh. Akad. Wiss. Gött.*, Phil.Hist. Kl. Dr. Folge, 97: 341-55

Frederiksen, M.W. (1981) 'I cambiamenti delle strutture agrarie nella tarda repubblica; la Campania', in Giardina and Schiavone (1981), 265-88

Freeman, D. (1973) 'Kinship, attachment behaviour and the primary bond', in Goody, J., ed., *The Character of Kinship*, Cambridge, 109-19

Frend, W.H.C. (1965) *Martyrdom and Persecution in the Early Church*. Oxford

Frend, W.H.C. (1984) *The Rise of Christianity*. London

Frere, S. (1978) *Britannia*. 2nd ed. London

Frézouls, E. (1959) (1961) 'Recherches sur les théâtres de l'Orient Syrien', *Syria* 36: 202-27; 38: 54-86

Friedlaender, L. (1908-13) *Roman Life and Manners under the Early Empire*, 7th ed. transl. J.H. Freese. London

Frier, B.W. (1982) 'Roman Life Expectancy: Ulpian's evidence', *HSCP* 86: 213-51

Frier, B.W. (1983) 'Roman Life Expectancy: the Pannonian evidence', *Phoenix* 37: 328-44

Fulford, M. (1984) 'Demonstrating Britannia's economic dependence in the first and second centuries', in Blagg and King (1984), 129-42

Gabba, E. (1986) 'La Sicilia Romana', in Crawford (1986), 71-86

Gagé, J. (1964) *Les classes sociales dans l'Empire romain*. Paris

Galsterer, H. (1986) 'Roman Law in the Provinces: some problems of transmission', in Crawford (1986), 13-28

Garnsey, P. (1968a) 'Trajan's Alimenta. Some problems', *Historia* 17: 367-81

Garnsey, P. (1968b) 'The Criminal Jurisdiction of Governors', *JRS* 58: 51-9

Garnsey, P. (1970) *Social Status and Legal Privilege in the Roman Empire*. Oxford

Garnsey, P. (1971) 'Taxatio and Pollicitatio in Roman Africa', *JRS* 61: 116-29

Garnsey, P. (1974) 'Aspects of the Decline of the Urban Aristocracy in the Empire', *ANRW* II 1 229-52

Garnsey, P. (1975) 'Descendants of Freedman in Local Politics: some criteria', in Levick, B., ed., *The Ancient Historian and his Materials. Essays in honour of C.E. Stevens on his 70th Birthday*, Farnborough, 167-80

Garnsey, P. (1976) 'Urban Property Investment', in Finley (1976), 123-36

Garnsey, P. (1978) 'Rome's African Empire under the Principate', in Garnsey and Whittaker (1978), 223-54, 343-54

Garnsey, P. (1979) 'Where did Italian Peasants Live?' *PCPhS* 29: 1-25

Garnsey, P. (1980a) 'Non-Slave Labour in the Roman World', in Garnsey, ed., (1980b), 34-47

Garnsey, P., ed. (1980b) *Non-Slave Labour in the Greco-Roman World*. Cambridge

Garnsey, P. (1981) 'Independent freedmen and the economy of Roman Italy under the Principate', *Klio* 63: 359-71.

Garnsey, P. (1983a) 'Grain for Rome', in Garnsey, Hopkins & Whittaker (1983), 118-30

Garnsey, P. (1983b) 'Introduction' and 'Famine in Rome', in Garnsey and Whittaker (1983), 1-5, 56-65

Garnsey, P. (1984) 'Religious Toleration in Classical Antiquity', in W.J. Sheils, ed., *Persecution and Toleration. Studies in Church History* 21: 1-28

Garnsey, P. (1986a) 'Famine in the ancient Mediterranean' *History Today* 36: 24-30

Garnsey, P. (1986b) 'Mountain Economies in Southern Europe: Thoughts on the early history, continuity and individuality of Mediterranean upland pastoralism', in Mattmüller, M., ed., *Wirtschaft und Gesellschaft in Berggebieten, Itinera* 5/6 (1986), Basel: 7-29

Garnsey, P., Hopkins, K., Whittaker, C.R., eds. (1983). *Trade in the Ancient Economy*. London

Garnsey, P., Saller R. (1982) *The Early Principate, Augustus to Trajan. Greece and Rome: New surveys in the classics* No. 15. Oxford

Garnsey, P., Whittaker, C.R., eds. (1978) *Imperialism in the Ancient World*. Cambridge

Garnsey, P., Whittaker, C.R., eds. (1983). *Trade and Famine in Classical Antiquity*. Cambridge

Gascou, J. (1972) *La politique municipale de l'empire romain en Afrique proconsulaire de Trajan à Septime-Sévère*. Paris

Gaunt, D. (1983) 'The property and kin relationships of retired farmers in northern and central Europe', in Wall et al. (1983)

Gauthier, Ph. (1985) *Les cités grecques et leurs bienfaiteurs. BCH* suppl. XII. Paris

Gentry, A.P. (1976) *Roman Military Stone-built Granaries in Britain. BAR* 32. Oxford

Gérard, J. (1976). *Juvenal et la réalité contemporaine*. Paris

Gerov, B. (1980) *Beiträge zur Geschichte der römischen Provinzen Moesien und Thrakien*. Amsterdam

Giacchero, M. (1974) *Edictum Diocletiani et collegarum de pretiis rerum venalium*. 2 vols. Genoa

Giardina, A., Schiavone A., eds. (1981) *Società romana e produzione schiavistica*. 3 vols. Rome

Giddens, A., Held, D., eds. (1982) *Classes, Power and Conflict*. London

Gilliam, J.F. (1950) 'Some Latin military papyri from Dura', *YCS* 11: 171-252

Giovannini, A. (1978) *Rome et la circulation monétaire en Grèce au IIe siècle avant Jésus-Christ*. Basel

Gold, B.K., ed. (1982) *Literary and Artistic Patronage in Ancient Rome*. Austin

Goodman, M. (1983) *State and Society in Roman Galilee, AD 132-212*. Totowa, New Jersey

Goody, J. (1976) *Production and Reproduction*. Cambridge

Goody, J. (1983) *The Development of the Family and Marriage in Europe*. Cambridge

Gordon, M.L. (1931) 'The freedman's son in municipal life', *JRS* 21: 65-77

Gordon, R.L. (1972) 'Mithraism and Roman Society', *Religion* 2: 92-121

Gordon, R.L. (1975) 'Franz Cumont and the doctrines of Mithraism', in J.R. Hinnells, ed., *Mithraic Studies: Proceedings of the First International Congress of Mithraic Studies*, 2 vols., Manchester: 215-48.

Goudineau, Chr. (1980) 'Sources et problèmes', in Duby, G., ed., *Histoire de la France urbaine*, I: *La ville antique*. Paris

Graindor, P. (1930) *Hérode Atticus et sa famille*. Cairo

Gratwick, A.S. (1984) 'Free or not so free? Wives and daughters in the Late Roman Republic', in E.M. Craik, ed., *Marriage and Property*, Aberdeen: 30-53

Gren, E. (1941) *Kleinasien und der Ostbalkan in der Wirtschaftlichen Entwicklung der römischen Kaiserzeit*. Uppsala

Grew, F., Hobley, B. (1985) *Roman Urban Topography and the Western Empire. CBA Res. Rept.* No. 59. London

Griffin, J. (1976) 'Augustan Poetry and the Life of Luxury', *JRS* 66: 87-105

Griffin, M. (1972) 'The Elder Seneca and Spain', *JRS* 62: 1-24

Griffin, M. (1976) *Seneca, a philosopher in politics*. Oxford

Hajnal, J. (1965) 'European marriage patterns in perspective', in Glass, D.V., Eversley, D.E.C., eds., *Population in History*, London: 101-43

Hajnal, J. (1983) 'Two kinds of pre-industrial household formation system', in Wall et al. (1983): 65-104

Hallet, J.P. (1984) *Fathers and Daughters in Roman Society: Women and the Elite Family*. Princeton

Halsberghe, G.H. (1972) *The Cult of Sol Invictus*. Leiden.

Halstead, P. (1981) 'From determinism to uncertainty; social storage and the rise of the Minoan palace', in A. Sheridan, G. Bailey, eds., *Economic Archaeology, BAR* Int. Ser. 96: 187-213

Hammond, M. (1957) 'Composition of the senate, AD 68-235', *JRS* 47: 74-81

Hands, A.R. (1968) *Charities and Social Aid in Greece and Rome*. London

Hansen, S.A. (1965) 'Changes in the wealth and the demographic characteristics of the Danish aristocracy, 1470-1720', in *The Third International Congress of Economic History* III, Munich: 91-102

Hardie, A. (1983) *Statius and the Silvae: Poets, Patrons and Epideixis in the Graeco-Roman World*. Liverpool

Harper, G.M. (1928). 'Village Administration in the Roman province of Syria', *YCS* 1: 105-68

Harrauer, H., Sijpesteijn, P.J. (1985) 'Ein neues Dokument zu Roms Indienhandel. P. Vindob. G 40822', *Anz. d. Öst. Akad. Wiss., Phil.-Hist. Kl.* 122: 124-55

Harris, W.V. (1980) 'Towards a study of the Roman slave trade', in D'Arms and Kopff (1980): 117-40

Harris, W.V. (1982) 'The theoretical possibility of extensive infanticide in the Graeco-Roman world', *CQ* 32: 114-16

Hatzfeld, J. (1919) *Les trafiquants italiens dans l'Orient hellénique*. Paris

Helen, T. (1975) *The Organization of Roman Brick Production in the First and Second Centuries AD. Annales Academiae Scientiarum Fennicae.*

Henig, M. (1984) *Religion in Roman Britain*. London

Hicks, R.D. (1911) *Stoic and Epicurean*. London

Hill, H. (1969) 'Nobilitas in the imperial period', *Historia* 18: 230-50

Hobson, D.W. (1985) 'House and Household in Roman Egypt', *YCS* 28: 211-29

Hopkins, K. (1965a) 'Age of Roman girls at marriage', *Population Studies* 18: 309-27

Hopkins, K. (1965b) 'Contraception in the Roman empire', *Comparative Studies in Society and History* 8: 124-51

Hopkins, K. (1966) 'On the probable age structure of the Roman population', *Population Studies* 20: 245-64

Hopkins, K. (1974) 'Elite mobility in the Roman empire', in Finley (1974), 103-20

Hopkins, K. (1978a) *Conquerors and Slaves*. Cambridge

Hopkins, K, (1978b) 'Economic Growth and Towns in Classical Antiquity', in Abrams, P., Wrigley, E.A., eds., *Towns in Societies*, Cambridge: 35-77

Hopkins, K. (1980) 'Taxes and Trade in the Roman Empire (200 BC – AD 400)', *JRS* 70: 101-25

Hopkins, K. (1983a) 'Introduction' in Garnsey, Hopkins & Whittaker (eds.) (1983), ix-xxv

Hopkins, K. (1983b) 'Models, ships and staples', in Garnsey, Whittaker (1983), 84-109

Hopkins, K. (1983c) *Death and Renewal*. Cambridge

Humbert, M. (1972) *Le remariage à Rome: Etude d'histoire juridique et sociale*. Milan

Humphreys, S.C. (1978) *Anthropology and the Greeks*. London

Hurst, H.R. (1985) *Kingsholm*. Gloucester

Huvelin, P. (1929) *Etudes d'histoire du droit commercial romain*. Paris

Jacques, F. (1984) *Le privilège de liberté: politique impériale et autonomie municipale dans les cités de l'Occident romain*. Paris

Jameson, M.H. (1977-78) 'Agriculture and Slavery in classical Athens', *CJ* 73: 122-45

Johne, K.-P., Köhn, J., Weber, V. (1983) *Die Kolonen in Italien und den westlichen Provinzen des römischen Reiches*. Berlin

Johnson, W.R. (1976) *Darkness Visible, a Study of Virgil's Aeneid*. Berkeley

Jolowicz, H.F., Nicholas, B. (1972) *Historical Introduction to the Study of Roman Law*. Oxford

Jones, A.H.M. (1940) *The Greek City from Alexander to Justinian*. Oxford

Jones, A.H.M. (1956) 'Slavery in the ancient world', *Ec.Hist.Rev.* 9: 185-99, repr. in Finley (1968), 1-15

Jones, A.H.M. (1960) *Studies in Roman Government*. Oxford

Jones, A.H.M. (1964) *The Later Roman Empire*. Oxford

Jones, A.H.M. (1971) *Cities of the Eastern Roman Provinces*. 2nd ed. Oxford

Jones, A.H.M. (1974) *The Roman Economy. Studies in ancient economic and administrative history*, ed. P.A. Brunt. Oxford

Jones, C.P. (1971) *Plutarch and Rome*. Oxford

Jones, C.P. (1978) *The Roman World of Dio Chrysostom*. Cambridge, Mass.

Jones, G.B.D. (1978) 'Concept and Development in Roman Frontiers', *Bull. Ryl. Libr.* 60: 116-44

Jones, G.B.D. (1984) 'Becoming different without knowing it. The role and development of vici', in Blagg and King (1984), 75-91

Jones, M.K. (1981) 'The development of crop husbandry', in Jones, M.K. and Dimbleby, G.W., *The Environment of Man: The Iron Age to the Anglo-Saxon Period, BAR* 87: 95-127

Jones, M.K. (1982) 'Crop Production in Roman Britain', in Miles, D., ed., *The Romano-British Countryside: Studies in Rural Settlement and Economy*, Pt.I, *BAR* 103: 97-108

Juster, J. (1914) *Les juifs dans l'empire romain: leur condition juridique, économique et sociale*. Paris

Kampen, N. (1981) *Image and Status: Roman Working Women in Ostia*. Berlin

Kaser, M. (1971-5) *Das römische Privatrecht*, 2 vols. 2nd ed. Munich.

Kaufman, R. (1974) 'The patron-client concept and macro-politics: prospects and problems', *CSSH* 16: 284-308

Kennedy, G. (1972) *The Art of Rhetoric in the Roman World*. Princeton

Kenney, E.J., ed. (1982) *The Cambridge History of Classical Literature, II: Latin Literature*

Kenney, E.J. (1984) *The Ploughman's Lunch: Moretum; a poem ascribed to Virgil*. Bristol

Keppie, L. (1983) *Colonisation and Veteran Settlement in Italy 47-14 BC.* London

Kloft, H. (1970) *Liberalitas Principis*. Boehlau

Klotz, A. (1931) 'Die geographischen commentarii des Agrippa und ihre Uberreste', *Klio* 24: 38-58, 386-466

Kolendo, J. (1980) *L'agricoltura nell' Italia romana. Tecniche agrarie e progresso economico dalla tarda repubblica al principato*. Rome

Kraut, B.H. (1984) 'Seven Heidelberg papyri concerning the office of exegetes', *ZPE* 55: 167-90

Kuehn, T. (1981) 'Women, marriage, and patria potestas in late medieval Florence', *RHDFE* 49: 127-47

Labriolle, P. de (1948) *La réaction paienne. Etude sur la polémique antichrétienne du Ier au VIe siècle*. 2nd ed. Paris

Lambrino, S. (1965) 'Les cultes indigènes sous Trajan et Hadrien', in *Les empereurs romains d'Espagne (Colloques Int. du CNRS)*, Paris: 223-39

Landels, J.G. (1978) *Engineering in the Ancient World*. London

Langhammer, W. (1973) *Die rechtliche und soziale Stellung der Magistratus municipalis und der Decuriones*. Wiesbaden

Laslett, P., ed. (1972) *Household and Family in Past Time*. Cambridge

Laslett, P. (1983) 'Family and household as work group: areas of traditional Europe compared', in Wall et al. (1983): 513-63

Lasserre, Fr. (1982) 'Strabon devant l'Empire romain', *ANRW* II.30: 867-96

Latte, K. (1960) *Römische Religionsgeschichte*. Munich

Le Gall, J. (1975) *La religion romaine de l'époque de Cato l'Ancien au règne de l'empereur Commode*. Paris

Leglay, M. (1966) *Saturne Africaine*. Paris

Le Roux, P. (1977) 'L'armée de la péninsule ibérique et la vie économique sous le

Haut-Empire', in *Armées et fiscalité* (1977), 341-72

Le Roux, P., Tranoy, A. (1973) 'Rome et les indigènes dans le nord-ouest de la péninsule ibérique. Problèmes de l'epigraphie et d'histoire', *Mel.Casa Vel.* 9: 177-231

Lesquier, J. (1898) *L'armée romaine d'Egypte d'Auguste à Dioclétien.* Paris

Letta, C. (1984) 'Amministrazione Romana e culti locali in età altoimperiale: il caso della Gallia', *Riv.Stor.Ital.* 96:1001-24

Leveau, Ph. (1983) 'La ville antique, "ville de consommation"? Parasitisme social et économie antique', *Etudes rurales* 89-91: 275-89

Leveau, Ph. (1984) *Caesarea de Maurétanie: Une ville romaine et ses campagnes.* Rome

Leveau, Ph., ed. (1985) *L'origine des richesses depensées dans la ville antique. Actes du colloque Aix-en-Provence 11-12 Mai 1984.* Aix-en-Provence

Levick, B. (1967) *Roman Colonies in Southern Asia Minor.* Oxford

Levick, B. (1982) 'Domitian and the provinces', *Latomus* 41: 50-73

Levick, B. (1983) 'The Senatus Consultum from Larinum', *JRS* 73: 97-115

Lewis, N. (1970) 'On paternal authority in Roman Egypt', *RIDA* 17: 251-8

Lewis, N., Reinhold, M. (1955) *Roman Civilization.* New York

Liebenam, W. (1900) *Städteverwaltung in römischen Kaiserreiche.* Leipzig

Liebeschuetz, J.H.W.G. (1979) *Continuity and Change in Roman Religion.* Oxford

Lightman, M., Feisel, W. (1977) 'Univira: an example of continuity and change in Roman society', *Church History* 46: 19-32

Lo Cascio, E. (1981) 'State and Coinage in the Late Republic and Early Empire', *JRS* 71: 76-86

Long, A.A., ed. (1971) *Problems in Stoicism.* London.

Lopuszanski, G. (1951) 'La police romaine et les Chrétiens', *Ant. Class.* 20: 5-46

Luttwak, E.N. (1976) *The Grand Strategy of the Roman Empire from the First Century AD to the Third.* Baltimore

MacDonald, W. (1965) *The Architecture of the Roman Empire I.* New Haven

MacMullen, R. (1963) *Soldier and Civilian in the Later Roman Empire.* Cambridge, Mass.

MacMullen, R. (1966) *Enemies of the Roman Order.* Cambridge, Mass.

MacMullen, R. (1971) 'Social history in astrology', *Ancient Society* 2: 105-16

MacMullen, R. (1974) *Roman Social Relations, 50 BC to AD 284.* New Haven

MacMullen, R. (1980) 'How big was the Roman Imperial Army?', *Klio* 62: 451-60

MacMullen, R. (1981) *Paganism in the Roman Empire.* New Haven

MacMullen, R. (1982) 'The epigraphic habit in the Roman empire', *AJP* 103: 233-46

MacMullen, R. (1984) *Christianizing the Roman Empire (AD 100-400).* New Haven

Macve, R.H. (1985) 'Some glosses on Greek and Roman Accounting', in Cartledge and Harvey (1985), 233-64

Magie, D. (1950) *Roman Rule in Asia Minor to the end of the Third Century after Christ.* 2 vols. Princeton

Malaise, M. (1972) *Les conditions de pénétration et diffusion des cultes Egyptiens en Italie.* Leiden

Mann, J.C. (1983) *Legionary Recruitment and Veteran Settlement during the Principate.* ed. M.M. Roxan. London

Marrou, H.I. (1956) *A History of Education in Antiquity*. Trans. G. Lamb. New York

Marsden, P. (1977) 'Celtic Ships of Europe' in McGrail, S., ed., *Sources and Techniques in Boat Archaeology, BAR* 29: 281-8

Marshall, A.J. (1975) 'Tacitus and the governor's lady: a note on *Annals* iii. 33-4', *G&R* 22: 11-18

Martin, R. (1971) *Recherches sur les agronomes latins et leurs conceptions économiques et sociales*. Paris

Martin, R. (1984) *L'urbanisme dans la Grèce antique*. 2nd ed. Paris

Matringe, G. (1971) 'La puissance paternelle et le mariage des fils et filles de famille en droit romain', in *Studi in Onore di Eduardo Volterra*, Milan, vol. 5: 191-237

Meiggs, R. (1973) *Roman Ostia*. 2nd ed. Oxford

Michel, J. (1962) *Gratuité en droit romain*. Brussels

Middleton, P. (1979) 'Army supply in Roman Gaul', in Burnham, B.C. and Johnson, H.B., eds. *Invasion and Response. BAR* 73: 81-97

Middleton, P. (1983) 'The Roman Army and Long-Distance Trade', in Garnsey and Whittaker (1983), 75-83

Miles, D. (1982) *The Romano-British Countryside: Studies in rural settlement and economy. BAR* 103. Oxford

Millar, F.G.B. (1963) 'The Fiscus in the First Two Centuries', *JRS* 53: 29-42

Millar, F.G.B. (1964) *A Study of Cassius Dio*. Oxford

Millar, F.G.B. (1966) 'The Emperor, the Senate and the Provinces', *JRS* 56: 156-66

Millar, F.G.B. (1967) *The Roman Empire and its Neighbours*. London

Millar, F.G.B. (1968) 'Local Cultures in the Roman Empire: Libyan, Punic and Latin in Roman Africa', *JRS* 58: 126-134

Millar, F.G.B. (1971) 'Paul of Samosata, Zenobia and Aurelian: The Church, local culture and political allegiance in third-century Syria', *JRS* 61: 1-17

Millar, F.G.B. (1977) *The Emperor in the Roman World*. London

Millar, F.G.B. (1981) 'The world of the Golden Ass', *JRS* 71: 65-75

Millar, F.G.B. (1982) 'Emperors, Frontiers and Foreign Relations, 31 BC to AD 378', *Britannia* 13: 1-23

Millar, F.G.B. (1983a) 'Empire and city, Augustus to Julian: obligations, excuses and status', *JRS* 83: 76-96

Millar, F.G.B. (1983b) 'The Phoenician Cities: a case-study of Hellenisation', *PCPhS* 29: 55-71

Millar, F.G.B. (1984) 'Condemnation to hard labour in the Roman empire, from the Julio-Claudians to Constantine', *PBSR* 52: 128-47

Millar, F.G.B., Segal, E., eds. (1984) *Caesar Augustus: Seven Aspects*. Oxford

Mitchell, S. (1976) 'Requisitioning transport in the Roman Empire: A new inscription from Pisidia', *JRS* 66: 106-31

Mócsy, A. (1967) 'Zu den Prata legionis', *Studien zu den Militärgrenzen Roms*: 211-14. Köln-Graz

Mócsy, A. (1970) *Gesellschaft und Romanisation in der römischen Provinz Moesia Superior*. Amsterdam

Mócsy, A. (1972) 'Das Problem der militärischen Territorium im Donauraum', *Acta Ant.* 20: 131ff.

Mócsy, A. (1974) *Pannonia and Upper Moesia: A History of the Middle Danube*

Provinces of the Roman Empire. London

Mócsy, A. (1983) 'The civilized Pannonians of Velleius', in Hartley, B., Wacher, J., eds. *Rome and her Northern Frontiers: Papers presented to Sheppard Frere*, 169-78

Mohler, S.L. (1931) 'The cliens in the time of Martial', in Hadzsits, G.D., ed., *Classical Studies in Honor of John C. Rolfe*, Philadelphia, 239-63

Momigliano, A. (1975) *Alien Wisdom: the limits of Hellenisation.* Cambridge

Morford, M. (1985) 'Nero's patronage and participation in literature and the arts', *ANRW* II 32.3: 2003-31

Morris, J. (1964) (1965) 'Leges Annales under the Principate', *Listy Fil.* 87: 316-37; 88: 22-31

Mouterde, R. (1964) 'Regards sur Beyrouth Phénicienne, Héllenistique et Romaine', *Mél. Univ. St. Joseph* 40: 149-90

Nash, E. (1968) *Pictorial Dictionary of Ancient Rome.* London

Neesen, L. (1980) *Untersuchungen zu den direkten Staatsabgaben der römischen Kaiserzeit (27 v. Chr. -284 n. Chr.).* Bonn

de Neeve, P.W. (1984) *Colonus: Private Farm-Tenancy in Roman Italy during the Republic and the early Principate.* Amsterdam

Newbold, R.F. (1974) 'Social tension at Rome in the early years of Tiberius' reign', *Athenaeum* 52: 110-43

Nicholas, H. (1962) *An Introduction to Roman Law.* Oxford

Nicolet, Cl. (1976) 'Le cens sénatorial sous la République et sous Auguste', *JRS* 66: 20-38

Nicolet, Cl. (1977) 'Les classes dirigeantes romaines sous la République: ordre sénatorial et ordre équestre', *Annales ESC* 31: 726-55

Nicolet, Cl. (1984) 'Augustus, government, and the propertied class', in Millar and Segal (1984), 89-128

Nippel, W. (1984) 'Policing Rome', *JRS* 74: 20-9

Nock, A.D. (1933) *Conversion: the old and the new in religion from Alexander the Great to Augustine of Hippo.* Oxford

Nock, A.D. (1937) 'The Genius of Mithraism', *JRS* 27: 108-13

Nörr, D. (1966) *Imperium und Polis in der hohen Prinzipatszeit.* Munich

North, J. (1976) 'Conservation and change in Roman religion', *PBSR* 44: 1-12

North, J. (1979) 'Religious Toleration in Republican Rome', *PCPhS* 25: 85-103

Nutton, V. (1971) 'Two notes on immunities: *Digest* 27, 1, 6, 10 and 11', *JRS* 61: 52-63

Nutton, V. (1978) 'The Beneficial Ideology', in Garnsey and Whittaker (1978), 209-21

Oliver, J.H. (1970) *Marcus Aurelius; Aspects of civic and cultural policy in the East.* Hesperia Supplement XIII

L'onomastique latine (1977) *L'onomastique latine, Paris 13-15 Oct. 1975: Colloques internationales du centre nationale de la recherche scientifique*, no. 564. Paris

Oswald, F., Davies Pryce, T. (1920) *An Introduction to the Study of Terra Sigillata from a Chronological Standpoint.* London

Otis, B. (1970) *Ovid as an Epic Poet.* 2nd ed. Cambridge

de Pachtère, F.G. (1920) *La table hypothécaire de Veleia.* Paris

Palm, J. (1959) *Rom, Römertum und Imperium in der griechischen Literatur der Kaiserzeit.* Lund

Pasquinucci, M. (1979) 'La transumanza nell'Italia Romana', in Gabba, E. and Pasquinucci, M., *Strutture agrarie e allevamento transumante nell'Italia Romana (III-I sec. A.C.)*, 79-182. Pisa

Patterson, O. (1982) *Slavery and Social Death*. Cambridge, Mass.

Pearce, T. (1974) 'The role of the wife as *custos*', *Eranos* 72: 16-33

Pédech, P. (1976) *La géographie des grecs*. Paris

Petracco Sicardi, G. (1969) 'Problemi di topographia Veleiate', *Atti del III Convegno di Studi Veleiati, 3 Maggio-2 Giugno 1967*, Milan, 207-18

Peyre, C. (1970) 'Tite-Live et la "férocité" gauloise', *REL* 48: 277-96

Pflaum, H.-G. (1948) *Le Marbre de Thorigny*. Paris

Pflaum, H.-G. (1950) *Les procurateurs équestres sous le Haut-Empire romain*. Paris

Pflaum, H.-G. (1960) *Les carrières procuratoriennes équestres sous le Haut-Empire romain*, 3 vols. Paris

Pflaum, H.-G. (1970a) 'La romanisation de l'ancien territoire de la Carthage punique', *Ant. Afr.* 4: 75-117

Pflaum, H.-G. (1970b) 'Titulature et rang social sous le Haut-Empire', in Nicolet, Cl., ed. *Recherches sur les structures sociales dans l'antiquité classique*. Paris

Pippidi, D.M., ed. (1976) *Assimilation et résistance à la culture gréco-romaine dans le monde ancien: Travaux du VIe Congrès International d'Etudes Classiques (Madrid, Sept. 1974)*. Bucharest and Paris

Pitts, L., St. Joseph, J.K. (1986) *Inchtuthil: the Roman legionary fortress*. Britannia Monograph Series No.6. London

Pleket, H.W. (1983) 'Urban elites and business in the Greek part of the Roman Empire', in Garnsey, Hopkins, Whittaker (1983), 131-44

Polanyi, K. (1957) *Trade and Market in the Early Empires: economies in history and theory*, Polanyi, K., Arensberg, C., Pearson, H.W., eds. Chicago

Polanyi, K. (1968) *Primitive, Archaic and Modern Economies: Essays of Karl Polanyi*, Dalton, G., ed. New York

Pollitt, J.J. (1966) *The Art of Rome c. 753 BC to 337 AD: Sources and Documents*. New Jersey

Pomeroy, S. (1975) *Goddesses, Whores, Wives and Slaves: Women in Classical Antiquity*. New York

Pomeroy, S. (1976) 'The relationship of the married woman to her blood relatives in Rome', *Ancient Society* 7: 215-27

Pomey, P., Tchernia, A. (1978) 'Le tonnage maximum des navires de commerce romains', *Archaeonautica* 2: 233-5

Potter, T.W. (1979) *Changing Landscapes in Southern Etruria*. London

Poulantzas, N. (1975) *Classes in Contemporary Capitalism*. London

Poulter, A. (1980) 'Rural communities (vici and komai) and their role in the organisation of the Limes of Moesia Inferior', in Hanson, W.S. and Keppie, L.J.F., eds. *Roman Frontier Studies* XII. 1979 *BAR* 71: 729-44

Price, S.R.F. (1984) *Rituals and Power: The Roman imperial cult in Asia Minor*. Cambridge

Purcell, N. (1983) 'The Apparitores: A Study of social mobility', *PBSR* 51: 125-73

Purcell, N. (1985) 'Wine and Wealth in Ancient Italy', *JRS* 75: 1-19

Rabello, A.M. (1980) 'The legal condition of the Jews in the Roman empire', *ANRW* II 13: 662-762

Rajak, T. (1984) *Josephus*. London

Rathbone, D.W. (1981) 'The Development of Agriculture in the "Ager Cosanus" during the Roman Republic: Problems of Evidence and Interpretation', *JRS* 71: 10-23

Rathbone, D.W. (1983) 'The Slave Mode of Production'. Review-discussion of Giardina and Schiavone (1981), *JRS* 73: 160-8.

Rawson, B.M. (1966) 'Family life among the lower classes at Rome in the first two centuries of the Empire', *CP* 61: 71-83

Rawson, B.M. (1974) 'Roman concubinage and other *de facto* marriages', *TAPA* 104: 279-305

Rawson, B.M., ed. (1986) *The Family in Ancient Rome: New Perspectives*. Ithaca, N.Y.

Rea, J.R. (1972) *Public Documents; the corn dole in Oxyrhynchus, and kindred documents. Pap. Oxy.* XL

Reardon, B.P. (1971) *Courants littéraires grecs des IIe et IIIe siècles après J-C.* Paris

Reinhold, M. (1971) 'Usurpation of status and status symbols in the Roman empire', *Historia* 20: 275-301

Reynolds, J.M. (1981) 'New evidence for the imperial cult in Julio-Claudian Aphrodisias', *ZPE* 43: 317-28

Reynolds, J.M. (1982) *Aphrodisias and Rome*. London

Richmond, I.A., McIntyre, J. (1934) 'Tents of the Roman army and leather from Birdoswald', *Trans. Cumb. Westmor. Arch. Soc.*: 62-90

Rickman, G.E. (1971) *Roman Granaries and Store Buildings*. Cambridge

Rickman, G.E. (1980) *The Corn Supply of Ancient Rome*. Oxford

Robert, L. (1941) *Les gladiateurs dans l'Orient grec*. Paris

Robert, L. (1974) 'Des Carpathes à la Propontide', *Studii Clasice* 16: 1-36

Robertis, F.M. de (1955) *Il fenomeno associativo nel mondo romano*. Naples

Rodriguez-Almeida, E. (1984) *Il monte Testaccio*. Rome

Rostovtzeff, M. (1910) *Studien zur Geschichte des römischen Kolonates*. Leipzig

Rostovtzeff, M. (1957) *The Social and Economic History of the Roman Empire*, 2nd ed. Oxford

Rougé, J. (1966) *Recherches sur l'organisation du commerce maritime en Méditerranée sous l'empire romain*. Paris

Rougé, J. (1980) 'Prêt et sociétés maritimes dans le monde romain', in D'Arms and Kopff (1980)

Rousselle, A. (1984) 'Concubinat et adultère', *Opus* 3: 75-84

Rowland, R.J. (1976) 'The very poor and the grain dole at Rome and Oxyrhynchos' *ZPE* 21: 69-72

Rowland, R.J. (1984) 'The case of the missing Sardinian grain', *The Ancient World* 10: 45-8

Ryberg, I.S. (1955) *Rites of the State Religion in Roman Art, MAAR* 22. Rome

de Ste. Croix, G.E.M. (1954) 'Suffragium: from vote to patronage', *Brit. Jl. Soc.* 5: 33-48

de Ste. Croix, G.E.M. (1956) 'Greek and Roman Accounting', in Littleton, A.C., Yamey, B.S., eds. *Studies in the History of Accounting*, 14-74. London

de Ste. Croix, G.E.M. (1974) 'Why were the early Christians persecuted?', in Finley (1974), 210-49, 256-62 de Ste. Croix, G.E.M. (1981) *The Class Struggle in the Ancient Greek World*. London

Saller, R.P. (1980) 'Patronage and Promotion in Equestrian Careers', *JRS* 70: 44-63

Saller, R.P. (1982) *Personal Patronage under the Early Empire*. Cambridge

Saller, R.P. (1983) 'Martial on patronage and literature', *CQ* 33: 246-57

Saller, R.P. (1984a) '*Familia, domus*, and the Roman conception of the family', *Phoenix* 38: 336-55

Saller, R.P. (1984b) 'Roman dowry and the devolution of property in the Principate', *CQ* n.s. 34: 195-205

Saller, R.P. (1986) 'Patria potestas and the stereotype of the Roman family', *Continuity and Change* 1: 7-22

Saller, R.P. (1987a) 'Men's age at marriage and its consequence in the Roman family', *CP* 82: forthcoming

Saller, R.P. (1987b) 'Slavery and the Roman family', *Slavery and Abolition* 8: forthcoming

Saller, R.P., Shaw, B.D. (1984a) 'Tombstones and Roman family relations in the Principate: Civilians, soldiers and slaves', *JRS* 74: 124-56

Saller, R.P., Shaw, B.D. (1984b) 'Close-kin marriage in Roman society', *Man* 19: 432-44

Salmon, E.T. (1971) *Roman Colonisation under the Republic*. London.

Sandbach, F.H. (1975) *The Stoics*. London

Sasel, J. (1982) 'Senatori ed appartenenti all'ordine senatorio provenienti dalle province romane di Dacia, Tracia, Mesia, Dalmazia e Pannonia', in *Atti del Colloquio Internationale AIEGL, Roma 14-20 maggio 1981, su Epigrafia e ordine senatorio*, vol. 2, 553-81. Rome

Schlumberger, D. (1970) *L'Orient hellénisé*. Paris

Schneider, H. (1974) *Wirtschaft und Politik; Untersuchungen zur Geschichte der späten römischen Republik*. Erlangen

Schürer, E. (1973-79) *The History of the Jewish People in the Age of Jesus Christ (175 BC – AD 135)*. Rev. ed. Vermes, G., Millar, F., Black, M. Edinburgh

Schulz, F. (1946) *Roman Legal Science*. Oxford

Semple, E.C. (1932) *The Geography of the Mediterranean Region. Its relation to Ancient History*. Constable

Setala, P. (1977) *Private Domini in Roman Brickstamps of the Empire. Annales Academiae Scientiarum Fennicae*

Shatzman, I. (1975) *Senatorial Wealth and Roman Politics*. Brussels.

Shaw, B.D. (1983) 'Soldiers and Society: the Army in Numidia', *Opus* 2, 1: 133-60

Shaw, B.D. (1984a) 'Water and Society in the Ancient Maghrib: Technology, Property and Development', *Ant. Afr.* 20: 121-73

Shaw, B.D. (1984b) 'Bandits in the Roman empire', *P & P* 105: 3-52

Shaw, B.D. (1985) 'The Divine Economy: Stoicism as Ideology', *Latomus* 44: 16-54

Shaw, B.D. (forthcoming a) 'The family in late antiquity: the experience of Augustine'

Shaw, B.D. (forthcoming b) 'The age of Roman girls at marriage: some reconsiderations'

Sherwin-White, A.N. (1939) 'Procurator Augusti', *PBSR* 15: 11-26

Sherwin-White, A.N. (1967) *Racial Prejudice in Imperial Rome*. Cambridge

Sherwin-White, A.N. (1973) *The Roman Citizenship*. 2nd ed. Oxford

Sieder, R., Mitterauer, M. (1982) *The European Family*. Cambridge

Sirago, A. (1958) *L'Italia agraria sotto Traiano*. Louvain

Slicher van Bath, B.H. (1963) *Yield Ratios 810-1820*

Smadja, E. (n.d.) 'Remarques sur les débuts du culte impérial en Afrique sous le règne d'Auguste', *Religions, pouvoir, rapports sociaux*, Centre de Recherches d'Histoire ancienne 32: 149-70

Smadja, E. (1978) 'L'inscription du culte impérial dans la cité: l'exemple de Lepcis Magna au début de l'empire', *DHA* 4: 171ff.

Smadja, E. (1985) 'L'empereur et les dieux en Afrique romaine', *DHA* 11: 541-55

Smallwood, E.M. (1976) *The Jews under Roman Rule*. Leiden

Smith, R.M. (1981) 'The people of Tuscany and their families in the fifteenth century: medieval or Mediterranean?', *Journal of Family History* 6: 107-28

Sommer, C.S. (1984) *The Military Vici in Roman Britain. BAR* 129. Oxford

Staerman, E.M. (1964) *Die Krise der Sklaverhalterordnung im Westen der römischen Reiches*. Berlin

Staerman, E.M. (1975) *La schiavitù nell'Italia imperiale*. Rome

Starr, C.G. (1982) *The Roman Empire, 27 BC – AD 476: A Study in Survival*. New York and Oxford

Stein, A. (1927) *Der römische Ritterstand*. Munich

Stone, L. (1965) *The Crisis of the Aristocracy 1558-1641*. Oxford

Stone, L. (1977) *The Family, Sex and Marriage in England, 1500-1800*. London

Strong, D.E. (1961) *Roman Imperial Sculpture*. London

Strong, D.E. (1966) *Greek and Roman Gold and Silver Plate*. London

Strong, D.E. (1976) *Roman Art*. London

Sullivan, J.P. (1976) *Propertius*. Cambridge

Syme, R. (1939) *The Roman Revolution*. Oxford

Syme, R. (1958) *Tacitus*. 2 vols. Oxford

Syme, R. (1971) *Emperors and Biography: Studies in the Augustan History*. Oxford

Syme, R. (1978) *History in Ovid*. Oxford

Tatum, J. (1979) *Apuleius and the Golden Ass*. Ithaca

Taubenschlag, R. (1955) *The Law of Greco-Roman Egypt in the Light of the Papyri*. 2nd ed. New York

Tchernia, A. (1980) 'Quelques remarques sur la commerce du vin et les amphores' in D'Arms and Kopff (1980), 305-12

Tchernia, A. (1985) 'Rêves de richesse, emprunts et commerce maritime', *Colloque Antibes, Oct. 1985* (to appear)

Tchernia, A. (1986a) *Le vin de l'Italie romaine: essai d'histoire économique d'après les amphores*. Paris

Tchernia, A. (1986b) 'Amphores et textes: deux exemples', in Empereur, J.-Y., Garlan, Y., eds. *Recherches sur les amphores grecques, BCH* Suppl. 13: 33-6

Thomas, J.A.C. (1976) *Textbook of Roman Law*. Amsterdam

Thomas, Y. (1980) 'Mariages endogamiques à Rome: patrimoine, pouvoir et parenté depuis l'époque archaïque', *Revue d'Histoire Français et Etranger* 58:345-82

Thomas, Y. (1981) 'Parricidium I. Le père, la famille et la cité', *MEFR* 93: 643-713

Thomas, Y. (1982) 'Droit domestique et droit politique à Rome. Remarques sur le pécule et les honores del fils de famille', *MEFR* 94: 527-80

Thomson, J.O. (1948) *History of Ancient Geography*. Cambridge

Toynbee, J.M.C. (1964) *Art in Roman Britain*. Oxford

Toynbee, J.M.C. (1971) *Death and Burial in the Roman World*. London

Treggiari, S. (1969) *Roman Freedmen during the Late Republic*. Oxford

Treggiari, S. (1975a) 'Jobs in the household of Livia', *PBSR* 43: 48-77

Treggiari, S. (1975b) 'Family life among the staff of the Volusii', *TAPA* 105: 393-401

Treggiari, S. (1976) 'Jobs for women', *Am.Jl. Anc.Hist.* 1: 76-104

Treggiari, S. (1979a) 'Questions on women domestics in the Roman west', in *Schiavitù, manomissione, e classi dipendenti nel mondo antico*, 185-201

Treggiari, S. (1979b) 'Lower class women in the Roman economy', *Florilegium* 1: 65-86

Treggiari, S. (1980) 'Women as property in the early Roman empire', in D. Kelly Weisberg, ed. *Women and the Law: A social history perspective*, vol. 2, 7-33

Treggiari, S. (1981a) '*Concubinae*', *PBSR* 49: 59-81

Treggiari, S. (1981b) '*Contubernales* in *CIL* 6', *Phoenix* 35: 42-69

Treggiari, S. (1982) 'Consent to Roman marriage: some aspects of law and reality', *EMC/CV* n.s. 1: 34-44

Treggiari, S. (1984) '*Digna condicio*: betrothals in the Roman upper class', *EMC/CV* n.s. 3: 419-51

van Berchem, D. (1937) *L'annone militaire dans l'Empire romain au IIIᵉ siècle*. Paris

van Berchem, D. (1977) 'L'annone militaire est-elle un mythe?' in *Armées et fiscalité* (1977): 331-9

Veyne, P. (1957, 1958) 'La Table des Ligures Baebiani et l'Institution Alimentaire de Trajan' *MEFR* 69: 81-135; 70: 177-241

Veyne, P. (1961) 'Vie de Trimalchio', *Annales ESC* 16: 213-47

Veyne, P. (1976) *Le pain et le cirque*. Paris

Veyne, P. (1978) 'La famille et l'amour sous le Haut-Empire romain', *Annales ESC* 33: 35-63

Vitucci, G. (1956) *Ricerche sulla Praefectura Urbi in Età Imperiale*. Rome

Volterra, E. (1948) 'Quelques observations sur le mariage des filiifamilias', *RIDA* 1: 213-42

von Petrikovits, H. (1974a) 'Römisches Militarhandwerk', *Anz d. Ost.Akad. d. Wiss.*, Phil.Hist., Kl. 111:1ff.

von Petrikovits, H. (1974b) 'Militärische Fabricae der Romer', in *Actes du IXᵉ Congrès International d'Etudes sur les Frontières Romaines 1972*: 399ff.

Wachter, K.W. et al. (1978) *Statistical Studies of Historical Social Structure*. New York

Walker, D.S. (1965) *The Mediterranean Lands*. London

Wall, R. et al., ed. (1983) *Family Forms in Historic Europe*. Cambridge

Wallace-Hadrill, A. (1981) 'Family and inheritance in the Augustan marriage laws', *PCPhS* 27: 58-80

Wallace-Hadrill, A. (1983) *Suetonius: The Scholar and his Caesars*. London

Waltzing, J.P. (1895-1900) *Etude historique sur les corporations professionelles chez les Romains*. Louvain

Wardman, A. (1982) *Religion and statecraft among the Romans*. London
Ward-Perkins, J.B., Claridge, A. (1976) *Pompeii AD 79, Exhibition Catalogue*. London
Watson, A. (1967) *The Law of Persons in the Later Roman Republic*. Oxford
Watson, A. (1975) *Rome of the XII Tables*. Princeton
Watson, G.R. (1969) *The Roman Soldier*. London
Weaver, P.R.C. (1972) *Familia Caesaris*. Cambridge
Weaver, P.R.C. (1974) 'Social mobility in the early Roman empire: the evidence of the imperial freedmen and slaves', in Finley (1974), 121-40
Wells, C. (1972) *The German Policy of Augustus*. Oxford
Wells, C. (1984) *The Roman Empire*. Glasgow
White, K.D (1963) 'Wheat Farming in Roman times', *Antiquity* 37: 207ff.
White, K.D. (1967a) *Agricultural Implements of the Roman World*. London
White, K.D. (1967b) 'Latifundia', *BICS* 14: 62-79
White, K.D. (1970) *Roman Farming*. London
White, K.D. (1984) *Greek and Roman Technology*. London
White, P. (1978) 'Amicitia and the profession of poetry in early imperial Rome', *JRS* 68: 74-92
White, P. (1982) 'Positions for poets in early imperial Rome', in Gold (1982), 50-66.
Whitehorne, J.E.G. (1980) 'New light on Temple and State in Roman Egypt', *Jl. Relig. Hist.* 11: 218-26
Whittaker, C.R. (1978) 'Land and Labour in North Africa', *Klio* 60: 331-62
Whittaker, C.R. (1980) 'Rural Labour in three Roman provinces', in Garnsey (1980), 73-99
Whittaker, C.R. (1985) 'Trade and the Aristocracy in the Roman empire', *Opus* 4: 1-27
Whittaker, C.R. (1986) 'Supplying the System: Frontiers and Beyond' (to appear)
Wierschowski, L. (1984) *Heer und Wirtschaft: Das römische Heer der Prinzipatszeit als Wirtschaftsfaktor*. Bonn
Wightman, E.M. (1970) *Roman Trier and the Treveri*. London
Wilken, R.L. (1984) *The Christians as the Romans saw them*. New Haven
Wilkes, J.J. (1969) *Dalmatia*. London
Williams, G. (1968) *Tradition and Originality in Roman Poetry*. Oxford
Williams, G. (1978) *Change and Decline: Roman Literature in the Early Empire*. Berkeley
Wilson, A.J.N. (1966) *Emigration from Italy in the Republican Age*. Manchester
Winkler, J.J. (1985) *Auctor and Actor: a narratological reading of Apuleius, The Golden Ass*. Berkeley
Wiseman, T.P. (1970) 'The definition of "eques Romanus" in the late Republic and early Empire', *Historia* 19: 67-83
Wistrand, E. (1976) *The So-called Laudatio Turiae. Introduction, text, translation and commentary*. Lund
Wörrle, M. (1971) 'Aegyptisches Getreide für Ephesos', *Chiron* 1: 325-40
Woodman, T., West, D. (1984) *Poetry and Politics in the Age of Augustus*. Cambridge
Wrightson, K. (1982) *English Society 1580-1680*. London
Xella, P. (ed.) (1976) *Magia: Studi in memorie di Raffaella Garosi*. Rome

224 *The Roman Empire*

Yavetz, Z. (1969) *Plebs and Princeps*. Oxford
Ziegler, R. (1977) 'Münzen Kilikiens als Zeugnis kaiserlicher Getreidespenden', *Jahrbuch für Numismatik und Geldgeschichte*, 27-67
Ziegler, R. (1978) 'Antiochia, Laodicea und Sidon in der Politik der Severer', *Chiron* 8: 493-514

Roman Emperors

From Augustus to Severus Alexander

Augustus (Imp. Caesar Augustus)	27 BC–AD 14
Tiberius (Ti. Caesar Augustus)	AD 14–37
Gaius (C. Caesar Augustus Germanicus)	37–41
Claudius (Ti. Claudius Caesar Augustus Germanicus)	41–54
Nero (Imp. Nero Claudius Caesar Augustus Germanicus)	54–68
Galba (Ser. Sulpicius Galba Imp. Caesar Augustus)	68–69
Otho (Imp. M. Otho Caesar Augustus)	69
Vitellius (A. Vitellius Augustus Germanicus Imp.)	69
Vespasian (Imp. Caesar Vespasianus Augustus)	69–79
Titus (Imp. Titus Caesar Vespasianus Augustus)	79–81
Domitian (Imp. Caesar Domitianus Augustus)	81–96
Nerva (Imp. Caesar Nerva Augustus)	96–98
Trajan (Imp. Caesar Nerva Traianus Augustus)	98–117
Hadrian (Imp. Caesar Traianus Hadrianus Augustus)	117–138
Antoninus Pius (Imp. Caesar T. Aelius Hadrianus Antoninus Augustus Pius)	138–161
Marcus Aurelius (Imp. Caesar M. Aurelius Antoninus Augustus)	161–180
Lucius Verus (Imp. Caesar L. Aurelius Verus Augustus)	161–169
Commodus (Imp. Caesar M. Aurelius Commodus Antoninus Augustus)	176–192
Pertinax (Imp. Caesar P. Helvius Pertinax Augustus)	193
Didius Julianus (Imp. Caesar M. Didius Severus Julianus Augustus)	193
Septimius Severus (Imp. Caesar L. Septimius Severus Pertinax Augustus)	193–211
Clodius Albinus (Imp. Caesar D. Clodius Septimius Albinus Augustus)	193–197
Pescennius Niger (Imp. Caesar C. Pescennius Niger Justus Augustus)	193–194
Caracalla (Imp. Caesar M. Aurelius Antoninus Augustus)	198–217
Geta (Imp. Caesar P. Septimius Geta Augustus)	209–211
Macrinus (Imp. Caesar M. Opellius Macrinus Augustus)	217–218
Diadumenianus (Imp. Caesar M. Opellius Antoninus Diadumenianus Augustus)	218
Elagabal (Imp. Caesar M. Aurelius Antoninus Augustus)	218–222
Severus Alexander (Imp. Caesar M. Aurelius Severus Alexander Augustus)	222–235

Some later emperors referred to in the text

Maximinus (Imp. Caesar C. Julius Verus Maximinus Augustus)	235–238
Philip (Imp. Caesar M. Julius Philippus Augustus)	244–249
Decius (Imp. Caesar C. Messius Quintus Traianus Decius Augustus)	249–251
Valerian (Imp. Caesar P. Licinius Valerianus Augustus)	253–260
Gallienus (Imp. Caesar P. Licinius Egnatius Gallienus Augustus)	253–268
Aurelian (Imp. Caesar Domitius Aurelianus Augustus)	270–275
Diocletian (Imp. Caesar C. Aurelius Valerius Diocletianus Augustus)	284–305
Constantine (Imp. Caesar Flavius Valerius Constantinus Augustus)	307–337

Index

administration, *see* bureaucracy, emperors, government

adoption, 124, 127, 144, 200

Aedui, 9, 166

Aelius Aristides, 15-16

aerarium, 24

Africa, Roman north, 9, 11, 19, 32, 38, 49, 55-8, 66-7, 79, 85, 87, 90, 95-6, 98, 111-12, 134, 167-9, 186-9, 191-2, 195-6, 202-3; Proconsularis, 21, 31-2, 96, 151, 165-6

agency, 54-5

Agricola, 18, 194

agriculture: and civilization, 12-13, 17; improvements in, 45, 52, 55-8, 62, 77-8, 197-8; predominance of, 43-6, 48-9, 51, 55, 197, productivity of, 43, 77-82; underdevelopment of, 6, 43-4, 51-2, 57, 63, 111, 197-8; *see also* crops; grain; investment; land; olives; wine

Agrippa, M., 7, 86

agronomists, 45, 58-9, 67, 78

Alexandria, 31

alimenta, 59-60, 65, 74-5, 77, 101

Alps, 7, 23

amphitheatres, 114, 117, 189-90

annona, see food supply; grain, public distribution of; prefect of the *annona*

Antioch, 32, 192

Antoninus Pius, 9, 29, 31, 37, 167

Aphrodisias, 28, 39, 191

apparitores, 116

Apuleius, 11, 111, 119, 121, 151, 158, 173, 180, 187-8, 192, 202-3

aqueducts, 33, 86

architecture, 183-6, 188-90, 194, 202; *see also* public works

aristocracy (imperial), economic values of, 45, 47-8, 57, 73-4, 197; social values of, 112-15, 118, 120-1, 123-4, 129, 134-5, 143-4, 150, 154, 156, 172, 179, 199; provincials in, 9-12, 15, 50, 96, 123, 152, 186; *see also* decurions; equestrians; senate and senators; status

army, 15, 33, 112, 137, 140, 149, 158, 185-6, 190, 193-4, 196-7, 201, 203; and political power, 16-17, 89, 107, 158; and religion, 167, 173; auxiliary units, 10, 22, 88, 96, 124; cost of, 20, 88-9, 94-6; legions, 10-12, 22, 88, 96, 124; officers, 10-11, 16, 22, 110, 124, 200; recruitment, 10, 16-18, 58, 75-6, 90, 112, 115, 124, 194; requisitions, 32, 40, 50, 56, 92-4; supply of, 44, 48, 50, 56-8, 83, 85, 88-96, 194, 196, 198; *see also* food supply; praetorian guard; veterans

Arretium (Arezzo), 44, 52

arts (visual), 183-6, 188-9, 191, 193-4, 202-3; *see also* architecture

Asia Minor, 9, 12, 15-16, 29-30, 37, 66, 94, 96, 98, 101, 111, 167, 190-1, 195; province of Asia, 21, 33, 102, 165

astrology, 173, 179

Augustales, 121

Augustine, 134, 187, 192-3

Augustus, 7, 12-14, 22-5, 28, 30, 34-5, 37, 51, 57-8, 61, 67, 72, 83, 85-8, 90, 93-4, 99, 107, 110, 112-13, 116-17, 121, 126, 130-2, 136-7, 143-5, 149-50, 158, 164-9, 171-5, 178, 180-1, 183-4, 189-91, 196, 198-203

banditry, 13, 159

banking, 52, 54-5

banquets, 117, 122, 151, 156-7, 199

Bithynia, 17, 36-7, 39, 165; *see also* Pliny the younger, as governor

bookkeeping, 52, 74; imperial, 24

Britain, 7, 16-19, 22, 28, 30, 55, 57-8, 78, 90-2, 96, 166-9, 189, 194-5

brothers, 127, 129, 146; *consortium*, 129

bureaucracy, 20-1, 23, 25-6, 31, 38-9, 150, 153, 168, 196-7

Caesar, C. Julius, 9, 14, 28, 81, 107, 163, 179, 189-90, 202

Calpurnius Fabatus, 65, 72, 131, 142

Caracalla, 30, 170, 201; citizenship edict of, 15-16, 115

Carandini, A., 60-1

Carthage, 21, 27, 31, 165, 187

Cassius Dio, 8, 16-17, 19, 113, 172, 176, 183

Casson, L., 98-100

Cato, 45, 71, 73-4, 90

Celts, 10, 13-14, 53, 169, 186, 189, 192-3, 195

census, 21, 64, 103, 113

children, 75, 81, 107, 127-30, 133-4, 136-41, 146; child-bearing, 138, 142-5, 155, 200; daughters, 127-8, 135, 140-2, 144, 200; generation gap, 138, 200-1; mortality of, 138-9, 142; 'right of three children', 88, 126, 130, 143; sons, 55, 113, 123, 126, 129, 136, 140-2, 144; *see also* infant exposure

Christianity, 29, 133, 146, 191, 201; persecution of, 36, 158, 170, 174-6, 202; rise of, 174-7

Cicero, 37, 45, 65, 68, 71, 79-82, 98, 114, 128, 133-4, 140, 146, 148, 155, 169, 182

cities: and culture, 119, 192-4, 203; consumer, 48-9, 55-8, 97-100, 103; finances of, 33-4, 36-8, 100, 188, 197; medieval, 48; statuses of, 15, 26-32, 36-7, 39, 102, 189, 203; urbanization,

11-13, 18-19, 26, 28-30, 32, 56-8, 103, 168, 178, 186, 188-90, 194-7, 202-3; *see also* decurions; government, local; Rome; taxes

citizenship, 15, 27, 35, 87-8, 107, 110-12, 115, 117-18, 120, 123-4, 146, 150-1, 190, 193, 200

class, 109-12, 199; and property, 71, 109, 111, 199

Claudius, 7, 9, 15, 23-4, 86, 88, 116, 120, 130, 166, 173, 202

climate, 5-6, 13-14, 17, 19, 71, 74, 86

clothing, 44, 50-1, 81, 84, 89, 91-3, 113, 116-17, 119, 121-2, 154, 199

coinage, 50; debasement of, 21

collegia, 36, 156-8, 201

colonate, 112, 199

coloniae, 26-7, 32, 39, 51, 167, 189-90

Columella, 45, 58-9, 62, 66-7, 71, 74, 76, 79-82, 111, 132

Commodus, 24, 61, 172

communications, 6, 14

consilium principis, 24

Constantine, 29, 143

consumption and demand, 43-4, 50-3, 56-60, 62, 68, 74, 81, 83-6, 89-90; conspicuous, 57, 121-2, 143; subsistence, 81, 84, 97-8; *see also* cities, consumer

corruption, 36, 39, 152, 197

craftsmen, 43, 52, 87, 90, 188-9, 191

Crawford, M.H., 50

Crook, J.A., 127

crops, 6, 56; cash, 56-8, 76, 96; mix, 63, 81-2, 100, 198; *see also* agriculture; grain; olives; wine

cultures: Graeco-Roman, 6, 12-16, 18-19, 26, 30-1, 119, 164, 167, 178, 182-3, 194, 196, 203; non-Mediterranean, 11-19, 196; rural, 192-5, 203

curatores rei publicae, 22-3, 34, 38-9

Dacia, 7, 185

Danube, Danubian region, 7, 10-11, 16-17, 19, 30, 93, 96, 193

daughters, *see* children

debt, 34, 55, 112, 140, 148-9, 155; debt-bondage, 67, 111

Decius, 39, 174-6

decurions, 11, 27-30, 32-4, 38-9, 50, 114-15, 117-18, 123, 152, 186, 194, 196, 199-200, 203; census of, 114; contributions and services of, 29, 33-4, 37-8, 92, 100-1, 110, 115, 121, 158, 181, 188, 197-8; recruitment of, 38-9, 45, 110, 114-15, 121, 124-5, 200; wealth of, 64-5, 71, 110-11, 124; *see also* euergetism; government, local

desert, 12-13

diet, 13, 17, 81, 84, 89-90, 97-8

Dio Chrysostom (of Prusa), 11, 37

Diocletian, 9, 16, 47, 95, 175

divination, 163, 168-9

divorce, 130-1, 133, 135-6, 139, 201

Domitian, 59-60, 167, 172, 179, 181, 184

dowry, 70-1, 130, 135, 146, 201

Druids, 168-9

economics, 21, 74

education, 10, 16-17, 26, 118, 120, 134, 139, 181, 186-8, 190, 194, 202

Egypt, 22-3, 31, 46-7, 49, 58, 66, 79, 85, 87, 92, 95-6, 98-101, 103, 107, 111, 119, 168, 172-3, 189, 191, 195, 201, 203

Elagabalus, 16

emperors, administrative policy of, 10-11, 20, 22-5, 29-30, 34-8, 94, 156, 179, 189, 196, 203; economic and social policy of, 12, 20-1, 51, 60, 62, 85-6, 107, 110, 112-13, 116, 122-3, 126, 143-4, 147, 157-8, 171, 178, 183, 199-200, 202; estates of, 8, 20, 23, 31, 62, 66, 87-8, 93, 95, 112, 152; origins of, 9, 16; jurisdiction of, 35-6; *mandata* of, 35-6; patronage by, 20, 24, 26, 60, 94, 102, 146, 149-51, 153-4, 156, 158, 178, 180-5, 188, 201-2; religious policy of, 163-6, 169, 171-7, 201-2; wealth of, 47; *see also* government; monarchy; ruler-cult

equestrians, 31, 118; as functionaries, 20, 22-6, 34, 93, 114, 123-4; as legionary commanders, 11, 22; as military officers, 10, 23, 199; 'public horse', 113-14, 117, 123; order of, 107, 113-14, 117, 119-22, 199; origins of, 9-10; recruitment of, 123-4, 153-4, 156, 200-1; wealth of, 64-5, 71, 114

euergetism, 33-4, 38, 101-2, 198

Evans, J.K., 81-2

families, 6, 55, 85, 107, 110, 116, 118-19, 123-5, 126-8, 144, 148, 153, 156, 181, 199-201; extended, 129, 140, 147, 200; *familia*, 127-8, 130, 141; life cycle, 75, 124, 131, 138-9; size of, 143-4, 147; *see also* children; house and household; mothers; *paterfamilias*; wives

famine, 50, 97, 99-100, 103, 175, 198

fathers, *see paterfamilias*

Finley, M.I., 46, 48, 74

fiscus, 24

food supply, 111; for armies, 48, 56-7, 83, 88-96, 198; for cities, 6-7, 56, 94, 97-102, 119, 158; for Rome, 8, 20, 23, 48-9, 56, 58, 60, 83-8, 95, 99, 150, 158, 198; *see also* grain; olives; wine

freedmen, 39, 44-5, 55, 67, 73-4, 76, 107, 110, 113-15, 124-5, 131, 134, 146, 199-200; imperial, 20-1, 23-6, 120, 122-3; status of, 120-1

friends, 128-9, 146, 148-50, 152, 154-6, 182, 201; differentiation of, 122, 149, 152-5; *see also* protégés

frontiers, 81, 10-11, 14, 16, 50, 92, 175, 193, 196

Fronto, 139, 142-3, 182, 187

Gaius, 87, 130, 136

Galen, 97-8, 183

Gaul, 7, 9-10, 13-14, 17-19, 28-30, 51, 55, 57-9, 62, 91, 93, 95-6, 107, 111, 119, 165-6, 168-9, 188, 195-6, 202; *see also* Narbonensis

geography, 7, 14-16

Germany, 7, 17, 96, 195; German tribes, 10, 14, 166, 169

government: financial policy, 21, 34, 37-8, 56, 103; goals of, 20, 26, 32, 38-9, 51, 56, 102-3, 186, 194, 196-8, 203; local, 13, 22, 26-33, 36-9, 101-2,

110, 115, 158, 194, 197-8; recruitment of, 10, 20, 24-5, 196, 201; size of, 20, 22-3, 25-6, 110, 196-7; *see also* bureaucracy; emperors; equestrians; food supply; manufacture; law; senate and senators; taxes; trade, 'administered'

governors, 21-3, 25, 88, 118, 134, 165, 194; as patrons, 151-2, 154-5; powers and duties of, 34-8, 40, 101, 197; *see also* legates; prefect of Egypt; proconsuls

grain: distribution of, 8, 48-9, 56, 83-7, 94, 100-1, 117, 151; production of, 31, 55, 57-60, 64, 67, 73, 78-82, 87, 91-2, 98-9; storage of, 86-7, 93, 97; trade in, 48-50, 52, 84-8, 99; yields, 78-82; *see also* food supply

grandfathers, 129, 131, 142, 145, 193

Greece, Greeks, 5-6, 11-13, 15-16, 28-31, 39, 66, 79, 94, 98, 158, 164-5, 167, 182, 188, 191-2, 196-7, 203; *see also* culture, Graeco-Roman; languages, Greek; literature, Greek renaissance

growth, economic, 43, 50-8, 62-3, 91, 197

Hadrian, 9, 22, 27, 31, 33, 36, 94, 102, 111, 115-16, 136, 167, 185, 188, 195, 202

hoarding, 101-2, 198

honestiores, 35, 111, 116, 118, 200

honour, 33, 44-5, 47, 57, 107, 114-18, 120-1, 148-51, 153, 155-6

Hopkins, K., 49-50, 53

Horace, 71, 180, 190, 202

house and household, 88, 98, 103, 119, 121-2, 133, 140-1, 148, 153, 155-6, 199; *domus*, 127-8, 134, 141-2, 144; imperial, 20, 24-5, 119, 149, 183-4; production in, 51-2, 72-3, 81, 132; *see also* families

humiliores, 35, 111, 116, 118, 152, 200

ideology, 107, 121, 149-50, 152, 167, 171, 180, 183, 199, 202

imperialism and conquest, 7-8, 14, 23, 100, 103, 115, 143, 152, 178, 183-5, 196

infant exposure, 72, 136, 138, 143

inflation, 94-5

inheritance, 20, 38, 65, 67-71, 87, 110, 113, 124, 126, 128, 135, 139, 141-2, 144, 150, 154-5, 193, 198-200; law of, 130, 135, 137, 141-3, 145; legacy hunting, 135, 144, 155; *see also* taxes

investment, 52, 74; in land, 43-5, 48-9, 56, 59, 64-7, 74, 77, 124, 197-8; in manufacture, 43-4, 47-8; in trade, 44, 47-50, 53; in urban property, 49

Isis, 170-3, 201

Italy, 8-10, 17, 19, 27, 30, 45, 50-2, 64-76, 79-82, 96, 111, 114, 121, 164, 173, 183, 189, 196; administration of, 22, 26; alleged decline of, 58-62, 67, 73, 198; environment of, 5, 6, 14; privileged status of, 9, 22, 56, 60, 96

iuridicus, 22

Jews, 31, 138, 169-70, 173-4, 176, 191, 202-3

Jones, A.H.M., 46-7, 72, 89-90

Judaea, 23, 98

jurists, 110, 147

kinship, 128-9, 140, 145-9, 156, 201; terminology of, 145-6

labour, 45, 51-2, 56, 71; compulsory, 29, 57; direct exploitation of, 111; division of, 109, 122; intensification of, 57, 63, 82, 198; temporary, 71, 76-7, 112; *see also* debt-bondage; *obaerarii*; peasants; slaves

land: attitudes to, 44-5, 64, 73-4, 198; concentration of, 66, 69-71, 74, 76; distribution and size of holdings, 51, 59, 64-71, 73-6, 109, 126, 143, 146, 198; management of, 59, 64, 70-5, 77, 80, 140, 155, 198; taxes on, 9, 21, 46-7, 51, 56-7, 66; *see also* investment; labour

languages: Greek, 182, 186, 189-91; Latin, 18, 186, 188-91, 193; local, 186, 191-3

latifundia, 66-7, 73, 198

law: administration of, 13, 22, 24, 34-6, 110, 152, 155, 181, 190-2, 194; and inequality, 109-12, 115-18, 120, 199; and order, 20, 32-3, 110, 157-9, 174, 196; commercial, 52-5; emperor as legislator, 24, 110, 147; local, 27, 33, 110; property rights, 49, 109-10, 135, 137, 140, 199; *see also* inheritance; marriage; *paterfamilias*; police; unrest

legates, imperial, 16, 22, 25, 35-9; *see also* governors

Lepcis Magna, 9, 27, 165, 186, 188, 192

Libya, 5, 9, 186, 192

life expectancy, 99, 138-9, 142, 146, 200-1

lineage, 123, 141-5, 200; agnatic, 127-9

literature, 108, 121, 125, 127-9, 132-4, 139, 178, 180-2, 191, 202; Greek renaissance, 182-3; history-writing, 180, 182, 187; poetry, 180, 186-7; *see also* emperors, patronage by; oratory; patronage of the arts

liturgies, *see* euergetism

loans, *see* debt; moneylending

Maecenas, 154, 172, 180

magic, 172-3, 176, 179

management, *see* land, management of

manufacture, 45, 47-8, 52, 56, 90-1, 191; state ownership of, 47, 92; trade in manufactured goods, 47, 90-1; underdevelopment of, 43-4, 46-7, 49, 52-3; *see also* clothing; craftsmen; pottery

manumission, 110, 115, 120, 124, 200

manus, 128, 130, 135, 138

Marcus Aurelius, 9-11, 39, 51, 66, 125, 167, 174-5, 179, 181-2, 185

marriage, 44-5, 70-1, 120, 127-36, 142, 145-7, 180, 198-9; age at, 131-2, 135-6, 138, 140-1, 147, 154, 200-1; imperial legislation on, 88, 113, 115, 126, 130, 143-4, 200; law of, 130-1, 135-8, 140-1, 146-7; values of, 132-4; *see also* wives

Martial, 71, 135, 151, 154, 180, 187

Marx, K., 109, 199

Mediterranean, 5-12, 14, 77-9, 100, 147, 178, 183, 196

metals, 7, 50, 89, 91-2

'middle class', lack of, 45, 109, 116

mines, 119-20
Mithras, 171-3
mobility, social, 44-5, 110, 120-1, 123-6, 155, 167, 199-200; *see also* decurions, recruitment; equestrians, recruitment; senate, recruitment
models, economic, 43, 45-6, 48-51, 53; simulation, 138, 146
Moesias, 16, 30, 90-1, 193
monarchy, 34, 36, 126, 163, 171, 178-81, 196, 202
money, 21, 50, 53, 68, 81, 93, 95-7, 117, 122, 154, 197-8
moneylending, 43-4, 47; bottomry loans, 44
mothers, 127-8, 139, 145, 147
mountains, 12-14, 159
municipium, 26-7, 31, 167

Narbonensis, 17, 19, 96, 166, 186-8
Nero, 10, 24, 66, 158, 179, 181, 184
Nile, 15, 99
nurses, wet-, 68, 139

obaerarii, 111
olives and olive oil, 13, 17, 50, 55, 58-9, 64, 86-7, 89-90, 94, 102
oratory, 132, 148, 151, 155, 181-2, 186-8
orders and rank, 107, 112-18, 199-200; display of, 113-14; 116-17, 199; inversion of, 107, 118, 120, 122-3
Ostia, 61
oxen, 52, 68

Pannonias, 10, 16-19, 193
partnership, 54
pastoralism, 13, 68
pasturage, 13, 65, 67-71, 73, 75, 198
paterfamilias, 113, 127-30, 134-41, 146, 153; *patria potestas*, 126-7, 130, 134, 136-8, 140-1, 147, 200-1
patricians, 123
patronage, 20, 24, 26, 107, 122, 125, 128, 134, 146, 148-56, 194, 196, 198-200; municipal, 31-2; of *collegia*, 157; of freedmen, 120, 125; of the arts, 154, 180, 189, 202; rural, 77, 98, 112; terminology of, 152-3; *see also* emperor, patronage by; friends; protégés
peasants, 43, 51, 59, 64, 75-7, 81-2, 97-8, 103, 109, 112, 124, 192-4, 198-9
peculium, 119, 137, 140
Persia, 7-8
Petronius, 44-5, 120-1, 180
Philip, 32, 175
philosophy, 121-2, 154, 173-4, 179, 183, 187, 202
plains, 7, 12-13
plebs, Roman, 56, 60, 85, 87, 89, 149-51, 156-8, 201
Pliny the elder, 5, 14, 19, 57-8, 65-7, 74, 95, 114
Pliny the younger, 59-60, 64-9, 71-2, 74, 112, 118, 120, 128, 143, 146, 149-50, 153-6, 181, 188, 202; as governor of Bithynia, 36-7, 39, 157-8; as husband, 131-4, 142
Plutarch, 11, 134, 153
Polanyi, K., 48
police, 23, 157-9

polis, *see* cities
Pontus, 12, 36, 39
population, 29-30, 108, 123; migration, 8, 19, 51, 56, 99-100, 103, 151, 186, 196-7; of Italy, 6, 51, 60; of Rome, 6, 8, 62, 83, 99-100
pottery, 44, 47, 52, 91-2, 188; amphorae, 53-4, 58, 60-1, 67
poverty, 13, 52, 75, 101, 112, 118, 157, 197
praetorian guard, 17, 23, 158
praetorian prefect, 22-4, 114, 118
prefect of the *annona*, 23, 86-8
prefect of Egypt, 7, 15, 22-3
prefect of the *vigiles*, 23, 158
prices, *see* inflation
priesthoods, 45, 115, 171; Egyptian, 168; of ruler-cult, 166; of state religion, 163-4, 167; provincial, 10, 15; *see also* Druids
proconsuls, 21-2, 25, 35-7, 102, 164-5
procurators, 10, 22-5, 112, 114, 124, 152
protégés, 149, 152-5, 201
provinces, administration of, 21-6, 34-5, 196-7
publicani, 21, 54, 87, 114
public works, 8, 20, 28, 33, 37-8, 56, 184-5, 188, 190, 197

quaestors, 21-2, 25
Quintilian, 181-2, 186-7, 202

rebellion, 17-18; *see also* unrest
reciprocity, 146, 148-55, 163, 165, 170, 175, 201
religion, state, 163-4, 167-9; conservatism of, 170-7, 201-2
religious cults, 156, 163-4, 167, 183, 193; native, 167-74, 191, 201-2; *see also* Christianity; ruler-cult; state religion
rent, 49-51, 57, 62, 72, 81, 86-8, 93, 95, 98, 198; share-cropping, 72; *see also* investment; tenants
Rhine, 7, 10, 57, 90, 92, 96
rivers, 5, 14, 52, 62
roads, 15, 29
Roma, cult of, 164-5, 190
Romanization, 15, 18-19, 26, 108, 110-11, 178, 186-9, 202-3; limits of, 12-19; 110-11, 178, 186, 189-96, 203; of religion, 164-8, 186, 202
Rome, city of, 17, 27, 31, 122, 151-2, 173, 178, 183-7, 189-90, 196, 201-2; administration of, 22-3, 26, 158; as consumer, 6, 8, 48-9, 56, 58, 60, 62, 83-8, 95, 99, 103, 198; population of, 6, 8, 62, 83, 99; *see also* plebs; Roma
Rostovtzeff, M.I., 59
ruler-cult, 10, 164-7, 190, 201-2

salutatio, 122, 151, 153
Sardinia, 23, 95, 98, 192
senate and senators, 27, 31, 103, 107, 114-15, 118, 131, 142, 179, 200-1; administrative functions of, 20-6, 34-6, 113, 120, 154-5, 163, 181; census of, 64-5, 69, 113, 116, 199; order of, 112-13, 116-17, 199; recruitment and provincialization of, 9-11, 16, 36, 66, 96, 107, 113, 123-4, 144-5, 152-4, 156, 171-2, 200-1; wealth of, 47-50, 64-7,

71, 74, 95-6, 114, 155; *see also* aristocracy; legates; proconsuls
Seneca the elder, 181-2, 187
Seneca the younger, 66-7, 74, 121-2, 134, 139, 141, 143, 146, 148-9, 154, 169, 179, 187
Septimius Severus, 8-9, 11, 15, 22, 27, 30, 32, 61, 85, 87-8, 90, 95, 185, 188-9, 191
Severus Alexander, 8, 16-17
ships, 20; and trade, 44, 49-50, 52-4, 88; and travel, 14; cost and size of, 49, 53
Sicily, 6, 15, 21, 58, 67, 79-80, 82, 95-6, 98, 100, 111, 192
sitones, 100
slaves, 83, 110, 118-19, 123, 173, 179, 200; alleged decline of, 72-3, 198; as a class, 109; as an order, 115-16; breeding of, 72; domestic, 107, 119-22, 124, 127-8, 132, 134, 139, 199; imperial, 20-1, 24-6; in agriculture, 52, 56, 59, 61-2, 67-8, 71-3, 76-7, 90, 111, 120; in commerce, 47, 55, 73, 119, 124; managerial, 72, 119, 132; sources and supply of, 72-3, 99, 138
social stratification, 107, 109-10, 112-14, 116-22, 136, 148-9, 154-5, 194-5, 199, 203
sons, *see* children
sophists, 15, 182, 187
sources, archaeological, 46, 53, 60-2, 76, 82, 91, 193; epigraphical, 108, 124, 127, 129, 131, 136, 193; legal, 108, 127, 136, 138, 147, 200; limitations of, 43, 46-9, 62, 75, 108, 127, 147, 191; *see also* geography
Spain, 7, 9, 13, 15, 17, 21-2, 27, 32, 36-7, 51, 55-6, 58, 61, 87, 90, 95-6, 117-18, 166, 168, 186-8, 192, 195-6, 202
spectacles, public, 8, 20, 33, 38, 150, 158, 188, 190; seating at, 113-14, 117, 121-2, 199; *see also* amphitheatre; theatre
status, 107, 111, 118-23, 126, 148-50, 194, 199, 203; and economic activity, 47-50, 57, 111; symbols, 107, 113-17, 119-22, 194, 199; *see also* honour; orders; social stratification
step-mothers, 139
Stoics, 173, 179, 182, 202
Strabo, 5, 6, 12, 14-16, 19, 29-30, 168-9
Suetonius, 60, 186-7
sumptuary laws, 122
supply, *see* food supply; trade
Syria, 8, 27, 30, 32, 90, 169, 172, 191, 195

Tacitus, 9, 17-19, 139, 148, 151, 155-6, 166, 169, 180, 182, 186-7
taxes, 8, 20, 32, 37, 39-40, 43, 50, 81, 86-7, 193-4, 196; and economic growth, 50, 53, 56, 62, 91, 197; *annona militaris*, 94-5; burden of, 9, 21, 23, 29, 33, 46-7, 49, 51, 56-7, 83, 90, 92-8, 103, 112, 198; capitation, 9, 29; *collatio lustralis*, 46-7; collection of, 13, 21, 23-4, 34, 39, 56-7, 87-8, 92, 115, 197; exemption from, 27-8, 32,

49, 58, 96; indirect, 21, 23, 47; inheritance, 23; *tributum*, 21; *see also* land, tax on
teaching, *see* education; oratory
technology, 43-4, 52-5, 57-9, 63, 77-8, 80, 197-8
temples, 164, 167-8, 190-1
tenants, 52, 59-60, 68, 71-3, 76-7, 98, 112, 152, 198; *see also* debt-bondage, *obaerarii*
textiles, *see* clothing
theatres, 107, 117, 158, 189-90
Tiberius, 23, 86, 94, 113-14, 116, 118-19, 122, 158, 166, 180, 184, 190-1
timber, 13, 50, 89
trade, 13, 40, 44-50, 52-6, 84-5, 91, 197; 'administered', 48-50, 85-8, 90-3, 95-6; in luxuries, 47, 62, 93; traders, 13, 44-5, 48-9, 85, 87-90, 93, 96, 115, 190; underdevelopment of, 44, 46-7, 50, 52-3; *see also* grain; wine
Trajan, 7, 9, 36, 38-9, 59-61, 66, 74-5, 77, 85, 87, 101, 150, 157-8, 167, 174, 184-5, 189
transport, 14, 32, 44, 52, 71, 90, 93; *cursus publicus*, 94; *see also* roads; ships; trade
tribes, 13-14, 18, 28, 32, 90, 166, 188, 193, 197
Trimalchio, *see* Petronius

Ulpian, 127-8, 136, 191-2
unrest, 157-9, 170, 175; *see also* rebellion
urban prefect, 22

Varro, 5, 45, 67-8, 71, 79, 81-2, 111, 169
Veleia, 65, 69, 70-2, 74-5
Velleius Paterculus, 18-19, 180
Verus, Lucius, 8, 167
Vespasian, 37, 103, 151, 166, 171-2, 181, 185, 202
veterans, 24, 27, 51, 58, 77, 81, 189; social mobility of, 110, 116, 124, 199-200
Veyne, P., 133
villages, 28-30, 90, 189, 195
villas, 61-2, 71, 185, 192, 194-5
Virgil, 154, 180, 190, 202; pseudo-Virgilian *Moretum*, 75-6
Vitruvius, 6, 184

wages, 71, 76-7, 111, 155
war, 56, 62, 72, 168; civil, 12, 27-8, 51, 58, 62, 76, 86, 94, 99, 107, 165, 171, 175
water supply and control, 29, 57-8, 78, 86, 150
wealth, 43-5, 51, 54, 64-6, 107, 109-13, 115, 118-24, 126, 134, 144, 200
Weber, M., 46, 48, 109, 199
wine, 13, 17; distribution of, 86-7, 89, 94, 157; production of, 55, 58-62, 64, 67-8, 73-4, 76; trade in, 50, 53-4, 59-62, 87, 93
wives, 107, 127-36, 200-1; imperial, 24
women, 120, 126, 128, 200-1; education of, 133-4; guardianship over, 130-1; property rights of, 130, 135-6, 138, 146, 201; *see also* families; house and household; *manus*; wives